D0734792

Managing Risk in Developing Countries

Managing Risk in Developing Countries

NATIONAL DEMANDS AND MULTINATIONAL RESPONSE

Barbara C. Samuels II

PRINCETON UNIVERSITY PRESS
PRINCETON, NEW JERSEY

Published by Princeton University Press, 41 William Street,
Princeton, New Jersey 08540

In the United Kingdom: Princeotn University Press, Oxford

Library of Congress Cataloging-in-Publication Data

Samuels, Barbara C., 1954–
Managing risk in developing countries: national demands and
multinational response / Barbara C. Samuels II.
p. cm.
ISBN 0-691-07826-2
1. Automobile industry and trade—Brazil. 2. Automobile industry
and trade—Government policy—Brazil. 3. International business
enterprises—Brazil. 4. Automobile industry and trade—Mexico.
5. Automibile industry and trade—Government policy—Mexico.
6. International business enterprises—Mexico. I. Title.
HD9710.B82S26 1990
338.8′81—dc20 89-36441
CIP

Publication of this book has been aided by the Whitney Darrow
Fund of Princeton University Press

This book has been composed in Linotron Caledonia

Princeton University Press Books are printed on acid-free paper,
and meet the guidelines for permanence and durability of the
Committee on Production Guidelines for Book Longevity of the
Council on Library Resources

Printed in the United States of America by Princeton University Press,
Princeton, New Jersey

10 9 8 7 6 5 4 3 2 1

TO MY FATHER AND MY DAUGHTER

Unknown to each other, united by this book

Contents

Figures

Tables

Acknowledgments

AS THIS BOOK was born of my Ph.D. thesis at MIT, I would first like to thank my thesis advisers, Professors Myron Weiner and Lucian W. Pye of the Political Science Department, and Professor Richard D. Robinson of the Sloan School of Management for their enduring patience, support, and encouragement. In the years since 1980 that I have been developing my ideas, many individuals (and their work) have been sources of support and inspiration. I would like to especially thank Raymond Vernon, Louis Wells, Samuel Huntington, Thomas Poynter, and Stephen Kobrin. I am also indebted to Maria Helena Moreira Alves, who was generous enough to share with me her three years of extensive research on labor in Brazil. Riordan Roett was a source of steady, good-hearted prodding. My special thanks go to Thomas A. Murphy, former Chairman of the Board of the General Motors Corporation, for his assistance in launching my research.

This book, however, could never have been written without the generous support of many, many people—nationals of Brazil and Mexico as well as executives of the multinational companies included in the study. Over eighty people contributed their experiences and perspectives in multiple interviews lasting several hours. (Their names are listed in the Appendix.) I hope this finished volume proves their time was well spent.

Many individuals assisted my research on the Brazilian subsidiaries throughout my visits in 1980, 1981, and 1982. I would like especially to acknowledge the late Joseph Sánchez, former Managing Director of General Motors do Brasil; Andre Beer, Executive Vice-President of General Motors do Brasil; Lloyd Halstead, former Managing Director of Ford do Brasil; Gunnar Lindquist, Managing Director of Saab-Scania do Brasil; Wolfgang Sauer, Managing Director of Volkswagen do Brasil; Karl-Heinz Gerber, Vice-President and Finance Director of Volkswagen do Brasil; and Werner Fritz Gerhard Jessen, former Managing Director of Mercedes Benz do Brasil. I am very grateful to those subisidiary staff members in industrial relations, who with great patience introduced me to their companies' policies: Herbert Brenner, Ereudy Fernandes, Antonio Alcantara (General Motors); Donald Kummer, Osmar Valentin, Salvadore Evangelista, Jr., Diego Alarcon Clemente (Ford); Louis Scheur, Pedro Proseurcin (Mercedes Benz); Inge Lunnerdal, Claudio Orlandi (Saab-Scania); and Admon Ganem, Laura Magalhaes C. Amorim, Mauro Marcondes Machado (Volkswagen). I would also like to thank the Directors of Strategic Planning, Production, and Public Relations at each subsidiary, especially Jens Kook-Weskott (Volkswagen); Antonio Romeu Netto (General Motors); Larry Kazanowski (Ford); and William Losh (General Motors).

Union officials were very generous with their time and viewpoints. I would especially like to acknowledge Jair Meneguelli, President of the São Bernardo Metalworkers Union.

Despite the particularly sensitive nature of the Mexican study, many company executives and Mexican government officials were very supportive. Of particular assistance were Marvin Runyon, Managing Director of Nissan Motor Manufacturing Corporation, USA; Issei Yoshino, Managing Director of Nissan Mexicana; William Slocum, Managing Director of General Motors de México; Michael Hammes, Managing Director of Ford de México; and Jack Parkinson, Managing Director of Chrysler de México. The Government Relations Directors of the subsidiaries were also very helpful, notably Mario Silva (General Motors) and Armando Carrillo (Volkswagen). Also Thomas Gilman, Director of Planning and Investments (Chrysler de México), and Jacob Hanneman, Manager of Business Planning and Development (Ford de México), were particularly generous with their time. Cesar Flores, Executive President of the automotive association (Associación Mexicana de la Industria Automotriz), and his staff were of great help in explaining issues and providing information.

My very special thanks also to Hiroshi Yoshioka, Coordinator of Commercial Relations for Nissan Mexicana; Juan Wolffer P., former Director of Development for Diesel Nacional, S.A.; and Amado Vega, former Assistant Director of the Automotive and Transport Industry (Ministry of National Resources and Industrial development). The assistance of Guadalupe Garza Escobar in searching the libraries of Mexico City was invaluable.

Post-research, both my employer Chase Manhattan Bank and I endured the challenge of completing this book while working full time. I would like to thank Chase Manhattan Bank and my managers for their generous support. Most understanding and encouraging was the former Executive of the Country Risk Policy Group, Francis L. Mason. I would also like to express my appreciation to John A. Hooper, the former Vice-Chairman, for providing me with the on-the-job experience that motivated my research, reinforcing the importance of this topic and the pragmatic value of the underlying arguments.

I am also grateful to those people whose support and guidance transformed this work into publication: Sandy Thatcher of Princeton University Press, Ted Moran, Douglas Bennett, and Roy Thomas. Many persons wrestled with the typing and ordering of this document. I would like to thank David Wells, Priscilla Davis, and especially Marie N. Celestin.

Finally, to my husband, Raul Luciano Katz, who shared my ideas, fatigue, and triumphs with great courage and patience, who improved the manuscript with his countless suggestions, who endured much and consoled more: *à la prochaine*!

Abbreviations

ABC	Industrial suburbs of São Paulo including the towns of Santo André, São Bernardo do Campo, São Caetano, and Diadema
AMIA	Asociación Mexicana de la Indústria Automotriz (Mexican Association of the Automotive Industry)
ANFAVEA	Associação Nacional dos Fabricantes de Veículos Automotores (National Brazilian Motor Vehicle Constructors Association)
DIEESE	Departmento Intersindical de Estatística e Estudos Sócio-Econômicos (Brazilian Inter-Trade Union Statistical and Socioeconomic Studies Department)
FIESP	Federação das Indústrias do Estado de São Paulo (São Paulo Federation of Industry)
IMF	International Metalworkers Federation
LDC	Less-developed country
MNC	Multinational company
SEPAFIN	Secretaría de Patrimonio y Fomento Industrial (Ministry of Patrimony and Industrial Promotion)
SINFAVEA	Sindicato Nacional de Indústria de Tratores, Caminhões, Automóveis e Veículos Similares (The Brazilian National Union of the Tractor, Truck, Automobile, and Like Vehicles Industry)
UAW	United Automobile Workers

Managing Risk in Developing Countries

CHAPTER 1

Introduction: Competing Issues—National Demands and Multinational Response

THE SPREAD of businesses across national boundaries is one of the most important phenomenons affecting our society, prompting much debate on the global competitiveness of multinational companies and national economies as well as on the sociopolitical implications. As the technological advances of communications, transportation, and production modes further cut through national boundaries, the very structure and fabric of the nation-state, international relations, and businesses are being revolutionized. Increasingly, the relevant parameters are not national but global, with national policymakers and business managers being forced to consider the impact of international variables on public policies and business strategies. Against this backdrop, the multinational company (MNC) reigns supreme, the creature of the internationalization of business, reaching around the world and through national boundaries with its global strategies. It is here, within the structure of the MNC, that the economic imperatives of globalization often run counter to the political imperatives of the individual nation-state, while at the same time the MNC is itself subject to the complexities and contradictions of operating across national boundaries. The conflict becomes acute in developing countries (LDC): as MNCs strive for cheaper labor and new markets, LDCs are particularly concerned with extracting benefits from MNCs to meet their own development objectives.

The trends of MNC strategies and LDC demands are contradictory: as MNCs face the economic imperatives of global competition and centralize their subsidiaries' activities, local pressures from within LDCs are pushing for increased decentralization and responsiveness from individual subsidiaries. From the MNC side, LDCs are assuming a larger role as growth markets as well as sites of competitive production. Competition and the relative importance of superior management in international integration are increasing with the continued globalization of business. Simultaneously, both LDC governments and local groups focus demands on MNC subsidiaries operating within their countries with the objective of influencing individual subsidiary behavior.

Despite critical importance to business managers, national policymakers, and the public at large, the crux of this phenomenon remains obscure: what do host countries demand of MNCs and how do they respond? This book zeros in on this critical intersection of the host-country-MNC relationship, focusing on the much-neglected dynamics of national demands in LDCs and the ability and willingness of MNCs to respond to those demands.

Multiple interested parties have grappled with this issue, each from its own, often conflicting, perspective. The MNC manager needs to manage across nations, enhancing his company's global competitiveness. Conversely, the host-country's policymakers strive to extract benefits from the MNC. Likewise, the policymakers of the MNC's home country struggle to retain benefits from the MNC. To complicate matters further, various interest groups such as labor and national business try to influence MNC decisions, sometimes joining forces beyond national boundaries to attain common objectives.

Despite (and partly due to) this plethora of interested parties and their varied perspectives, scholars and business managers have tended to concentrate on the wrong questions. MNCs and LDCs are often seen from generalized, static, and polarized perspectives. From the LDC perspective, multinationals are commonly thought of and portrayed as monolithic entities, stereotyped with no or little differentiation of individual behavior and derived benefits. Likewise, from the MNC perspective, most research and practice have concentrated on macrogeneralizations about LDCs, asking what the "country risk" of a foreign investment is, with no consideration of the MNC's own behavior. As a result, despite the great importance given to the issue, these partial and static approaches have dominated the debate over the last decades, and the questioning of all parties has reached a dead end with few operative, applicable answers. In short, our knowledge and understanding lag seriously behind the challenge. This book attempts to attack this stalemate head on: What is the relationship of the MNC to LDC demands? What variables shape MNC response to those demands? What are the implications for the risks to the MNC and benefits to the LDC?

The argument speaks to the individuality of MNCs: within this dynamic of MNC-LDC conflict, MNCs differ systematically in their will and capacity to deal with host-country demands. Further, to understand conflict between MNCs and LDCs, we must concentrate not on each entity itself but on the relationship between the two, in particular the specific relationship of MNC policies to the LDC's development process. This analysis of MNC policies must be framed within a dynamic historical view of the LDC's development process and must also consider whether those policies are perceived by LDC groups as advancing their objectives. As this study shows, LDC demands on MNC policies do not appear suddenly but evolve over long periods of time, building up until eruption.

Within this dynamic context, MNCs inadvertedly act as "levers for change," implicit agents in the creation of both country risk to themselves and benefits to the host country. In other words, MNCs do not just encounter risk in the host country, but call out risk as a result of their own specific, distinctive presence and behavior. Further, when faced with the same LDC demands, the behavior of MNCs differs. Even before the eruption of conflict, MNCs often differ in their ability to identify escalating demands. Then, at the point of crisis, the degree of conflict differs due to company-specific characteristics. The outcome—the subsidiary's response to LDC demands—is also distinctly shaped by the particular characteristics of the MNC. Understanding these dynamics is significant for both parties: business managers can manage country risk to their own competitive advantage, and LDC groups can develop strategies on how to optimize MNC response to their demands.

The Case Studies

Two case studies of actual conflict between MNCs and host-country demands will help to illuminate these dynamics. If knowledge lags behind reality and we are to develop useful answers, then the best means is to study actual occurrences. In the first case, LDC national groups pressured MNC subsidiaries for changes in their local labor policies. In the second case, the host LDC government established regulations that affected the global investment and sourcing strategies of the subsidiaries' parent companies.

For both cases, field research with the MNC subsidiaries and national interest groups included extensive literature reviews and multiple intensive interviews. From 1980 to 1984 over three hundred interview sessions were conducted with more than eighty people (see Appendix for listing of interviewees). Given the prime objective of understanding MNC behavior, the focus was on interviewing a wide range of executives in each of the subsidiaries included in the study. Relevant members of senior management participated, and the managing directors of all subsidiaries completed in-depth questionnaires.

To break through the generalizations on MNCs, LDCs, and country risk, each case study is composed of different MNC subsidiaries in the same environment: subsidiaries operated in the same industry and faced the same demands in the same country. The automotive industry is used for both studies; given its ranking as one of the first international, and perhaps most integrated, industries with large production centers throughout the world, it provides us with the most advanced stage of

MNC centralization, subject to diverse host-country pressures. The countries selected were Mexico and Brazil. As two of the more advanced LDCs and key automotive producers, their experiences are most likely to typify future issues in the less-advanced LDCs and host countries in general. (See table 1–1.)

The cases differ in focus to substantiate overall generalizations: the Brazilian case study deals with MNC conflict with a local interest group, the Mexican case study concerns MNC conflict with the host government. Likewise, to illustrate the broad generalizations on MNC responsiveness, the case studies include conflict with both autonomous and centralized MNC decisions: the Brazilian case involves demands on labor-relations policies, usually as determined by the subsidiary; the Mexican case entails demands on trade-balance policies, usually the result of parent MNC decisions on global investment and sourcing strategies.

The research illuminates the issues at hand and seeks to provide insights that are applicable across industries and countries. In both cases, does an examination of the historical relationship of MNC policies to the LDC development process show an interactive process in which MNCs contribute to the creation of both country risk and host-country benefits? In both cases, do individual subsidiaries differ in their ability and willingness to respond, with MNC subsidiaries in the same industry faced with the same LDC demands responding differently? If the answers are positive, the implications for business strategies and national policies are enormous, demonstrating that latitude does exist for MNC managers to mitigate country risks and for LDC groups to extract benefits from responsive MNCs.

The Issues

First of all, the great majority of LDC governments envision the MNC as a possible mechanism to further their countries' economic development; the use of government regulations and performance requirements toward this end is well documented. In addition, numerous other LDC interest groups such as labor, local business, and opposition political parties often perceive MNC subsidiaries in their countries as crucial in aiding or endangering their own political and economic objectives. For LDC governments and interest groups, therefore, MNC subsidiaries may become priority targets of pressure for advancing their respective agendas.

Moreover, greater competition between MNCs to penetrate foreign economies has provided LDC governments with the opportunity of making discriminating demands. This, added to the LDC policymakers' accumulating experience, has led to a growing proliferation of ever-more-sophisticated and effectively expressed LDC demands. Regardless of any

TABLE 1–1
Automotive World Production (thousands of units)

Countries	*1960*	*1965*	*1970*	*1975*	*1980*	*1982*	*1964–1982*[a]
Japan	482	1,876	5,289	6,942	11,043	10,737	530.7
United States	7,095	11,138	8,284	8,987	8,010	6,985	(25.0)
West Germany	2,055	2,977	3,842	3,186	3,878	4,063	84.2
France	1,369	1,642	2,750	2,861	3,378	3,149	94.9
USSR	524	616	922	1,964	2,197	2,210	266.4
Italy	645	1,176	1,354	1,459	1,612	1,453	33.0
Canada	398	847	1,160	1,424	1,374	1,236	84.2
United Kingdom	1,811	2,177	2,099	1,648	1,313	1,157	(50.4)
Spain	58	229	536	814	1,182	1,070	500.4
Brazil	**133**	**185**	**416**	**930**	**1,165**	**861**	**370.2**
Mexico	**50**	**97**	**193**	**361**	**490**	**473**	**420.8**
Australia	326	408	474	456	364	409	0.8
Sweden	129	206	311	367	298	345	87.6
Others	493	971	1,523	1,867	2,056	2,588	252.4
Total	16,377	24,542	29,687	33,265	38,361	36,733	66.9

Source: Automotive News, 1982 Market Data Book Issues, 28 April 1983, p. 2; *Automotive News*, 1983 Market Data Book Issues, 27 April 1983, p. 4.

[a] % change.

disagreements on the capacity of MNCs to contribute to development in LDCs, in actuality the great majority of LDC governments today aggressively seek foreign investment. In the current global business environment, MNCs are rarely expropriated; on the contrary, host governments seek to attract, capture, and control. Despite the recent accelerated interest in attracting foreign investment, the trend toward the establishment of LDC national control systems that are increasingly more effective and discriminating is indisputable. Indeed, liberalization of foreign investment regulations often translates into targeting individual subsidiaries or industry groups, resulting in tailor-made demands and performance requirements yielding host-country benefits.[1] The primary objective of LDC governments and groups remains intact: once MNCs are captive, how can benefits be extracted?

The most important trend is that these host-country demands—whether they be from its government or a group such as labor—are increasingly targeted against a specific subsidiary or group of subsidiaries. LDC groups actively and aggressively target MNC policies based on their perception of potential benefits. The avoidance of risk requires the individual subsidiary to modify its behavior given the pertinent LDC groups' objectives. In short, economic nationalism has shifted from the blanket targeting of all MNCs to the pragmatic stand of corporate specificity, with individual subsidiaries being pressured to become autonomous from their parent headquarters and respond to specific LDC demands. As a result, MNCs are challenged to increase their capacity for local responsiveness.

Conversely, MNCs are encountering a growing disadvantage: as they are targeted by more specific LDC demands, the intensified globalization of strategies requires more centralization and coordination across national boundaries. Success in international business means efficient management across countries. Each MNC is faced with the dilemma inherent within the nature of the MNC organization itself—its subsidiaries are committed to a common strategy outlined by the parent; yet they are subjugated to national ruling bodies whose interests often conflict with the overall design of the parent. Furthermore, it must not be forgotten that the parent also operates under the subjugation of its own government.

And not only governments put pressure on the MNC parent—the MNC parent is also subject to influences and pressures from various in-

[1] For example, despite the much-acclaimed recent liberalization of Mexico's economy, the requirement that all foreign investment be in joint ventures with majority Mexican ownership remains largely unchanged. Even IBM with its obvious attractiveness had to negotiate over many years and to overcome intensive debate within the Mexican government before obtaining special permission for establishing a wholly owned subsidiary.

terest groups in its home country as well as all the host countries in which it has subsidiaries. Interest groups also pressure the subsidiaries. As a result, the parent company and the host countries of its subsidiaries may have few shared interests, bonds, traditions, or objectives except for competing claims on subsidiaries. As portrayed in figure 1–1, each MNC subsidiary may be envisioned as "floating" between (1) the claims of the parent company and its home country and (2) the claims of its host country, its government and interest groups.

The changing pattern of global competition over the last decade has intensified the problem of competing claims on the subsidiary. In order to remain competitive and develop new markets, MNCs have moved production centers overseas. For many MNC industries, other countries and LDCs in particular have relatively lower costs of production and higher market growth potential than their home countries. MNCs have increased dramatically their share of revenues and profits from overseas

FIGURE 1–1
Competing Claims: The "Floating" of an MNC Subsidiary between the Parent Company and the Host Country

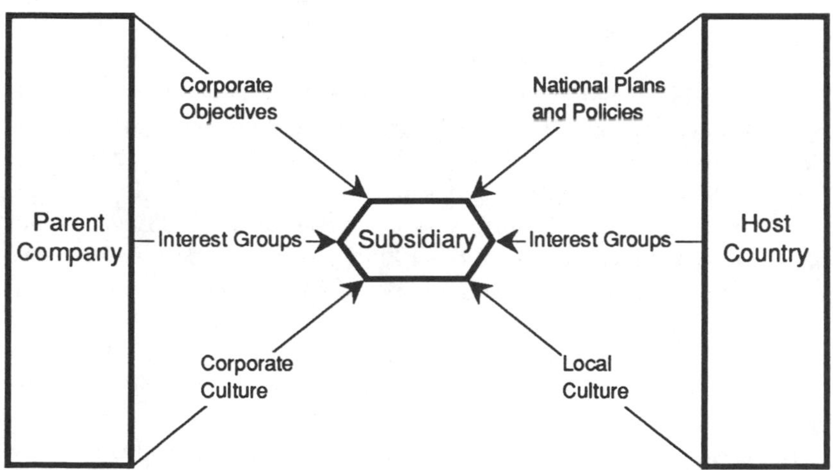

markets, investing more of their assets in these countries. This geographical fragmentation has resulted in dramatically escalating the importance of subsidiaries within the parent's global strategy and their contribution to overall profitability, and strengthening the role of the parent in centralizing and coordinating the policies and activities of these subsidiaries.[2] Therefore, MNC managers have increasingly to deal with issues re-

[2] For example, see Yves L. Doz and C. K. Prahalad, "An Approach to Strategic Control in MNCs," *Sloan Management Review* 22, no. 4 (Summer 1981): 5–13; and idem, *The Mul-*

lating to coordinating more important subsidiaries located in a growing array of country environments.

Besides the expanding problem of coordinating its overseas activities, the MNC must also contend with the growing conditioning forces in its own home country. The shift of MNC investment from the home country to overseas has resulted in a debate within labor, governments, business, and academia on the effects upon the home country's balance of payments situation, employment, tax revenues, international political relations, national security goals, and domestic antitrust policies. Some argue that home-country controls must be applied to MNCs in order to protect home-country interests. Furthermore, home-country groups, especially labor, may join forces with those in host countries in attempts to change MNC policies.[3] The most visible example today is undoubtedly that of MNCs operating in South Africa. Therefore, MNCs, by virtue of their very organization and importance to various groups, are prone to be affected by a multitude of pressures inside their home countries as well as in their subsidiaries' host countries. The successful MNC must manage these complex pressures within the formulation of its overall global strategy and in regard to its product and geographical components.

Moreover, competition between global MNC operations is stiffening and becoming more complex as the MNC activities of other countries such as Germany and Japan expand. U.S. MNCs that had enjoyed little competition in world markets now face competition from other MNCs. For example, in 1971, 280 of the 500 largest multinationals and 58 of the largest 100 multinationals in the world were U.S.-based. In 1979 the U.S. for the first time in history lost its majority lead: 281 of the 500 largest multinationals and 53 of the 100 largest multinationals were non–U.S.-based.[4] The overall result of increased international business is greater competition among MNC subsidiaries, with greater diversity between the subsidiaries in terms of parent nationality, products, objectives, and size—and, consequently, ability to respond to host-country pressures.

Increased MNC competition for Third World markets and production means amplifies the respective risks and benefits for MNCs and LDC

---

tinational Mission: Balancing Local Demands and Global Vision (New York: The Free Press, 1987).

[3] For example, see Sol C. Chaiken, "Trade, Investment and Reindustrialization: Myth and Reality," *Foreign Affairs* 60, no. 4 (Spring 1982): 836–51; and Robert J. Flanagan, "Introduction," in *Bargaining without Boundaries: The Multinational Corporation and International Labor Relations*, ed. Robert J. Flanagan and Arnold R. Weber (Chicago: University of Chicago Press, 1974), p. xiv.

[4] "Study Finds Majority of Biggest Firms Are Foreign," *Wall Street Journal*, 8 April 1981, p. 18.

groups. MNC subsidiaries must often compete against a greater number and level of diversity of MNCs in the same industry for the same market. Furthermore, given the larger supply of MNCs, LDC groups have greater latitude in their treatment of individual MNCs according to perceived benefits of each.

In summary, several factors escalate the MNC-LDC dilemma: the focus of LDC policies has shifted from blanket economic nationalism to corporate specificity, resulting in LDC demands targeted on individual subsidiaries; and MNCs, facing a more competitive world, seek to further utilize the cheaper production means of LDCs and capture their growth markets but must contend with the difficulties of coordinating worldwide operations as well as the growing conditioning forces of their home countries. Therefore, both MNC managers and LDC groups are confronted with a similar analytical task: how will subsidiaries in an LDC differ in their responses when facing similar pressures? Only the respective vantage points of MNC managers and LDC groups differ: risks versus benefits.

The State of the Art: Country-Risk Management

Over the last decade, the notion of country risk has received great fanfare. Dramatic cases have been heralded with references to the foreign debt crisis, the anti-apartheid South Africa campaign, Union Carbide's accident in Bhopal (India), and most recently Europe's 1992 quest for economic integration and deregulation. However, country risk is not confined to these well-publicized exceptions, but endemic to an international marketplace in which global competitiveness is recognized as the foremost business challenge and host-government relations as critical variables driving competitive advantage. There is a growing recognition that the complex global business environment requires not defensive reaction post-crisis, but ongoing day-to-day management of each host-country environment. However, as competition heightens and LDCs become more sophisticated in their bargaining and performance requirements, MNCs have not advanced significantly in their ability to manage the ongoing economic and sociopolitical risks associated with operating across national boundaries.

This stalemate has resulted from the static and piecemeal approach dominating company policies. Actual company policy concerning risk for MNCs in LDCs has not focused specifically on the capacity of individual subsidiaries to respond to pressures in the LDC environment, but rather on the characteristics of the LDC itself. MNC managers tend to ask for an analysis of the risk associated with an investment in a particular country independent of the MNC's own specific role within that country.

This kind of approach to country risk analysis is mirrored in the organizational structure of MNCs. As companies expanded internationally, they developed separate centralized country-risk functions with the responsibility of assessing the economic and political factors that could interfere with their global reach. Today, there is a growing understanding that these centralized units cannot, in isolation, manage country risk. In streamlining their organizations many MNCs have reduced or eliminated these units; however, only in a few cases are MNCs beginning to operationalize the country-risk function by systematically integrating it with management functions such as strategic planning, marketing, or government affairs. The problem has not yet been solved: key management functions of the MNC have not incorporated country-risk considerations as part of their ongoing operations—in effect, the internationalization of company functions lags behind the actual need of global marketplaces and cross-country production strategies.[5]

Meanwhile, with the passing of each day, MNC managers are faced with increasing complexity in global economics and politics, and country-risk issues multiply. A plethora of risk services and consultants travel the MNC circuit, selling their judgments on countries and global issues. The need to analyze economic and political factors is acknowledged, but MNC executives are cynical; despite many resources and much effort, results have been negligible, and besides, no one can predict the future, so why bother?

The issue, however, is not forecasting the future but rather hands-on management of country risk by the subsidiary in that host country itself—management of those economic and sociopolitical factors that affect or potentially affect every aspect of business operations. Centralization of this function at the parent level alone (i.e., head office unit) results in ineffectiveness—an imperative complement is that the management functions in subsidiaries consider how to manage those various economic and sociopolitical factors that may potentially influence profits. Namely, how does the MNC subsidiary effectively operate in its host-country environment given its particular economic and sociopolitical context?

Academic research is ahead of company practice in answering this pragmatic question. However, the bulk of research is partial and general, ranging from the view of the MNC as a crucial instrument of economic growth in LDCs that is at once adaptive and innovative, to the notion

[5] This study is not concerned with risk techniques of international finance, but the recent internationalization of teaching materials in key management functions such as finance and marketing should be noted. See for example, David K. Eiteman and Arthur I. Stonehill, *Multinational Business Finance* (Reading, Mass.: Addison-Wesley Publishing Co., 1987); and Subhash C. Jain, *International Marketing Management* (Boston, Mass.: Kent Publishing Co., 1987).

that MNCs create dependent development due to inflexible policies.[6] Both the pro-MNC and dependency schools tend to envision the MNC-LDC relationship in macroabsolutist terms. These general viewpoints have spurred simplistic assumptions by scholars and managers alike that the role of MNCs in LDCs is similar, with similar risks to MNCs and similar benefits to LDCs. Much of the dialogue is not focused on the specific interaction between a particular MNC and a particular LDC, but rather on generalizations across the board about either MNCs or LDCs. In particular, many management scholars have concentrated on macro-generalizations of LDCs. Dependency scholars, on the other hand, have tended to emphasize general structural issues related to MNCs. Instead of tracing the specific MNC-LDC relationship in a historical fashion, many of the studies and conclusions have been aimed at static absolutist generalizations: management scholars, of the LDC; and dependency scholars, of the MNC.

More recently, certain scholars have developed dynamic views of the MNC-LDC relationship and, to a certain extent, have differentiated between MNCs. For example, noting the "lack . . . of comprehensive analyses which effectively relate the complex aspects of the interaction . . . of the MNC and LDC nationalism," Fayerweather stressed the importance of studying the continuing dynamic relationship of individual MNCs and individual nations.[7] Bergsten, Keohane, and Nye underlined the complexity of the international economic system of a "politically diverse and decentralized world" wherein countries vary in their "national policy preferences and national situations."[8] LDC governments were pre-

[6] Examples of the dependency school include: F. H. Cardoso et al., *Dependency in Latin America* (Los Angeles: University of California Press, 1979); Andre Grunder Frank, *Capitalism and Underdevelopment in Latin America: Historical Studies of Chile and Brazil* (New York: Monthly Review Press, 1969); S. Bodenheimer, Chile and Brazil (New York: Monthly Review Press, 1969); S. Bodenheimer, "Dependency and Imperialism: The Roots of Latin American Development," in *Readings in U.S. Imperialism*, K. Fann and D. Hodges, eds. (Boston: Porter Sargent, 1971); and Osvaldo Sunkel, "Big Business and 'Dependencia': A Latin American View," *Foreign Affairs* 50, no. 3 (April 1972): 517–31.

Excellent discussions of the dependency school and other main views on foreign investment in LDCs can be found in Theodore H. Moran, "Multinational Corporations and Dependency: A Dialogue for Dependentistas and Non-Dependentistas," *International Organization* 32 (Winter 1978): 79–100; and Raymond Vernon, "Multinational Enterprise in Developing Countries: Issues in Dependency and Interdependency," in *The Multinational Corporation and Social Change*, David E. Apter and Louis Wolf Goodman, eds. (New York: Praeger, 1976).

[7] John Fayerweather, "A Conceptual Scheme of the Interaction of the Multinational Firm and Nationalism," *Journal of Business Administration* 7 (1975): 67–89. Also, see *The Multinational Corporation and Social Change*, Apter and Goodman, eds.

[8] C. Fred Bergsten, Robert O, Keohane, and Joseph Nye, "International Economics and

sented as discriminating among MNCs. For example, Franko argued that LDC governments preferred European MNCs over U.S. MNCs: "The welcome was greater, since the names of Continental enterprises carried no echo, however distant, of American diplomatic or military influence. . . . Other multinationals not only brought alternative products and processes, they brought alternative home-country flags."[9] Governments had different objectives and perceived differences in the ability of MNCs to advance those objectives.

At the same time that academics introduced a dynamic view of the MNC-LDC relationship, several of these scholars also identified significant differences between MNCs. Parent nationality, in particular, was singled out as a significant variable. For example, Franko identified "the distinctive personality of Continental European Multinational Enterprise," citing differences that included products, behavior, history as well as conflicts with host governments, home- and host-country interest groups, and the home country. European subsidiaries were reported as having "little trouble adapting to the pressures for local ownership" compared to those of U.S. origin and as responding differently to competitive threats.[10] Variables such as MNC ownership (e.g., public or private) were cited as differentiating behavior. Fayerweather characterized MNCs in terms of their performance vis-à-vis functions as a business entity (external control, profit extraction), in socioeconomic roles (resource transmission, cultural-change agent, global rationalization), and as an agent of their home nation.[11] A 1975 Senate Report pointed out that MNCs differ in many important respects, with certain characteristics affecting conduct and power: absolute size, degree of international conglomeration, internal organization, intrafirm integration in ownership, finances, intrafirm trade, research and development, and finally, position in market structure (i.e., concentration of sellers, barriers to entry, and product differentiation).[12]

Out of the pro-MNC school, a large body of literature often referred to as "the bargaining power school" emerged. The static view of the

---

International Politics: A Framework for Analysis," *International Organization* 29, no. 1 (January 1975): 36.

[9] Lawrence G. Franko, *The European Multinationals* (Stamford, Conn.: Greyloch Publishers, 1976), p. 220.

[10] Franko, *The European Multinationals*, pp. 21, 118, 123, 133, 213. Also, see Raymond Vernon, *Sovereignty at Bay: The Multinational Spread of U.S. Enterprises* (New York: Basic Books, 1971).

[11] Fayerweather, "A Conceptual Scheme," pp. 67–89.

[12] U.S. Congress, Senate, *Multinational Corporations in Brazil and Mexico. Structural Sources of Economic and Non-Economic Power: Report to the Subcommittee on Multinational Corporations of the Committee of Foreign Relations*, prepared by Richard S. Newfarmer and Willard F. Mueller (Washington, D.C.: GPO, 1975).

MNC was enhanced with a dynamic framework for explaining the MNC-LDC relationship in the obsolescing bargain model.[13] The bargaining power of the MNC decreases after committing the substantial initial investment; the host country's bargaining power increases since the MNC is now captive and has less to offer.

A number of scholars attempted to identify variables that account for the variance in bargaining power among MNCs and external stakeholders such as host governments. Cited variables include: the organizational structure of the MNC; the perceived contribution of the MNC and its strategies/policies; the relationship of the MNC to its industry and market; the home country of the MNC; the policies of the parent's home government; and the external relationships of the MNC.[14] Scholars such as Kobrin found that—irrespective of industry—maturity of technology, relatively low research and development spending, and a lack of global integration increase vulnerability to expropriation.[15] A later study by Poynter argued that government intervention can be explained by the relative bargaining power of the company and the host nation using certain variables, such as the operational and managerial complexity of the subsidiary, the amount of sourcing with affiliated companies, company

[13] See Theodore H. Moran, *Multinational Corporations and the Politics of Dependence: Copper in Chile* (Princeton: Princeton University Press, 1974); and Vernon, *Sovereignty at Bay*.

[14] See, for example, *International Political Risk Assessment: The State of the Art*, ed. Theodore H. Moran, Landegger Papers in International Business and Public Policy (Washington, D.C.: Georgetown University, 1981); Michael Porter, *Competitive Strategy* (New York: The Free Press, 1980); Yves L. Doz, *Government Control and Multinational Strategic Management: Power Systems and Telecommunication Equipment* (New York: Praeger, 1979); Yves L. Doz and C. K. Prahalad, "Headquarters Influence and Strategic Control in MNCs," *Sloan School of Management* 23, no. 1 (Fall 1981): 15–29; idem, "An Approach to Strategic Control in MNCs," pp. 5–13; idem, "How MNCs Cope with Host Government Intervention," *Harvard Business Review* 58, no. 2 (March–April 1980): 149–57; Stephen J. Kobrin, *Managing Political Risk Assessment: Strategic Response to Environmental Change* (Los Angeles: University of California Press, 1982); idem, "Assessing Political Risk Overseas," *Wharton Magazine* 6, no. 2 (Winter 1981–1982): 24–31; idem, "The Environmental Determinants of Foreign Direct Investment: An Ex Post Empirical Analysis," *Journal of International Business Studies* 11, no. 3 (Fall 1976): 29–42; idem, "Global Strategy and National Politics: The Integration of Environmental Assessment and Strategic Planning," in *Managing International Political Risk: Strategies and Techniques*, Fariborz Ghadar, Stephen J. Kobrin, and Theodore H. Moran, eds. (Washington, D.C.: Georgetown University, 1983), pp. 142–52; idem, "Political Risk: A Review and Reconsideration," *Journal of International Business Studies* 14, no. 1 (Spring 1979): 67–80; idem, "Firm and Industry Factors Which Increase Vulnerability of Foreign Enterprise to Forced Divestment: A Cross-National Empirical Study," Sloan School of Management, Working Paper, 1022–78 (1978); Richard D. Robinson, *International Business Management: A Guide to Decision-Making* (Hinsdale, Ill.: The Dryden Press, 1978).

[15] See Kobrin, "Firm and Industry Factors Which Increase Vulnerability," p. 32.

exports, and the proportion of foreign nationals in managerial and technical positions.[16]

The most specific work done in the area of MNC risk refers to the varying degrees of political risk based on the type of industry. Extensive studies on the extractive industries indicated higher levels of political risk than for manufacturing industries regardless of the host country.[17] The reason lies in the greater ability of the manufacturing industries to meet the demands of the host country, whether by increasing local content, transferring technology, or greater exports.

However, while the work done to date is very instrumental in identifying variables that may influence subsidiary response, it does not give us a framework that explains the different responses of subsidiaries to common host-country demands. The bargaining power school, while it emphasizes the differences between MNCs, is not concerned with providing complete answers to our questions. Its domain is dynamic and historical but narrow in scope: while the overall general decline of subsidiary bargaining power in the LDC is well documented, it excludes the complexity of LDC demands and their relation to the entire MNC organization. In this study, the paradigm is considerably broadened: What will LDC demands be, and what are the implications for each subsidiary? Beyond its bargaining strengths and weaknesses, how will each subsidiary be affected? What key variables not only determine each subsidiary's ability and willingness to respond, but also shape the response itself? In the next section, two major arguments are presented that address these issues, drawing on ideas from the recent research on country-risk management as well as from the fields of public policy, political development, organization, culture, and decision-making.

Argument 1: MNC Subsidiary Policies as "Levers for Change"

The first argument is that country risk cannot be assessed without taking into account the MNC's behavior, as represented by its policies. These policies must be viewed against the particular development process of

[16] Thomas A. Poynter, "Government Intervention in Less-Developed Countries: The Experience of Multinational Companies," *Journal of International Business Studies* 17, no. 1 (Spring/Summer 1982): 9–25.

[17] For example, Moran, *Multinational Corporations and the Politics of Dependence*; Franklin Tugwell, *The Politics of Oil in Venezuela* (Palo Alto: Stanford University Press, 1975); Richard L. Sklar, *Corporate Power in an African State: The Political Impact of Multinational Mining Companies in Zambia* (Berkeley: University of California Press, 1975). Also, Stephen Kobrin's study on expropriation concluded that when selective, the extractive and banking sectors were most vulnerable (see Kobrin, "Firm and Industry Factors Which Increase Vulnerability").

the host LDC. Depending on the specific relationship between the MNC and the LDC, certain policies by their very nature are, regardless of any intent, likely to be principal influences in the LDC's development process and to act as "levers for change."

First, MNC subsidiaries play a developmental role within LDCs that is defined by their policies. Just as persons are defined by their character traits, subsidiaries make their imprint through consistent behavior as embodied in their policies. This is the first premise and basic building block of the argument: (1) LDC pressures are targeted on subsidiary policies, (2) which policy is targeted is a function of the development process, and (3) all subsidiary policies are vulnerable. While this first premise underlies some of the literature, it is not a truth lodged in either the academic work or the world of managers and needs to be reinforced and explicitly spelled out. Agreeing that host countries target subsidiary policies, rather than subsidiaries in general, allows us to argue later that the reformulation of subsidiary policy is also the appropriate management response to host-country pressure.

Second, we must relate subsidiary policies to the LDC's development process. As the country's economic and political structures evolve over time, perceptions of benefits to be derived from changes in MNC policies will also change, along with the willingness and ability to effectively target those policies. In other words, the key starting point has to be the behavior of the subsidiary, as represented by its policies, and the degree to which it fits within the country's ongoing development.

Given the perceived developmental role of MNCs in LDCs, a natural outgrowth is the buildup of pressure on specific subsidiary policies. MNC subsidiaries are not only usually larger than national companies, they enjoy resources and command markets, technology, and expertise not possessed by national companies. As a result, MNC subsidiaries tend to become models for the introduction, development, and testing of new policies to the LDC before adoption by national companies. By their very definition, MNC subsidiaries provide a possible conduit to the outside world that is always vulnerable to the pressures of their host LDC.

However, the LDC development process is intensely dynamic; the policies of subsidiaries operating within that environment must be in sync and must also evolve dynamically. LDCs are in the throes of a multilevel change in their political institutions, social structures, culture, and economies. MNC subsidiaries are an intrinsic part of the development process, transferring ideas, resources, products, and transforming the economic and social fabric. Given its foreign status and large economic role in LDCs, the MNC subsidiary is especially open to the varying demands of LDC groups for implementing their objectives. Many scholars, such as Aharoni and Baden, argue that the MNC is expected to play a role in social change: "As per capita income increases, as levels of education increase and as the growth in communications technology increases awareness of alternative lifestyles, there are rising expectations with regard to matters such as housing, welfare, recreation, and medicine. These public welfare functions have traditionally been considered the province of public agencies. . . . But as corporations are intimately involved with the growth of the economy—*they are perceived by many as the most effective levers for change*, and, they too will become—*by choice or by force*—involved in implementing these changes."[18] Therefore, MNC subsidiaries are especially vulnerable, with host-country interest groups likely to push for changes in government policy or directly pressure subsidiaries into roles as agents of change.

Consequently, as the MNC subsidiary's environment changes, its policies must also change. How policies should change is determined by the particular LDC's development process and the perceived role of its policies with that process. Crises rarely occur overnight; on the contrary, they are preceded by long histories. Depending on the history of the country's particular development process, certain subsidiary policies are especially vulnerable to LDC targeting. The type of policy under pressure is determined by the LDC's development process and by the perception of LDC interest groups of the policy's potential role in advancing their objectives. LDC interest groups are particularly important to MNC subsidiaries due to the high rate of social change common to LDCs and the uncertainty of the impact of new societal forces on government policies or directly on the subsidiary itself. MNC subsidiaries may be caught in LDCs undergoing radical social change between conflicts of opposing groups in the society and the government.

Pressure can be applied by LDC interest groups or by the host government itself. Often, interest groups that have political clout indirectly pressure subsidiaries by successfully pushing for new government legislation. For example, host-country businessmen are frequently even stronger in their support for selective national controls over subsidiaries than labor unions, student groups, or the local intelligentsia.[19]

Local groups sometimes directly pressure subsidiaries for change in their policies. In the extreme case, outright conflict between local groups and the government may result in political instability and economic crisis, thereby raising questions of possible expropriation, reduced investment, or divestment. However, the impact of local groups is not likely to

[18] Yair Aharoni and Clifford Baden, *Business in the International Environment* (Boulder, Colo.: Westview Press, 1977), p. 2. Emphasis added.

[19] For example, see Jorge I. Dominguez, "National and Multinational Business and the State in Latin America" (Center for International Affairs, Harvard University, Jan. 1979, Xeroxed).

produce these extreme situations; extreme nationalism or social revolution leading to expropriations are relatively rare events today. A more likely scenario resulting in direct local group pressure on subsidiaries might be public opinion, criticisms voiced by opposition parties, or at worst, strikes and sabotage carried out by their work force. Subsidiaries may, for example, be under public pressure to reduce layoffs or pay higher wages.

Group pressures such as these are distinctly different in their effect on the subsidiary than regulations established by the LDC government. First, demands from local groups directly on the subsidiary may not be endorsed by the government. If the demands are counter to the government's policies, then the subsidiary is placed in the difficult position of go-between and diplomat. In contrast, government pressure usually requires eventual and certain, if modified, compliance. Second, because of the overriding nature of government regulations, pressures are more apt to affect subsidiary policies related to the overall parent strategy. The pressure of local groups, however, will be most likely limited to directly influencing local subsidiary policies (such as labor relations) which are usually decentralized and do not require the day-to-day involvement of the parent. Therefore, the source of pressure on the MNC subsidiary will also largely determine the type of policy that can potentially be subjected to significant pressure.

The range of policies potentially targeted is also defined by the LDC environment. Any subsidiary policy, even if it is formulated outside the country by the parent, may be perceived as providing benefits to the LDC pressuring group. Subsidiaries, therefore, may serve as captive targets for LDC groups seeking to change the policies of their parent companies. As a result, the development process in LDCs and subsequent targeting of subsidiary policies can directly affect the MNC parent in its home country.

In both case studies in this volume, the approach chosen to prove this argument is by necessity historical, mapping the evolution of LDC demands on a particular policy until eruption, and begins with an historical overview of the selected policy in the context of the country's overall development process: What was the role of this subsidiary policy in the context of the overall development process? How was the policy seen by key LDC actors? Were changes in the subsidiary's policy seen as having an actual or potential impact on furthering the LDC actors' objectives? Did pressure on the specified policies build up over time or did crisis erupt mysteriously? Then, LDC pressure on policies is contrasted by selecting the extreme ranges: a local policy usually adapted to the host country (labor relations) and a parent policy usually dictated by global external requirements (investment and sourcing). Are both types of policies open to LDC targeting, and vulnerable to change?

Argument 2: The Differing Response Capacities of MNC Subsidiaries

The second main argument focuses on the individual character of the MNC subsidiary. In the first argument, MNC subsidiary policies were differentiated on the basis of their role within the LDC's development process; the second argument goes further, submitting that individual MNC subsidiaries vary systematically in their will and capacity to deal with host-country demands. The range of variables underlying this argument includes those of the bargaining power school but expands to include the characteristics of the entire MNC organization. Each subsidiary's policy reformulation process—the identification and response to pressures before crisis, the degree of conflict between their policies and the LDC demands, and the type of response—is a function of a multitude of specific subsidiary characteristics: structures, strategies, policies, practices, individuals, relationships, philosophies, products, production requirements, and market position.

Recent literature goes beyond the strengths and weaknesses of relative bargaining positions, acknowledging the importance of the MNC organization itself. For example, Doz and Prahalad categorized LDC pressures as constituting "problems of internal organization [for the MNC] as serious as those of external competitive posture."[20] And the organizational problem is subsidiary-specific: each subsidiary, facing its own specific kind and level of LDC demands, must be organized with effective management systems and structures that match those specific demands.

Building an effective subsidiary organization, however, is a complex, comprehensive exercise. In the context of increased pressures for subsidiary autonomy, Doz and Prahalad addressed the need for "rebuilding headquarters influence."[21] Their answer lay in administrative mechanisms that encompass multiple levels of the MNC organization, from information-gathering to human resources, policies, corporate culture, and decision structures. In a similar vein, Poynter mapped out optimum behavior strategies to defend the subsidiary based on the particular company characteristics. He referred to the importance of developing in-country relationships, having politically attuned executives, and the tim-

[20] Doz and Prahalad, "How MNCs Cope with Host Government Intervention," p. 156.

[21] Doz and Prahalad, "Headquarters Influence and Strategic Control in MNCs," pp. 15–29.

ing of investments.[22] Kobrin emphasized the organizational issue of the political risk function, suggesting that institutionalization results in more effective country assessment.[23] In fact, in order for a firm to effectively exploit its environment, there must be a strategic fit between its strategy and its environment; hence, environmental assessment must be an integral part of the planning process.[24]

In reviewing the literature and management practice, a gap in our knowledge is readily apparent. While there are scattered bits and pieces of other variables cited by scholars of diverse origins to fill this gap, the challenge remains: given the complexity of the MNC organization, how can we identify the range of subsidiary characteristics that constitute its individuality and determine its behavior when pressured with LDC demands?

In each case study, the complexity of factors affecting subsidiary behavior is examined with a chronological examination of the policy reformulation process: Do significant differences exist (1) before crisis in subsidiary detection and response to the buildup of pressure, (2) at crisis, in the degree of conflict between the subsidiaries and the pressuring LDC group, and finally (3) between subsidiaries, in the types of responses? (See figure 1–2.) Using this basic approach, we will examine the policy reformulation process for each subsidiary, highlighting the specific subsidiary characteristics that affect behavior. Illustrating the complexity of

FIGURE 1–2
LDC Demands and MNC Response: The Policy Reformulation Process

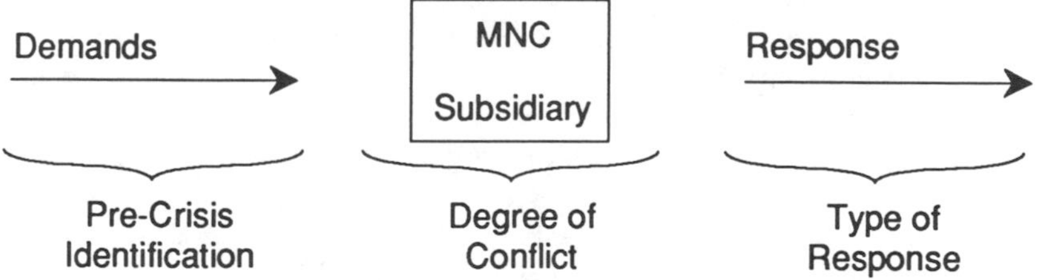

subsidiary behavior and the importance of differing subsidiary characteristics will, it is hoped, convince others of the need to enlarge the existing paradigms and management practices to account for these differences within the current challenges of risk management, strategy development, and policymaking.

Within this context, we are concerned with the more specific task of

[22] Thomas A. Poynter, "Managing Political Risk: A Strategy for Defending the Subsidiary" (March 1984, Mimeographed).

[23] See Kobrin, *Managing Political Risk Assessment*.

[24] Kobrin, "Global Strategy and National Politics," pp. 142–52.

highlighting common variables that affect subsidiary behavior. Relationships are a key determinant in subsidiary behavior. First, despite the level of autonomy, the subsidiary's relationship with its parent influences subsidiary response throughout its policy reformulation process, albeit in different ways. Second, the subsidiary's relationships with in-country groups, in particular the host government, also influence its response.

By breaking the policy reformulation process into three separate parts, we create a framework enabling the specification of common variables that serve to differentiate subsidiary behavior. These variables serve as benchmarks against which we can compare subsidiary behavior throughout the different phases of LDC demands and MNC response. As benchmarks, they provide a structure for the comparison of that complex multitude of subsidiary characteristics that differentiate MNC response.

Pre-Crisis Identification of LDC Demands

The first aspect of policy reformulation is the subsidiary's identification of LDC demands before crisis. The argument is that a subsidiary's ability to identify and respond before crisis varies according to specific characteristics related to internal management policies, relationships in-country, and parent intervention in its policies. (See figure 1–3.) A variety of studies indicates the significance of inherent differences between subsidiaries in their ability to identify and respond before crisis. In terms of internal management policies, senior management must have the ability to perceive changes in their environment, study the implications of those changes, and have the resources and latitude to make the desired adjustments. Gladwin and Terpstra stated in their study of cultural environments: "As cultural environments grow more variable, complex, hostile, heterogeneous, and inter-dependent, they demand more attention from the organization. Since the organization will respond only to what it perceives, it is important to have an accurate perception. . . . The organization's ability to adapt will depend on: (1) its ability to monitor the environment in a distortion-free manner; (2) its ability to diagnose the implications of changing environmental demands; and (3) its capacity for changing organizational strategies and structures."[25] Their work singled out approaches that improve the organization's ability to have accurate perception, sound diagnosis, and appropriate adaptation: language training, empathy to break down ethnocentric mental sets, and social interest-group analysis. Literature concerned with how companies scan their environments effectively also stresses the importance of management ini-

[25] Thomas Neil Gladwin and Vern Terpstra, "Introduction," in *The Cultural Environment of International Business*, ed. Vern Terpstra (Cincinnati: South Western Publishing Co., 1978), p. xxiii.

FIGURE 1–3
Key Variables Determining Pre-Crisis Identification of Host-Country Demands

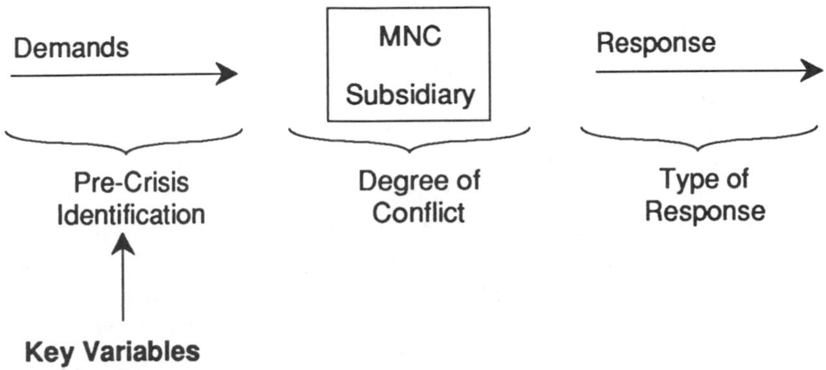

tiative, resources, and authority.[26] While this literature is largely concerned with domestic companies, its emphasis on the firm-environment interface underlines the importance of the subsidiary, rather than the parent, in understanding its own environment.

In terms of in-country relationships, close subsidiary contact with key LDC actors can increase the subsidiary's ability to diagnose its environment. As Gladwin and Walter stressed, the quality of relationships will play a major role in subsidiary interpretation of the environment.[27] They argued that good relations help prevent conflicts; negative relations are usually the result of ethnocentrism and nationalism.[28] Likewise, in his work on global competitiveness, Porter emphasizes the strategic impor-

[26] See, for example, H. Igor Ansoff, "Strategic Issue Management," *Strategic Management Journal* (1980): 131–48; Eli Segev, "How to Use Environmental Analysis in Strategy Making," *Management Review* (March 1977): 5–12; and John D. Stoffels, "Environmental Scanning for Future Success," *Managerial Planning* (Nov.–Dec. 1982): 4–12.

[27] Thomas N. Gladwin and Ingo Walter, "How Multinationals Can Manage Social and Political Forces," *The Journal of Business Strategy* 1, no. 1 (Summer 1980): 54–68.

[28] Gladwin and Walter stated: "Ethnocentrism reflects an inability to appreciate the viewpoint of others whose cultures have, for example, a different morality, religion, or language, and leads to an unwillingness to see their common problems. . . . Nationalism, as an extension of ethnocentrism, adds a strong chauvinistic and emotional component to many conflicts involving multinationals." Gladwin and Walter, "How Multinationals Can Manage Social and Political Forces," pp. 54–68.

tance of government relations and the resulting need for competitive strategy to include actions specifically designed to build political capital.[29] The relationships of each MNC subsidiary with LDC actors have specific and important implications for its capacity to perceive and manage its host LDC environment.

The degree of parent intervention also appears to be a key variable differentiating subsidiary ability to identify and respond before crisis. Doz and others argue that, as organizational theory would indicate, the autonomy of the subsidiary from its parent increases its responsiveness. The problem is how to reconcile local autonomy in decision-making with the global interests of the parent. Some authors such as Singh have suggested that with increased emphasis by LDCs on control, parent-subsidiary relations may need to change substantially, with greater autonomy and decentralization of decision-making.[30]

Autonomy itself, however, is only part of the answer. Autonomy only partially describes parent-subsidiary relationships; parents intervene in other ways that affect subsidiary responsiveness. For example, in their comparison of German, Japanese, and U.S. subsidiaries, Negandhi and Baliga found that the type of headquarters-subsidiary relationship varied significantly.[31] The overall subsidiary-parent relationship encompassed

[29] Porter, *Competitive Strategy*, p. 292.

[30] Rana K.D.N. Singh, "Policy Issues and Trends in Parent-Affiliate Relationships in Developing Countries," in *The Management of Headquarters-Subsidiary Relationships in Multinational Corporations*, ed. Lars Otterbeck (New York: St. Martin's Press, 1981).

Some general work on subsidiary autonomy has been done. For example, Brooke and Remmers found that the autonomy of a subsidiary decreased with the size of the parent company. However, Hedlund submits the opposite: autonomy increases with the size of the subsidiary. Hedlund also found in his study of Swedish MNCs unusual subsidiary autonomy due in part to "the historically evolved mother-daughter structure of organization, by the mode of early internationalization of the larger companies, and the strong Swedish tradition of emphasizing individual responsibility, a lack of feudal patterns of land ownership and an absence of respect for organizational hierarchies." See M. Z. Brooke and H. L. Remmers, *The Strategy of Multinational Enterprise* (New York: Elsevier, 1970); and Gunnar Hedlund, "Autonomy of Subsidiaries and Formalization of Headquarters-Subsidiary Relationships in Swedish MNCs," in *The Management of Headquarters-Subsidiary Relationships in Multinational Corporations*, ed. Otterbeck, p. 33.

For other work on autonomy, see P. R. Lawrence and J. W. Lorsch, *Organization and Environment: Managing Differentiation and Integration* (Boston: Graduate School of Business Administration, Harvard University, 1967); M. Ajiferuke and J. Boddewyn, " 'Culture' and Other Explanatory Variables in Comparative Management Studies," *Academy of Management Journal* (June 1970): 153–63; R. Peccei and M. Warner, "Decision-Making in a Multinational Firm," *Journal of General Management* (1976): 66–71; and Franko, *The European Multinationals*.

[31] Anant R. Negandhi and B. R. Baliga, *Tables Are Turning: German and Japanese Multinational Companies in the United States* (Cambridge, Mass.: Oelgeschlager, Gunn & Hain, 1980).

more than autonomy: the parent's consideration of the subsidiary's viewpoints, even if informal, made a critical difference, increasing the subsidiary's ability to respond. They state: "In contrast to such apparent tension and misgivings between the managers of the U.S. subsidiaries and their head offices, the European and Japanese managers felt very comfortable in their relationship with their head offices. Although there was relatively far less formal reporting in the European and Japanese MNCs, the overseas managers felt that they were involved in and informed about the major strategic decisions undertaken back home and that their own voices and viewpoints were seriously considered in formulating major policies affecting their operations. They also felt they had considerable latitude in running their operations. In this respect, most of the American expatriate managers we interviewed felt that their role and duties were very narrowly defined; they were simply just another cog in the corporate machine."[32]

Furthermore, the parent relationship could transmit distinctive parent and home-country characteristics. For example, many scholars have pointed out that Japanese companies tend to extend their philosophy as well as the Ringi consensual decision-making system to their subsidiaries.[33] It has also been suggested that subsidiaries inherit a time orientation for their operations from their parents. For example, Negandhi concluded that Japanese and European subsidiaries have longer-term profit horizons (or payback periods) than their U.S. counterparts, confirming Vogel's conclusions on Japanese subsidiaries and Franko's on European.[34] However, the Japanese were perceived as being more cautious or slower.

Besides unintended parent influences, parents often have head-office staffs devoted to supporting their subsidiaries. When confronted with host-country issues, their role is to consult, recommend, and advise. Therefore, parent intervention in the subsidiary—whether it be ad hoc policy changes in crisis or day-to-day participation in policies—is a key variable influencing the subsidiary diagnosis of the LDC environment.

Therefore, many factors bearing on the subsidiary relationship to the host country and its parent could determine its ability to identify and respond before crisis to a changing LDC environment. It is submitted here that MNC subsidiaries that have (1) managers with considerable de-

[32] Negandhi and Baliga, *Tables Are Turning*, p. 13.

[33] See M. Yoshina, "Emerging Japanese Multinational Enterprises," in *Modern Japanese Organization and Decision-Making*, ed. E. F. Vogel (Berkeley: University of California Press, 1983); and Negandhi and Baliga, *Tables Are Turning*. Pascale, however, found little evidence of the Ringi system in Japanese subsidiaries located in the U.S. R. T. Pascale, "Communication and Decision-Making Across Cultures: Japanese and American Comparisons," *Administrative Science Quarterly* 23, no. 1 (March 1978): 99–109.

[34] Negandhi and Baliga, *Tables Are Turning*, p. 25.

cision-making authority, (2) close relationships with LDC actors, and (3) parents that support responsiveness, are likely to be at a competitive advantage in identifying and responding before crisis to a changing LDC environment. In our case studies we illustrate the importance of these characteristics, highlighting the central question: what are the implications of subsidiary relationships and decision roles for pre-crisis response?

The Degree of Conflict

The second aspect of policy reformulation examined is the degree of conflict between the subsidiary and the host country at the point of crisis. The argument is that the degree of conflict is not uniform for subsidiaries, but varies as a function of differing subsidiary characteristics, related to the subsidiary's historical policy performance, the pressuring group's perception of the subsidiary, and parent interests. (See figure 1–4.)

First, subsidiary policies differ significantly in whether they conflict with the LDC group's objectives, and if so, the degree to which they conflict. The LDC pressuring group discriminates on the basis of subsidiary policies, targeting those subsidiaries with policies relatively more out-of-line with their demands. Second, the LDC group also perceives differences between subsidiaries in terms of their capacity to respond as

FIGURE 1–4
Key Variables Determining Degree of Conflict between MNC Subsidiary and LDC Group

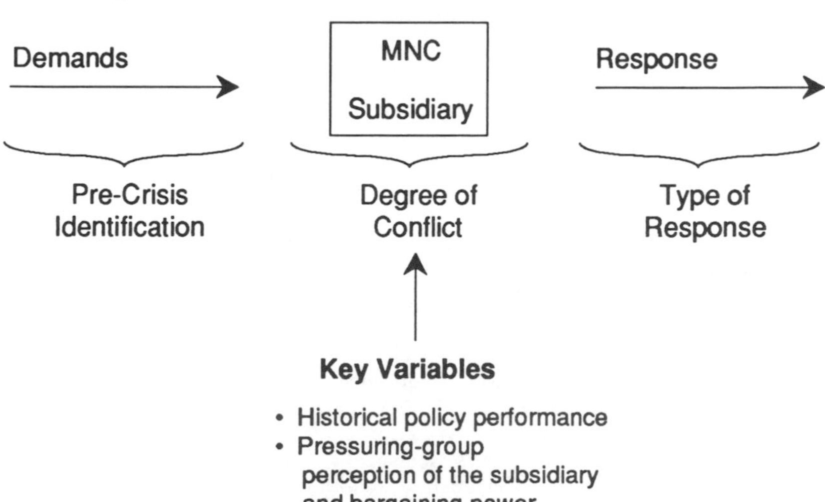

well as their overall value. Third, a parent's particular interests can become a key distinguishing factor.

The parent can increase or decrease the pressure felt by the subsidiary; the subsidiary is, in effect, potentially sandwiched between the parent and the LDC group. If the parent reinforces the subsidiary's stance, the subsidiary will be under less pressure. Parents and subsidiaries, however, do not always agree on the correct stance. If a home-country group linked to the parent joins forces with the LDC group against the subsidiary, or if the subsidiary agrees with the pressuring group in conflict with the parent, the degree of conflict escalates for the subsidiary.

Parent interests may be driven by home-country pressures, the parent philosophy, and its overall strategy. Pressure can also originate from within the subsidiary and the MNC structure itself. In crisis, the standard routinized parent-subsidiary relationship disintegrates, as parent and associated interest groups intervene.[35] This phenomenon underlines the importance of studying dynamic cases, which turn expected outcomes based on static observations upside down.

The degree of conflict, therefore, is not solely a function of the external environment, but of the interaction between the subsidiary and its environment, including its parent and home country, over time. In the case studies in this volume, these propositions are tested: At crisis, does the degree of conflict differ between subsidiaries? And if so: (1) Does historical policy performance make a difference? (2) Do the LDC group's perceptions of the subsidiary matter? (3) Do parent interests affect the pressure on subsidiary policies?

Type of Subsidiary Response

The third aspect of policy reformulation examined is the outcome: the type of subsidiary response. The argument is that subsidiary responses vary according to characteristics related to parent preferences, subsidiary relationships with LDC groups, and the first policy responses set forth. (See figure 1–5.)

Despite the degree of parent-subsidiary autonomy, the parent is likely to impose its own preferences, intentionally or unintentionally, on the subsidiary. Parent preferences may be a function of the parent's own involvement in designing the subsidiary's response. The subsidiary may adopt parent practices or be influenced by the parent's philosophy con-

[35] The literature on decision-making in MNCs documents how parent influence on subsidiary policies varies according to the type of policy in question and supports the view that a subsidiary's parent has the greatest influence in areas related to the parent strategy, such as investment strategy, and the least in local policies adapted to the local environment, such as labor relations. For example, see Robinson, *International Business Management*.

FIGURE 1–5
Key Variables Determining Subsidiary Response to LDC Demands

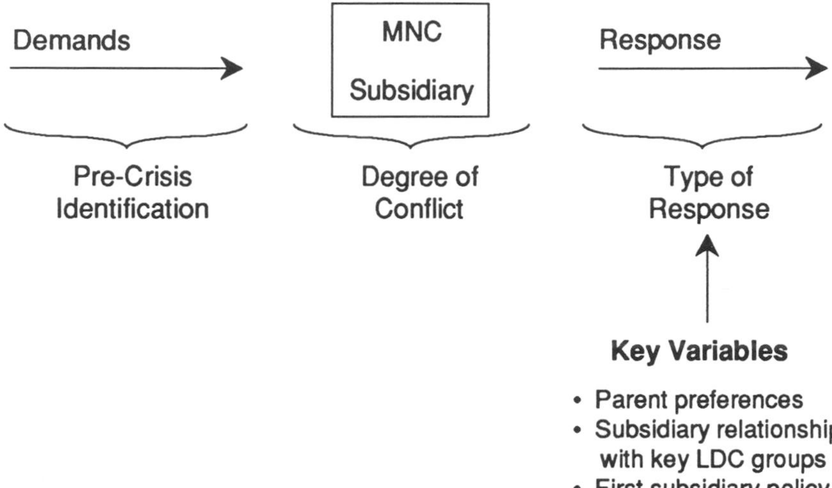

cerning the proper response. The parent may also have preferences that are imposed by its own external environment and, in effect, act as a vehicle for home-country pressures that shape subsidiary response.

Second, the subsidiary's immediate environment and its particular position within that environment influence its response. The nature of the subsidiary's relationships with key LDC groups affects its willingness to adopt the advocated changes. Subsidiaries may become captive to relationships they have nurtured over the years and lose flexibility in shaping their own policy response.

The competitive structure is also a key factor: just as there are price and quality leaders that set the parameters for industry-wide strategies, policy "response leaders" set the parameters for the policy responses of other subsidiaries. While separate research has confirmed the interactive effects of industry behavior, responsiveness to host-country demands as a competitive factor has not been explored. Several scholars, however, have noted the role of excessive competition in increasing host-government bargaining power.[36] Here we focus on the subsidiaries themselves

[36] For example, concerned with offsetting country risk in project vulnerability assessment, Moran identified key variables of projects constituting strength or weakness: the size of the required fixed investment, the technology, the importance of product differentiation via advertising, vertical integration, and the extent of competition. Theodore H. Moran, "International Political Risk Assessment, Corporate Planning and Strategies to Offset Polit-

and submit that the subsidiary that responds first (the "response leader") to host-country demands elicits a burgeoning phenomenon: other subsidiaries follow with defensive policy adaptation. The "response leader" sets the pattern for the defensive policy adaptation of other subsidiaries, potentially gaining competitive advantage.[37]

In the case studies, we will examine the propositions: Do parent preferences affect subsidiary response? How does the subsidiary's relationships with key LDC groups affect its response? Do certain subsidiaries take the role of "response leaders," and what is the impact on the other subsidiaries?

To illustrate the arguments two case studies are presented—the Brazilian automotive industry faced with local labor demands, and the Mexican automotive industry faced with host-government demands. Each case study is discussed in three sequential chapters which cover, first, the historical mapping of the automotive industry within the country, then the development of each subsidiary's policies, and finally, each subsidiary's organization and relationships. These chapters follow the arguments in sequence, for Brazil and Mexico respectively, from a macrohistorical examination illuminating our first argument (Chapters 2 and 5) to a microcomparison of subsidiaries for the second argument that is historical (Chapters 3 and 6) and then structural (Chapters 4 and 7). The conclusion (Chapter 8) suggests implications for MNC managers and LDC groups.

---

ical Risk," in *Managing International Political Risk*, Fariborz Ghadar et al., eds., pp. 158–66.

[37] This is not unlike the notions set forth by Knickerbocker and Kindleberger for the foreign investment process. Frederick T. Knickerbocker, *Oligopolistic Reaction and Multinational Enterprise*, (Boston: Harvard University School of Business, 1973). Charles Kindleberger, *American Business Abroad: Six Lectures on Direct Investment* (New Haven: Yale University Press, 1969). Also, see Marvin B. Lieberman and David B. Montgomery, "First-Mover Advantages," *Strategic Management Journal* 9 (1988): 41–58.

PART 1

Host-Country Group Demands and Subsidiary Response: The Case of the Brazilian Automotive Industry

CHAPTER 2

MNCs within a Changing Sociopolitical Environment

MULTINATIONALS, by definition, operate in differing national environments, which due to their very nature, inevitably undergo social and political changes. Typically, the MNC faced with a changing sociopolitical environment considers only a narrow range of economic and political issues, analyzing these external factors constituting so-called country risk with a removed and generalized macro-oriented approach. This approach to analyzing industry environments is, we argue, piecemeal at best, often misleading, and represents a potential liability in the process of defining and implementing global competitive strategies. Any comprehensive analysis must be interactive and dynamic, encompassing the role of the MNC itself within the particular country's development process and focusing on specific subsidiary characteristics. The often forgotten reality is that MNCs themselves may create the conditions for change, their behavior shaping the type and level of conflict with the host country. In short, country risks and host-country benefits are a function of individual MNC characteristics and behavior within the specific context of a country's economic and sociopolitical environment.

In this chapter the sufficiency of the generalized country-risk approach is challenged by examining a case study of five MNC subsidiaries in the same industry and facing the same threat: increased labor demands. We examine the overall evolution of labor demands and the role of the subsidiaries: was the emergence of this country risk a truly independent and mysterious phenomenon or did the subsidiaries themselves participate inadvertently in the very creation of that risk? These labor demands did not, in fact, represent a uniform risk for *all* MNC subsidiaries operating in the country; why were demands targeted specifically on these five subsidiaries? Furthermore, how did the responses of these specific subsidiaries, in turn, affect the evolution of labor demands within the country?

In the two subsequent chapters we will move from macro to micro, contrasting how each of the five MNC subsidiaries behaved during the same time period. First, each subsidiary's ability to read its shared environment is evaluated: Before the crisis, were there differences in detecting the oncoming future conflict? If so, why? Second, we consider whether the subsidiaries were equally vulnerable to labor demands: at the point of crisis, were there differentiating subsidiary characteristics that accounted for differing degrees of conflict with labor? Finally, in terms of outcome, the responses of the subsidiaries are compared: Who did what and why? Why did subsidiaries in the same industry facing the same host-country demands have different responses? What were the implications for them and the host country?

The Case

The MNC Subsidiaries

In 1978, when the first massive outbreak of strikes in over fifteen years occurred in Brazil, the five automotive subsidiaries under consideration had been operating in Brazil for more than two decades. The American subsidiaries of *Ford* and *General Motors* entered earliest in the years 1919 and 1925 respectively, followed by the European subsidiaries of *Mercedes Benz* and *Volkswagen* (Germany) in 1953 and *Saab* (Sweden) in 1957. The major manufacturing plants of the subsidiaries were clustered in the industrial suburbs of São Paulo, a small area known as the ABC area.[1] In 1979 these five MNC subsidiaries as a group accounted for 85 percent of total vehicle production in the Brazilian automotive industry.

The Host Country

The sociopolitical environment in Brazil had been undergoing dramatic changes since 1974.[2] National groups such as the opposition political party, labor, and the Catholic Church publicly demonstrated against the authoritarian military government installed in 1964 and advanced ideas promoting the democratization of Brazil. In 1977 the military government announced a policy of *abertura*, or political liberalization: government policies would be liberalized and the country would be prepared for a return to democracy. Reforms included the end of press censorship, the return of political exiles, and increased citizen participation in general elections.

Political liberalization in Brazil was accompanied by new social forces

[1] The ABC area includes the towns of Santo André, São Bernardo do Campo, São Caetano, and Diadema.

[2] In the congressional elections of November 1974, the opposition party, Movimento Democratico Brasileiro (MDB) made sweeping gains. The MDB called for an end to military government. See Peter Flynn, *Brazil: A Political Analysis* (Boulder, Colo.: Westview Press, 1978), p. 475.

demanding a greater sharing of economic benefits.[3] This included the open questioning of government policies on labor relations. Confrontation between outspoken labor leaders and hard-line military leaders was inevitable.

The battlefield for this historic confrontation in Brazil was the foreign-owned automotive industry. The subsidiaries of the major automotive multinationals became the national targets of labor unrest, criticism from political opposition groups, and pressure from the military government. In 1978 the largest strike in over fifteen years started at the Saab-Scania do Brasil automotive plant and signaled the beginning of a new era of widespread labor unrest. Riding the crest of the political liberalization process, the labor movement, in concert with opposition forces, challenged the military government. Since then, the automotive industry has been the central target for labor strikes, with the longest strike in Brazilian history (forty-one days) occurring in 1980 and reportedly costing the automotive industry U.S. $444 million in lost sales. (See figure 2–1.)

As a result of this conflict, the automotive subsidiaries finally complied with labor's demands for union-based worker-representation systems; acting as "levers for change," the subsidiaries heralded the introduction of new labor practices, bringing about fundamental change in Brazilian labor relations. The automotive industry had been swept into the transitional forces of social change. In 1985 the military government's *abertura* policy of political liberalization was concluded, and after twenty-one years of military rule, Brazil returned to democracy under a civilian government. The very lawyer who had represented the striking unions against the military government and the automotive subsidiaries was appointed Minister of Labor. The tables had turned: labor was being courted by the civilian government in Brazil's new democracy.

THE CHANGING SOCIOPOLITICAL ENVIRONMENT

Clearly, the Brazilian environment in which the automotive subsidiaries operate had undergone significant political changes. This chapter discusses the evolution of Brazilian labor demands on the automotive industry and illustrates the first main argument: *country risk does not evolve*

[3] On 25 January 1979 the Minister of Finance, Mario Henrique Simonsen, announced in-coming President Figuereido's goal of *abertura econômica* (economic liberalization) as "one of the direct consequences of political liberalization" (author's translation). "Simonsen define a abertura econômica," *O Estado de São Paulo*, 26 Jan. 1979, p. 1. As stated by the noted Brazilian economist Geraldo Carlos Langoni, "These modifications would enlarge the responsiveness of the economic system to the legitimate aspirations of the different social groups." Geraldo Carlos Langoni, "Decentralization and Development," *Econômia Brasileira e Suas Perspectivas* XVII (Rio de Janeiro: APEC Editora S.A., Aug. 1978): 175–84.

FIGURE 2–1
The Brazilian Automotive Industry: Production and Strikes, 1978–1980

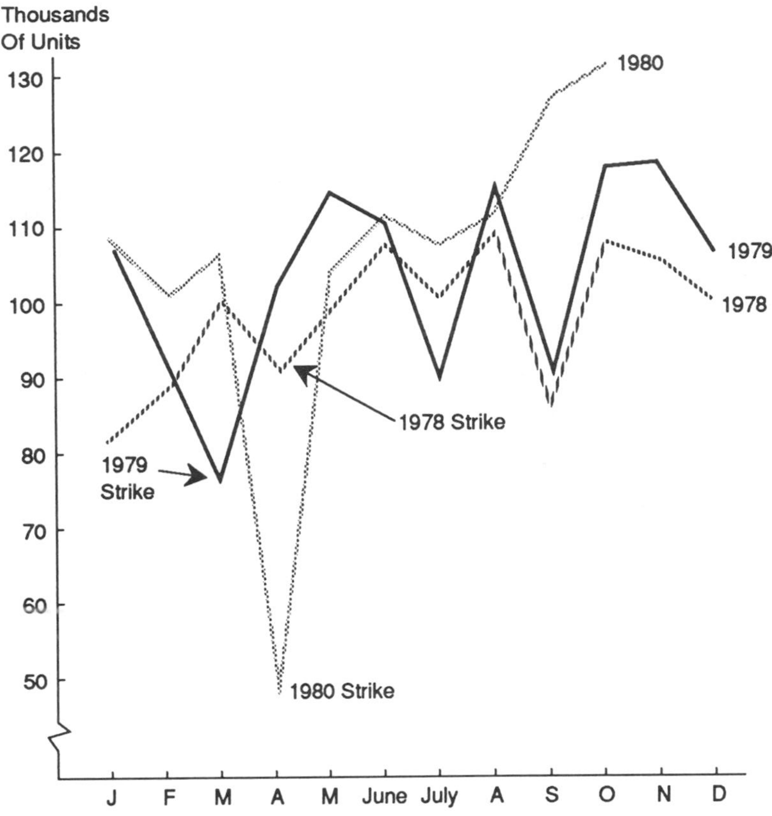

Source: ANFAVEA.

independently from MNCs, but rather is the result of interaction between LDC groups and MNCs themselves. Specific groups of MNC subsidiaries help to create the conditions for social change. As a result, specific policies of theirs are singled out for targeting by interest groups. Which policy is targeted and by whom is a function of the country's particular development process and whether key LDC groups perceive particular MNC subsidiary policies as advancing their objectives. At the point of outward conflict, an individual subsidiary breaks from the pack and acts as a "response leader," taking policy actions that will affect the evolution of future demands and determine the range of responses of other subsidiaries, and in so doing charts a course which will have a potentially significant impact on that particular issue for the entire country.

In the Brazilian automotive industry, the MNC subsidiaries themselves inadvertedly created the conditions for increased labor demands. The targeting of this industry was not chance but a logical outcome of specific subsidiary behavior and characteristics within the context of Brazil's development process. The following sections illustrate this view, mapping the evolution of Brazilian labor demands, then concluding with the actual MNC-LDC conflict—the outbreak of strikes and the responses of the MNC subsidiaries.

Industry Adaptation to the Environment

The foreign-owned automotive industry never intended to be innovative in Brazilian labor relations. Yet the industry created the conditions for change. The MNC subsidiaries could not deny what they were: modern international organizations with different values and production modes imported from their home countries—but operating in a developing country where they would inevitably create modern workers with modern demands.

The explicit labor policy of the MNC subsidiaries had been to conform to policies practiced in the host country. Historically, policy adaptation in the area of industrial relations had been practiced by the automotive subsidiaries in ways not dissimilar to locally owned firms. The subsidiaries had developed government contacts, participated in the employers' association of the industry, and exchanged information on industrial-relations policies. Not one of the five subsidiaries had a labor-relations function, as was customary in the parent organization. Instead, modeled after local Brazilian firms, industrial relations were dominated by the personnel, legal affairs, and security departments, the main activities being legal representation in the law courts and the maintenance of security forces throughout the plant. The narrow involvement of both national and foreign companies in labor relations had been due to extensive legislation by the Brazilian government outlining major aspects of such employee issues as wages, benefits, training, grievance procedures, and strike activity.

However, Brazil's foreign-owned automotive industry had generally conformed to the pattern of MNCs in LDCs by providing benefits and wages superior to those of national companies.[4] For example, as shown

[4] Many studies have shown that MNC subsidiaries in LDCs tend to provide higher wages and more benefits than national companies. For example, in a worldwide analysis of the textile industry, the US Tariff Commission reported significantly lower labor costs for national firms than for MNC subsidiaries. U.S. Congress, Senate, *Implications of Multinational Firms for World Trade and Investment and for U.S. Trade and Labor: Report to Committee on Finance* (Washington, D.C.: GPO, 1973), pp. 765, 803. Also, see Obei G. Wichard, "Employment and Employee Compensation of U.S. Multinational Companies in 1977," *Survey of Current Business* (Feb. 1982): 37–50.

FIGURE 2–2
Distribution by Income Groups: The Total Brazilian Work Force and Automotive Industry Work Force in 1980

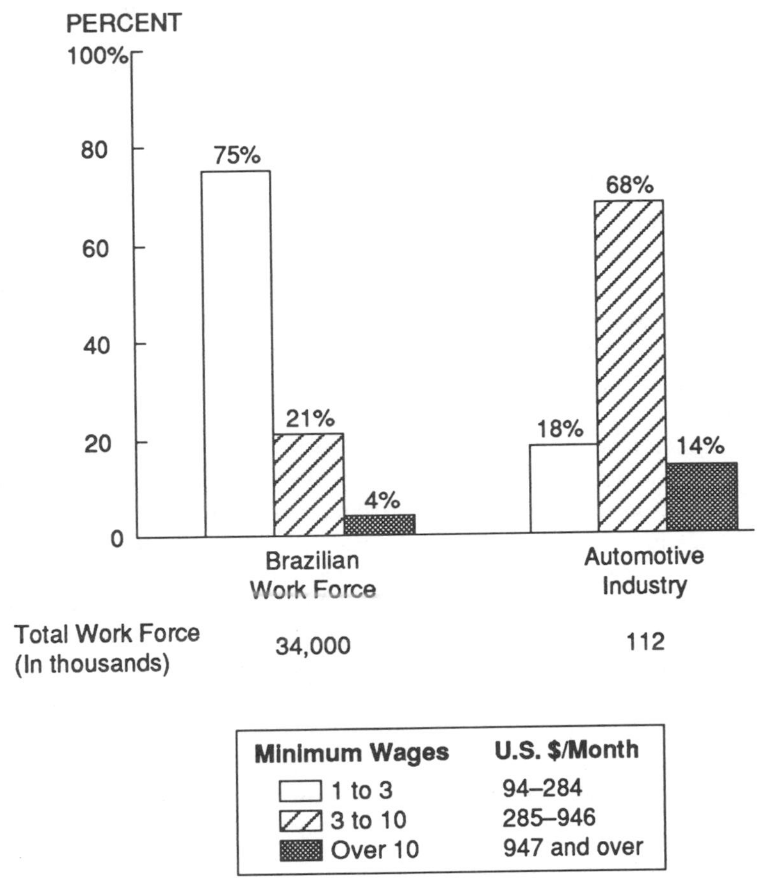

Source: Compiled by the author on the basis of information given by the subsidiaries.

in figure 2–2, in 1980 while 75 percent of Brazilian workers earned 1 to 3 minimum wages a month (U.S. $94–U.S. $284), 68 percent of the automotive workers earned between 3 to 10 wages (U.S. $285–U.S. $946).[5] In terms of benefits, the average for the automotive industry was also significantly above (21 percent) the national average. The degree of unionization in the MNC subsidiaries was also higher than in most na-

[5] The exchange rate in 1980 was fifty cruzeiros per U.S. dollar (compiled by the author based on information provided by the automotive subsidiaries).

tional firms, varying from a low of 26 percent (Volkswagen) to a high of 39 percent (General Motors) in 1980. Union membership was still a novelty throughout most of Brazil, however, and paternalistic employment practices dominated.[6]

Indeed, the MNC subsidiaries, particularly the automotive, introduced the preconditions for disintegrating the traditional paternalistic practices with collective worker organization. While the automotive subsidiaries had largely followed the practices of national firms, their industrial-relations policies had distinctly multinational characteristics—in addition to superior wages and benefits, modern management practices eroded traditional paternalism.[7] Because the plants were large, employees were concentrated and worked together collectively. As a result, Brazilian workers came to have not only higher expectations of the labor policies of the automotive subsidiaries but also the means to forcefully make demands. The modern automotive industry by its very nature provided a natural birthplace for labor unrest.

The Brazilian Industrial-Relations System

The corporatist labor structure was specified in the labor law of 1939, modeled on the labor system of fascist Italy and introduced in Brazil under the "Estado Novo" dictatorship of Getulio Vargas. The Estado Novo

[6] Aggregate data on Brazilian national firms is not available. However, multiple studies confirm the widespread absence of union members in national firms. (Union data on the automotive industry provided by the automotive subsidiaries in this study.)

[7] Humphrey stated the case well: "The modern factory is not merely modern because of the technology that it uses but because of its management practices. In the case of the [Brazilian] auto industry, the uniqueness of its role in the development of industrial relations and trade unionism was attributable to both use-value aspects (the size of the plants, the concentration of workers, and the nature of the work performed) and exchange-value aspects (the pressure for productivity and cost control) of production. . . . This resulted in a specific pattern of organization of work and control of labor which broke down paternalism and encouraged collective workers' resistance." John Humphrey, *Capitalist Control and Worker's Struggle in the Brazilian Auto Industry* (Princeton: Princeton University Press, 1982), pp. 99, 219.

The lawyer for the São Bernardo Union who later became the Minister of Labor for the new civilian government, Amir Pazzianotto, also explained the phenomenon: "The automobile worker is different from other workers. He is acutely conscious of his importance in the production process and acts with substantial independence. I know of workers who, after working twenty-five years at Nitroquímica, come and make twice as much at Volkswagen. It is natural that these workers learn to value their real importance. . . . I believe that many of the differences are dictated by the type of industry established in São Bernardo. *They are modern businesses in which the worker acquires more easily a consciousness of his value.*" Author translation with emphasis added, from "Um Doutor em Greves," *Veja* (21 May 1980): 6.

For a discussion of worker expectations, see Humphrey, *Capitalist Control*, p. 76.

period ended in 1945, and successive governments differed greatly in their use of the corporatist structure and control system. During the period of open political competition (1945–1964), many of the control measures were not used. However, when the military assumed control in 1964, the control measures were again implemented, and hundreds of militant and radical labor leaders were removed from office. The Labor Party was abolished along with all other parties.

As is common in LDCs, the Brazilian government was carefully controlling wage increases, strike activity, and contact between employers and employees. On the negotiation level, all contracts between unions and employers were officially controlled through specified legal procedures involving interaction between the Minister of Labor and Social Welfare, the Ministry of Finance, the judicial courts, government-paid lawyers, and employer and worker organizations.[8] The Labor Court System (*Justiça do Trabalho*), as the official conflict-resolution mechanism of the Brazilian industrial-relations system, performed most of the functions associated in the United States with collective bargaining and handling grievances.

Labor court decisions and collective contracts were limited almost exclusively to wage issues. Hours, working conditions, and fringe benefits were regulated in great detail in the labor law. The issue with greatest potential for mobilizing Brazilian workers was higher wages. On the first of May every year, the Brazilian government announced an increase in the minimum wage that allegedly was intended to match the inflation rate.

However, in 1975 the Union's research organization, Departamento Intersindical de Estatística e Estudos Sócio-Econômicos (DIEESE), published a study that claimed significant decreases in real wages: the government's adjustments to the minimum wage were far below the actual inflation rate. In fact, between 1964 and 1966 the military government engineered a 28.5 percent decline in the average real value of the minimum wage. Real wages in 1974 were roughly only 70 percent of the 1964 level.[9] In 1977 unions publicly accused the government of manipulating

[8] For more details on these relationships, see Maria Helena Moreira Alves, "Reformation of the National Security State: The State and the Opposition in Military Brazil" (Ph.D. diss., Massachussets Institute of Technology, 1982); Humphrey, *Capitalist Control*; Kenneth S. Mericle, "Conflict Regulation in the Brazilian Industrial Relations System" (Ph.D. diss., University of Wisconsin, 1974); and idem, "Corporatist Control of the Working Class: Authoritarian Brazil since 1964," in *Authoritarianism and Corporatism in Latin America*, ed. James Malloy (Pittsburgh: University of Pittsburgh Press, 1977).

[9] Departamento Intersindical de Estatística e Estudos Sócio-Econômicos (DIEESE), "Estudos Sócio-Econômicos: Dez Anos de Política Salarial," São Paulo (Aug. 1975). The study claims that the real wages of São Paulo metalworkers in 1974 were 74 percent of their 1964 level (p. 60). DIEESE also claimed that the 1978 minimum wage was sufficient only

cost-of-living index figures and of deliberately decreasing the value of real wages.

The government, however, had been very careful in setting official policies that deflated wage demands. Until October 1979 the fixed formula used by the Ministry of Finance in determining the National Wage Policy had included terms of trade, monetary correction, and productivity as well as rates of historic and expected inflation.[10] Some of the inputs, such as the historic inflation index, were state secrets, while others, such as productivity, were fixed officially. Beginning on 1 November 1979 the government adjusted wages semiannually on the basis of the National Index for Consumer Prices (INPC). Once a year, the parties negotiated a real productivity increase which was added to the INPC stipulated semiannual increase. If the parties failed to reach an agreement on the productivity increase, the case was referred to the Labor Courts which set a percentage. Collective bargaining was thus systematically controlled by key governmental bodies in the formulation of national policies.

The Brazilian government had traditionally held great power over strike activity and considered it as an act of aggression punishable with imprisonment. For example, the Constitution of 1937 prohibited strikes as being incompatible with the "superior interests of national production."[11] According to Article 723 of the Labor Law, all strikes were to be authorized first by the Regional Labor Court. Penalties for unauthorized strikes included suspension or firing of striking workers, removal of union leadership from office, fines for the union, and cancellation of the union's registration. After 1964, labor courts only authorized strikes if an employer had not paid workers' salaries for an extended period of time or if an employer had failed to conform to court-established salary levels. Political and solidarity strikes were illegal. Behavior during strikes was regulated and explicitly forbade sit-downs, sabotage, aggressive picketing, and the blockage of nonstriking workers. Workers found guilty of such behavior could be fined or criminally prosecuted.

In the Ministry of Labor and Social Welfare, the major agency responsible for policymaking and direct intervention in conflict situations was the Ministry's National Department of Labor, which performed a law-enforcement function and mediated labor-management disputes. Most

---

to pay for 70 percent of a subsistence diet for one person. For an analysis of the Brazilian government's labor and wage policy, see Mericle, "Conflict Regulation."

[10] In 1978 the Finance Minister, then Mario Henrique Simonsen, attributed the success of wage policy to the fact that "wage levels are not decided by pressures and strikes but by a rapid mathematical calculation." Quoted in "Brazilian Regime Stores up Labour Movement Trouble," *Latin America Economic Report* VI, no. 18 (12 May 1978): 144.

[11] Article 139 of the 1937 Constitution of the United States of Brazil. Araujo Castro, *A Constituição de 1937* (São Paulo: Editora Freitas Bastos, 1941), pp. 407, 561.

visible, however, was the Minister, who usually served as the official spokesman and negotiator for the government. In this way, labor relations were controlled by the government, with little unregulated dialogue between workers and firms on wage increases or other labor-relations issues.

Strike History and the Automotive Industry before 1978

While Brazil passed through different political stages, the government had been generally successful in using repressive methods to maintain control. A tradition of paternalism, rather than collective action, dominated company employee relations. However, there were specific indicators pointing to probable change. First, before the military regime was established, there had been numerous strikes in the São Paulo as well as other industrial areas. Furthermore, during the military regime, there had been political strikes that indicated a significant strengthening in worker organization. With the military regime's promise of political liberalization and a return to democracy, its continued willingness to employ repressive methods was not certain.

Strikes in the São Paulo industrial area of the automotive industry had occured before the imposition of military rule in 1964. A study of firms located in the ABC area during the period from 1955 to 1961 revealed that nearly all of the local unions for manufacturing industries had called strikes. A few solidarity strikes had occurred during this period. Indeed, a 1963 study reported that 60 percent of São Paulo's union members believed that solidarity strikes should be permitted.[12] Most of the industrial unions in São Paulo had joined a massive strike in 1963.[13]

State repression had been common against both economic and political strikes throughout the 1950s and early 1960s. Repressive acts had included physical intimidation, infiltration of union meetings, armed occupations of union facilities, and mass arrests of union leaders and strikers. In response, labor leadership had developed nonofficial labor organizations. However, these nonofficial bodies had no direct link with the rank and file and were therefore incapable of organizing workers effectively.[14]

Also, because of the nature of the working class itself—most of the workers were of rural origin, passive, individualistic, and uneducated—

[12] J. V. Freitas Marcondes, *Radiografia da Liderança Sindical Paulista* (São Paulo: Instituto Cultural do Trabalho, 1964), p. 72, as cited in Mericle, "Conflict Regulation."

[13] Kenneth P. Erickson, *The Brazilian Corporative State and Working-Class Politics* (Berkeley: University of California Press, 1977).

[14] Mericle, "Conflict Regulation," p. 120.

its members had difficulty articulating their interest in union issues. In a study of a São Paulo factory in 1957, Lopes found that 64.3 percent of the workers were migrants from the Northeast of Brazil, the states surrounding São Paulo, and the interior of the state of São Paulo.[15] An automobile factory studied in 1963 by Rodrigues reported that 53 percent of semi- and unskilled workers and 17 percent of skilled workers had had previous jobs in agriculture. Thirty-six percent of his sample had not completed primary education.[16]

These studies also suggested workers had low levels of union identification, solidarity, and confidence in the efficacy of strikes. One contributing factor was the lack of labor organization at the shop level.[17] A second related factor was the cultural mode defining workers' traditional bonds with paternalistic employers: the social hierarchy was accepted as valid and any opposition was deemed illegitimate.[18] Thus, union leadership had had to convince the rank and file of its authority. Political figures and other opinion leaders were recruited to participate in union activities, particularly picketing, in order to provide protection against repression and to enhance the union's authority with workers.

Primarily because of workers' passivity, unions relied on using pickets on large firms within concentrated industrial areas. First, halting a large firm's production was an important accomplishment. It increased the union's bargaining power with the employers' association and the courts and had great symbolic value. By halting a large firm, the spread of the strike to other firms was more likely. Second, firms in concentrated industrial areas with large working-class neighborhoods were more attractive targets for spreading strikes and, therefore, more strike-prone than isolated factories. Location was a key variable.

After the military takeover in 1964, there was an almost complete halt in strike activity as the military took immediate steps to repress those labor leaders who had been active. All militant union leaders were removed from office, the Labor Party was abolished along with all other political parties, and the labor-control legislation in the labor codes was reimplemented. The military also issued a decree regulating the right to

[15] Juarez R. B. Lopes, *Sociedade Industrial no Brasil* (São Paulo: Difusão Européia do Livro, 1968), p. 94, as cited in Mericle, "Conflict Regulation," p. 212.

[16] Leoncio M. Rodrigues, *Industrialização e Atitudes Operárias* (São Paulo: Editora Brasileira, 1970), p. 56.

[17] Lopes, *Sociedade Industrial*, as cited in Mericle, "Conflict Regulation," p. 80.

[18] Lopes explained the issue well: "What predominates among workers is a remoteness from class problems, an absence of the tradition of collective action, of united and open opposition to the authority of those who occupy dominant positions in the social hierarchy. Thus, in order that the authority of management be challenged, the challenge must be made by another 'authority,' that of the union leadership." Lopes, *Sociedade Industrial*, as cited in Mericle, "Conflict Regulation," p. 214.

strike and giving the federal government extensive power to intervene in all strikes. Political and solidarity strikes continued to be illegal, with legal strikes limited to contract-enforcement disputes in which wage clauses were being violated or whenever a firm was delinquent in wage payments.

In 1968, however, there were two important strike movements—important because they indicated the emergence of worker organization previously lacking and required for successful strikes. The military police were needed to repress these strikes. The first, organized in the state of Minais Gerais, involved the rank and file in such activities as picketing. The second wave of strikes began in the city of Osasco, an industrial community bordering on São Paulo. This movement differed from the pre-1964 strikes in that the rank and file had organized themselves at the factory level and demanded an end to specific government economic policies and the antistrike law. Both strike movements were given significant support by the middle class and students.

In sum, during the military regime strike activity that would disrupt production had been largely contained by the Brazilian conflict-regulation system. However, before the military regime, between 1960 and 1964, there had been significant strike activity, largely concentrated in the most industrialized area of Brazil, where the automotive subsidiaries were located. Obviously, the firms had been expected to support the government's repression of labor activity and to refrain from any divergent response. Strike activity did not seem to be a function of the individual company's personnel policies; a firm's proneness to strikes depended on its visibility and the ability of the local union. The strike movements in 1968, however, had been very significant, indicating that in a period of political liberalization it would be more difficult to repress strikes, and that a different employee-employer relationship might result.

Industry-Environment Integration

The automotive industry had been closely integrated with the Brazilian labor environment and local policies in industrial relations. Subsidiaries, in their relationships with the environment, went through three specific stages of development. First, strong individual relationships with the government predominated before manufacturing legislation in 1956. After 1956 coordination within the industry developed with the establishment of an industry association (ANFAVEA) and the organization of national firms as auto-parts suppliers. Finally, since 1974 the harmonious industry relationship with the government has been severed, and the automotive industry has increased the use of its industry association and its federation (FIESP) in government lobbying.[19] The automotive industry has entered a period of development where effective government lobbying requires more extensive contact with national firms, the industry association, and business groups.

The previous closeness of the automotive industry with the Brazilian government had been based on extensive interaction which had determined the nature and structure of the automotive industry itself. The Brazilian government had played a very large role in developing the automotive industry into one of the most dominant sectors of its economy. From 1956 to 1960 government decrees had prohibited automobile imports and had prompted foreign investors to decide instead to manufacture locally. As a result of this governmental intervention, the automotive subsidiaries transformed their Latin American sales, service, and assembly operations into full-fledged manufacturing facilities. Governmental pressures towards vertical integration had succeeded in separating the automotive industry into two distinct product groups—a foreign-dominated one of finished vehicles and a national-dominated group producing vehicle parts and accessories.

All of the subsidiaries in our study reported that individual contact between subsidiary management and the host-country government was extensive. The most extreme case was one managing director who claimed to have spent 55 percent of his time lobbying the government and meeting with his staff on government-related issues.[20] Several executives from different subsidiaries felt that a significant component of the automotive industry–government relationship was the exchange of information on workers and related developments. In three of the five subsidiaries included in the study, ex-members of the military or the government had been employed or had occupied important positions in the area of security. Likewise, many of the industrial-relations staff interviewed referred to the importance of government, military, and business contacts in maintaining correct up-to-date information on both worker and government actions.

The most important group in government lobbying was undoubtedly ANFAVEA, the association of the automotive industry. Because this was the official organization, its members were required by law to present

[19] The *Federação das Indústrias do Estado de São Paulo* (FIESP) was the official representative of all the employers' associations in the state of São Paulo. While for all pratical purposes ANFAVEA was the center of automotive collaboration on all issues (including labor), the official and legally constituted vehicle-producers' union—and member of FIESP—was SINFAVEA (Sindicato Nacional da Indústria de Tratores, Caminhões, Automóveis, e Veículos Similares).

[20] Questionnaires were given to each managing director of the automotive subsidiaries in the study.

industry-related issues or requests to the government through official ANFAVEA channels. A subsidiary document in the study explained the creation of ANFAVEA as resulting from "the country's continuous industrial evolution. . . . Employers were forced together in order to face the ever-increasing demands made by trade unions in addition to being represented before the governmental entities."[21] Examples of various continuing issues through the years were: pricing, import quotas, export programs, personnel policies, and the production of vehicles that would run on alcohol.

Personal contacts with the government became progressively less effective in lobbying, especially after the beginning of the 1970s. Top management interviewed in our study at two of the subsidiaries attributed recent difficulty in lobbying by individual firms to changes in the government's objectives and attitudes. Possible explanations given were: (1) the effects of industrialization on the creation of less-personalized business-government relations, (2) the pressure of national groups and public opinion on the government, and (3) specifically, the impact of the then-current oil crisis on Brazil and the resulting visibility of the automotive industry. Despite different viewpoints, executives agreed that it was generally more difficult to deal effectively with the Brazilian government on a personal basis. The increased importance of ANFAVEA in government lobbying is illustrated by the active participation of the major subsidiaries on its board of directors since 1974.

Using ANFAVEA as a rallying point, the subsidiaries acted as a group in adopting policies in areas such as industrial relations. The association provided a forum for the exchange of information on specific policies between firms and on the formulation of industry policies. As one subsidiary document explains, "in matters affecting a specific group of represented companies, the Industry Association has always shown the advantages of adopting common actions by the companies involved."[22] In each firm, the directors and staff members of areas such as public relations and industrial relations participated regularly in policy-area discussion groups.

ANFAVEA and the individual subsidiaries relied on several information sources for developing and testing industrial-relations policies compatible with national firms, their suppliers, and the government. Besides studies done by ANFAVEA and the subsidiaries themselves, the government and other associations analyzed in detail the industry and individual firms in terms of turnover, wages, and employee transfers. One association, the Associação Brasileira de Administração de Pessoal, provided

[21] Quoted directly from a document supplied by one of the subsidiaries.

[22] Quoted directly from a document supplied by a subsidiary in the study.

quarterly analyses of industries by geograpahical region and sector. In addition, individual firms did annual wage surveys.

The subsidiaries also reported regular direct contact with the government, state companies, national firms, their suppliers, and the other subsidiaries in the automotive industry, on two levels—through personal contacts and by association. Industrial-relations policies might be the subject of a telephone conversation or a group meeting. All of the subsidiaries had industrial-relations staffs who were members of industrial-relations groups. Certain groups in particular were considered valuable since membership included key government officials and national firms: the subsidiaries could get not only information on other firms' policies but also feedback on their own policy ideas.[23]

The Industry in Isolation: Political Change

Although the automotive subsidiaries maintained close ties as a group through their industry association (ANFAVEA) and had had extensive contacts with the government, neither individual subsidiaries nor their industry association had cultivated close relationships with national groups such as unions, opposition political parties, or the Catholic Church. This fact was significant in a changing sociopolitical environment with shifts in the allegiances and power of interest groups and the resulting impact on the power structure.

Political liberalization in Brazil meant the end of official censorship and more open communication between national groups as well as with groups outside the country. National groups, such as opposition political parties and the Catholic Church, organized in support of labor. Also, groups outside the country, such as foreign labor unions, supported Brazilian unions with training, funds, and company information. Antigovernment national groups strongly associated the automotive industry with the military government and publicized that perception to their memberships and to supportive groups outside the country.

In 1978 the most massive strike in Brazilian history occurred in the São Paulo industrial area where the automotive industry was concentrated. In response to the strikes, one automotive subsidiary defined the problem in a company document which read in part:

—unions without leadership but firm objectives
—employers unprepared with undefined objectives
Which route?[24]

[23] Information obtained in author interviews with subsidiary management.

[24] Quoted directly from a document supplied by a subsidiary in the study.

There was general consensus in the automotive industry that the automotive unions had prepared themselves exceptionally well over the last few years, while the automotive subsidiaries and the business community in general had "undefined objectives" as to how to respond.

Workers had built an effective and powerful organization. This organization permitted quick, coordinated, and sustained strike action. For example, when the workers again voted to strike just before midnight on 12 March 1978 the first factories began to stop operations only minutes after. At General Motors, one section of workers whistled to the next until all machines had stopped. This same commitment to joint action was responsible for the continuance of the strike even after government intervention.

A major development strengthening worker organization was the alliance between the Catholic Church and unions. As the largest Catholic country in the world, Brazil has been the focus of extensive grass-roots institution-building by the Church. Bonilla stated that both the "military and the Church lay claims . . . to being the only genuinely national institution" in Brazil.[25] The unique ability of the Church, however, lay in its integration function, itself the receptacle and instrument of a moral and spiritual unity that binds Brazilians together in ways political loyalties have never matched.

The Church thus provided a grass-roots ideological and organizational basis for collective action by groups with conflicting ideologies.[26] The 1979 strike was able to continue even after government intervention because the Catholic Church had organized with the *Pastoral Operaria*, or workers parish. For almost two years prior to the strike, "the seventy-two parishes in the ABC region were transformed into union meeting rooms."[27] During the strike, support from the Church's "basic communities," in addition to union strike funds and food programs, had been responsible for feeding and clothing workers. With strike funds now de-

[25] Frank Bonilla, "Brazil," in *Education and Political Development*, ed. James S. Coleman (Princeton: Princeton University Press, 1965), p. 226.

[26] Examples of the contrasting groups in support of the strikes include: the Communist Party, the Movement of the Cost of Life (Movimento do Custo de Vida), opposition leaders, liberal government officials, businessmen, and workers.

Pedro Casaldaglia, bishop of a huge 150,000 sq km diocese in the north of Mato Grosso, explained the development of the Church-union alliance in an interview: "A few years ago, the Church was the voice of the oppressed peasant families. Today they are acting on their own initiative, using their own organizations. The Church has become aware that it is not going to solve the land problem, but that it must organize the people so that, as a class or category, they can find their own solutions. Today we talk about trade unions in the same tone of voice we use for Our Lady." "Fears of Peasant Warfare in Amazon," *Latin America Weekly Report* WR–80–23 (13 June 1980): 7.

[27] See "O que a Greve Ensinou," *Istoé E* (4 April 1979): 4.

clared illegal, the Church delivered six tons of food daily for the striking workers. Under the charismatic support of a bishop from Santo Andre, rallies and meetings were held in churches. Church workers moved in with the family of the imprisoned labor leader, Lula (Luis Inácio da Silva), with the publicly stated purpose of protecting his wife and children from the military.

Another strike in 1980 lasted forty-one days despite government intervention and the arrest of labor leaders. The workers by this time had a sophisticated organization that extended from the plant level to union leadership, and alternative leaders simply took the place of those arrested. At the plant level, 425 members of a "salary committee" had been elected by the workers. As de facto shop stewards, they continued to organize meetings and assemblies in churches. Coordination was still provided by strike commands, even though the top two (of the five strike commands), composed of twenty-four well-known labor leaders, had been arrested. The strike reportedly continued under the leadership of the labor leader Lula, even though he was in jail.[28]

Therefore, the significance of the 1978, 1979, and 1980 strikes lay in the convergence of different interest groups, all supportive of the demands of the most dominant interest group, the working class. The 1980 metalworkers' strike brought together the most disparate elements of the opposition in a forceful condemnation of the military government's handling of the strike and also its overall economic policies. The prolongment of the strike under government repression resulted in cohesive public stands. A joint manifesto, signed by all opposition parties, denounced government action.[29] Elected government officials and well-known Brazilian leaders made public statements supporting the strike and criticizing government behavior. Deputy João Cunha was charged under the National Security Law for allegedly saying "half a dozen generals [were] acting like a bunch of clowns" during the strike.[30] Teotonio Vilela, the best-known senator in the largest opposition party, Partido do Movimento Democrático Brasileiro (PMDB), issued a call for all opposition parties to merge in order to defend themselves. The widespread acceptability of the underlying issues, and their infiltration into the mainstream of political discussion, was reflected in the emergence of *co-gestão*

[28] "Strike Underlines Need for New Arbitration Machinery," *Brazil Business* (May 1980): 9.

[29] Even the most right-wing of the opposition parties, the Partido Popular (PP), signed the manifesto. Second only to the government party in congressional representation, the PP traditionally backed the government on most issues.

[30] See "Congress Refuses to Toe Golbery Line," *Latin America Weekly Report* WR–8–25 (27 June 1980): 7.

(worker participation in management) as a central issue even endorsed by the progovernment party, the Partido Democrático Social (PDS).[31]

The labor movement became the key issue of debate between the military government and organized opposition groups in Brazil. As evidenced by the strikes, traditional control-variables in the conflict-regulation process had undergone significant alteration. External controls and those internalized by workers themselves were modified by the *abertura* process of political liberalization.

External controls were eroded by open discussions of political reforms and by the mobilization of interest groups. Traditional notions of class and patron-client relationships were supplanted with an increasing sentiment of collective social responsibility. The use and threat of force was curtailed by the government's promise of a return to a nonauthoritative system of democracy. In turn, the government admitted to the necessity of legal reform for the conflict-resolution of strikes, and its own political party endorsed and thus legitimized key worker-demands.

Environmental factors that had traditionally acted as controls on labor (such as the lack of communication infrastructure and geographical fragmentation) had been modified by the manifestations of economic development itself. The concentrated industrial areas of the country (e.g., São Paulo) had become populated with the subsidiaries of MNCs and large Brazilian firms requiring large numbers of laborers. Workers, unions, employers, and other organizations could easily and discreetly communicate with each other and between themselves, given the development of mass media, communications, and transportation systems.

Controls internalized in the workers (e.g., low levels of education, traditional notions of class relationships) were greatly altered by the industrial working environment. The solidarity of the ABC metalworkers' unions in strike actions could be partly attributed to the erosion of traditional corporatist attitudes and the development of an industry culture focused around automobile firms. As discussed in the first section, despite attempts to adapt to the local labor practices, the automotive industry itself had contributed to change in Brazil between employees and employers. The MNCs had built new factories with management practices that were distinctly "modern," thus breaking down paternalism and encouraging collective worker organization. Thus, the *abertura* dialogue and the resulting integration of values and objectives resulted in a weakening of the traditional conflict-regulation process.

The result was a breakdown in the Brazilian government's ability and willingness to control labor unrest. During the first strike in 1978, FIESP, the organization representing all the industrial firms of the São

[31] See "Business Outlook: Brazil," *Business Latin America* (6 Aug. 1980): 254.

Paulo area, sent a telegram to President Geisel warning that if strikes were to spread throughout the country, they would be a serious threat to national security. FIESP members said that events were out of their control and called for action from the government.[32] However, the government "offered the firms the political power to repress the strikes, but the firms felt that repression was a direct duty limited to the government."[33] Ignoring the automotive companies' demands for intervention, the government decided not to interfere.

By the time of the 1980 strike, the conflict between government and business interests had become more pronounced. According to various reliable sources, the government's predominant objective was political and concerned primarily with controlling the growth of the labor movement under the union leader Lula. Before the strike, on 27 and 28 March, the Brazilian Minister of Labor held a private, closed-door meeting with about twenty of the major firms, national and multinational, in the São Paulo area. The Minister firmly dictated company behavior for the expected upcoming strike:

1. The companies could not grant more than a 5 percent salary increase.
2. The Labor Court would be "instructed" to declare the strike illegal.
3. The companies would not be permitted to negotiate.
4. The companies would have to fire all employees considered militants, including union officers.

The Minister assured all the company directors that the Brazilian government would take the necessary steps to ensure order in the area. As one participant stated: "Not one person contradicted Murilo [the Labor Minister]. Each realized they had to cooperate in the political war against Lula. The employers were to be used as the instrument of the government."[34] The outcome of the government's political strategy was a strike lasting forty-one days, in which the business community and particularly the automotive industry suffered significant losses. The automotive strikes had affected each subsidiary's bottom line, and country risk was not merely an abstraction: the changing sociopolitical environment in Brazil was costing these companies almost $U.S. 500 million dollars in lost sales.[35]

[32] See "Brazilian Strike Heralds New Era in Labor Relations," *Latin America Economic Report* VI, no. 24 (22 June 1978): 188.

[33] Translated by the author from "Os Operíos, a Oposição e a Política," *Movimento* (12 June 1978): 7.

[34] Author interview with senior management of one of the subsidiaries in the study.

[35] The first twenty-four days of the 1980 strike resulted in business losses totaling more than 70 billion cruzeiros (U.S. $1.4 billion). The 1980 strike hurt many other industries throughout the state, especially auto-parts manufacturers and assemblers of household ap-

The MNC Subsidiaries as "Levers for Change"

The foreign-dominated automotive industry, irrespective of intent, acted as an agent of change within Brazil's political liberalization process. As discussed, due to its modern nature, the MNC and subsidiaries had introduced large-scale production processes that replaced traditional paternalism with collective worker organizing. And their employees expected the MNC subsidiaries to yield to their increasingly sophisticated demands. The story goes further, however. In crisis, the MNC subsidiaries imported—again unintentionally—home-country influences, transmitted initially from outside the firm, but later, intentionally, from within the firm itself.

Outside Support: International Labor Relations

There was general consensus that a major factor in the emergence and strengthening of the automotive union had been support from groups outside the country, such as national labor unions abroad and the International Metalworkers Union (IMF). The home unions of the parent companies of the automotive subsidiaries had been involved in training and financing the activities of their Brazilian counterparts. The chairman of the IG Metall Union of Germany (also the key labor representative on Volkswagen's Board of Directors) reportedly met with local labor leaders in Brazil every six months after 1975. The United Auto Workers (UAW) was also reported to have given substantial financial support to the Brazilian automotive unions. In addition, according to two reliable sources, both the IG Metall and the UAW not only put direct pressure on parent companies to change the labor policies of their subsidiaries but also to lobby the Brazilian government.[36]

The International Metalworkers Federation (IMF) publicly acknowledged extensive support of the Brazilian automotive unions and took credit for changes in the local policies of MNCs. As one of seventeen international trade secretariats, the IMF is the most advanced in the coordination and implementation of international efforts.[37] It has a com-

pliances. The São Paulo State Industrial Center (CIESP) in São Bernardo do Campo estimated a 40 percent decline in expected earnings over the following six months for many of these companies. Carlos Fannchi, president of SINFAVEA, termed the impact of the strike "a mini-recession." See "Cost of the Strikes," *Brazilian Business* (May 1980): 10; and "Challenge of Future Will Be Innovative Industrial Relations," *Brazilian Business* (May 1980): 8.

[36] Author interviews with subsidiary management and the President of the São Bernardo Metalworkers Union.

[37] The IMF reported a membership of 11.5 million workers in sixty-five countries. David D. Hirschfield, *The Multinational Union Challenges the Multinational Company* (New York: The Conference Board, 1975), p. 10.

puter-bank on wages and working conditions at forty-seven representative plants of fifteen world automobile companies. The UAW research department, with IMF and other union cooperation, prepared detailed analyses of the leading corporations' production, plant locations, profit, and union-contract provisions, which "as company booklets serve as guides for automotive bargaining throughout the world."[38]

As early as 1953 the IMF organized for multinational bargaining by setting up separate subgroups across nations for each major automotive employer. Permanent world auto-councils were established for Ford, General Motors, Chrysler, Volkswagen, Daimler Benz, and British Leyland in 1966, followed by Renault-Peugeot and Fiat Citröen in 1971, Toyota and Nissan in 1973, and Volvo-Daf-Saab in 1977. The auto-councils have reportedly been successful in promoting a "Detroit psychology" among local unions in LDCs, especially in South American countries.[39] In our Brazilian case study, the automotive subsidiaries unintentionally served as transmitters of home-country influences, because of the ideas and resources flowing from these international labor organizations.

Change from within the Subsidiaries

Later, however, the subsidiaries themselves became voluntary "levers for change." As Humphrey pointed out, given the strength of their workers, the automotive employers may have been the first in Brazil to recognize the need for coming to terms with the union's new power and seeking a new relationship.[40] Given the subsidiary management's more progressive home-country labor relations, they also had the background to understand and accept these changes. Indeed, some executives actually felt that Brazil had reached the point where direct negotiation with unions had to be accepted.[41] One subsidiary, *Ford do Brasil*, led the rest of the country into a new era of labor relations. When the Brazilian government demanded that its workers be fired for striking, Ford refused: the company felt that workers intrinsically had the right to strike. During a 1982 strike, its workers demanded a union-based worker-representation system. Despite the Brazilian government's long-standing overt opposition

[38] Herbert H. Northrup and Richard L. Rowan, *Multinational Collective Bargaining Attempts* (Philadelphia: The Wharton School, 1979), p. 36. For information on the IMF and international trade unionism, also see Charles Levenson, *International Trade Unionism* (London: Allen and Unwin, 1972).

[39] Northrup and Rowan, *Multinational Collective Bargaining*, p. 4. Such activities seem to have had effects on management in that, in 1975, 10 percent of a sample of 134 U.S. MNCs reported that they had already encountered international union solidarity. See Hirschfield, *The Multinational Union Challenges the Multinational Company*, pp. 7–9.

[40] Humphrey, *Capitalist Control*, p. 170.

[41] See Humphrey, *Capitalist Control*, pp. 170, 224.

to such a scheme, the Ford subsidiary acceded to the workers' demands, thus establishing the country's first union-based worker-representation system. For the first time in the history of Brazilian industrial relations, a union had been let into a company; years of demands for the workers' participation in decision-making (*co-gestão*) had at last accomplished a major breakthrough. Following Ford's lead, the other subsidiaries one by one set up union-based worker-representation systems.

Indeed, by the end of 1984 Brazil's sociopolitical environment had changed considerably. Labor even formed its own political party, which was much sought after as an ally. The managing director of Volkswagen do Brasil—once considered the military government's major supporter in aggressively opposing the union-based system—now publically applauded the unions and the automotive sector for leading the way to dialogue: "*in the process of democratization, the metalwork industry and its significant automobile sector led the way to dialogue, through their employee representative bodies, helping to relieve social tensions.*"[42] The MNC subsidiary's managing director who had previously been one of those most resistant to labor's demands now publically underscored the importance of the automotive industry in the successful transition to democracy, claiming that the "foreign automotive industry has played a prominent role in the democratization process of an originally paternalistic society."[43] In sync with the new sociopolitical environment, companies across-the-board adopted labor strategies that recognized the demands of the more powerful unions. Besides setting up union-based worker-representation systems, companies granted more frequent wage increases, allowed larger benefits, and made donations to employee social organizations. Key groups, such as church groups, were courted, with invitations to visit plants. The movement gained force, even within the government. The Labor Ministry introduced a bill that would institutionalize labor representation. The country's labor-relations system was to be significantly modified, one major change being the authorization to form "negotiation units" with both worker and management representatives.

Labor forces joined forces with their traditional foes as Brazil successfully completed its transition from political liberalization to democracy. President-elect Tancredo Neves appointed the São Bernardo union's lawyer, Amir Pazzianotto, to the position of Minister of Labor. The Minister's first announcement was the call for a "social pact," and he declared his intention to reform the labor laws and to liberalize those governing

[42] Wolfgang Sauer, "Manufacturing in Latin America in a Period of Economic Crisis" (24 May 1984, Geneva, manuscript provided to the *Financial Times*, Mimeographed).

[43] Sauer, "Manufacturing in Latin America."

strikes. Shortly thereafter, Pazzianotto permitted all labor leaders who had been banned from labor activity by the military government to return to their unions, and he promised never to use again the State's power to "intervene" (i.e., disposing of labor union directors who conducted "illegal" strikes). The celebrated hero of the automotive strikes, Lula—whom the military government had banned and jailed—became the leader of the workers' first political party and was allowed to return to the São Bernardo Union. Only ten years after the first automotive strike in 1978, Lula would become one of the most powerful politicians in the new democracy and one of the strongest candidates for the presidency of Brazil.

The automotive subsidiaries, because of their MNC nature, played an important role as "levers for change" in Brazil's transition to democracy. The development of the Brazilian automotive industry was distinguished by its close integration with the government as well as by its isolation from national groups such as labor, opposition political parties, and the Catholic Church. As Brazil entered a period of political liberalization, the automotive industry had major difficulties in maintaining its harmonious relationship with the government; the military government, in its turn, was not able or willing to regulate conflicts between workers and employers over its policies.

Political liberalization had in the meantime resulted in greater communication between national groups and groups outside the country, leading to significant support of Brazil's automotive labor unions. The automotive industry's ability to adapt to the Brazilian labor environment was complicated by its differing relationships with the government and national groups and by the growth, magnitude, and change of contending forces. (See figure 2–3.) Yet by their very presence, the automotive subsidiaries, in response to labor demands, involuntarily (i.e., through no formulated intent) acted as "levers for change," actually provoking and accelerating social change.

Therefore, the MNC subsidiaries themselves helped to create the conditions for change. Labor demands were aimed at the labor policies of the automotive subsidiaries because key LDC groups perceived the subsidiaries as advancing their objectives—and indeed the subsidiaries *had* increased worker expectations by introducing modern management practices that eroded traditional paternalism, followed by new ideas and resources from their home-country's own labor leaders. Conversely, the Brazilian government expected the automotive industry to endorse its position. Conflict occurred not because of the subsidiaries themselves, but because of the specific way in which their labor-relations policies and behavior fit into the competing agendas of LDC groups within a dynamic

FIGURE 2–3
The "Floating" Automotive Subsidiary in an LDC: Internal and External Influences on Local Policies

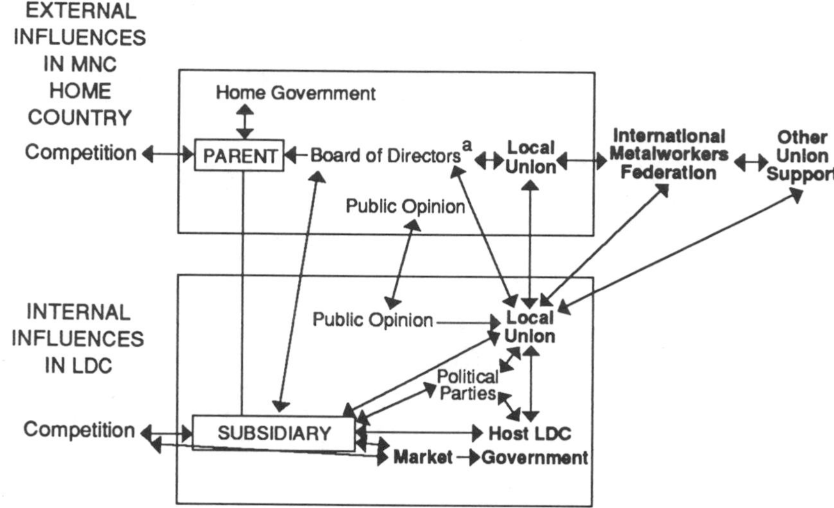

Source: Compiled by the author.

[a] The Board of Directors may be an important influence in those countries, such as Germany and Sweden, where labor representatives are members.

development process. The buildup of labor demands on MNC policies was therefore not sudden or mysterious but clearly evident. When analyzed within the historical evolution of the overall sociopolitical environment, the buildup of labor pressures was inevitable, the role of the MNC automotive subsidiaries as "levers for change" foreseeable. In the next chapter we will shift from the macro to the micro, focusing on the individual automotive subsidiaries, to ask: Why were there differences between the five subsidiaries in perception, risk, and response? Why did Ford do Brazil become the ultimate "response leader," leading the rest of the industry and the country into a new era of employee-employer relations?

CHAPTER 3

Individual Subsidiary Response: The Reformulation of Labor Policy

CHAPTER 2 MAPPED the evolution of labor demands on the subsidiaries of automotive MNCs, showing the role of their labor policies as "levers for change" in Brazil's transition to political liberalization. There, MNC subsidiary policies were differentiated on the basis of their role within the LDC's development process. However, within this process, the behavior of individual subsidiaries differed—*Ford do Brasil* became the ultimate "response leader," complying with labor's demands, thus setting the pace for the other automotive subsidiaries and then, inevitably, for all companies throughout the country. This chapter and the next will delve into the dynamics determining individual subsidiary behavior, to illustrate the second main argument: *MNC subsidiaries vary systematically in their will and capacity to deal with host-country demands.* In further examining the labor conflict between Brazilian unions and the Brazilian automotive industry, we will question broad generalizations about MNC behavior through an in-depth comparison of the five automotive subsidiaries.[1]

As noted, our examination of these five subsidiaries will be twofold. This chapter is devoted to a chronological portrayal of how each subsidiary behaved over the time period covered in the previous chapter (1972–1982). Subsequently, the following chapter probes for further explanations of differing subsidiary behavior with a structural analysis of each subsidiary's internal organization and its relationships with key actors: If the risks and benefits were not similar, what explanations resided within MNC subsidiaries themselves?

THE FRAMEWORK

Despite the fact that all five automobile subsidiaries in the study shared adaptive industrial-relations policies, they responded in significantly different ways and at different times to the changing labor environment.

[1] Information in this chapter, unless noted otherwise, was obtained from personal interviews with subsidiary management and labor leaders of the Brazilian automotive industry. In addition, comparative data was drawn from answers to a detailed questionnaire given to each of the subsidiaries' managing directors. See the Appendix for a list of interviewees.

Here we begin our examination of the individual subsidiaries by focusing on their behavior from 1972 to 1982. In order to preserve the dynamic nature of the subsidiaries' responses, their behavior is presented chronologically in a comparative framework. As discussed in Chapter 1 (see figure 1–2), three aspects of the policy reformulation process of each subsidiary are analyzed: (1) the identification of a changing labor environment and response before crisis, (2) the degree of conflict between the subsidiary and labor at crisis, and (3) the subsidiary's type of response. These aspects are discussed in greater detail in the following sections.

The first section, pre-crisis identification, specifically examines subsidiary behavior before the 1978 outburst of strikes: before the onset of crisis, were there differences between subsidiaries in the detection of a changing labor environment and measures taken to prepare for change? The second section focuses on the degree of conflict between the subsidiary and labor: were there significant differences in union pressures on subsidiaries and in each subsidiary's vulnerability to pressure? In the third section, type of response, the outcomes are explored: how did each subsidiary respond to labor demands? The answer to section three brings us full circle to the major questions posed in this case study: Was each subsidiary equally vulnerable to labor pressures, and did each contribute uniform benefits in response to labor demands? What do these findings suggest for our overall understanding of the role of MNC subsidiaries in LDCs: are there uniform risks and benefits or must a complex range of alternatives based on individual subsidiary characteristics be considered?

Pre-Crisis: Detection of the Changing Labor Environment

In the early 1970s all five automotive subsidiaries shared the same operating environment, participated in the same national market with similar products, and collaborated closely in their industry organization. Yet the case study shows that the subsidiaries varied considerably in their detection of impending labor changes in Brazil and in the measures they took to prepare for these. Three key variables differentiated subsidiary ability to identify and respond before crisis: (1) *internal management policies*, (2) *relationships with key LDC actors*, and (3) *parent intervention and influence*. A brief chronological survey of subsidiary behavior before the first 1978 strike illustrates the primacy of these variables in explaining differences in subsidiary ability to identify and prepare for a changing labor environment.

Volkswagen do Brasil's first move was geared to improving the information on its enormous work force, thereby sharpening its ability to monitor labor developments and issues. The subsidiary's managing director claimed to have taken the initiative: his close friends in the Brazilian government has warned him of the potential for increased, more effective labor demands. In 1972 the Volkswagen subsidiary added the Economics Group, consisting of eight employees, to its Industrial Relations Department. The new group, reporting to the director of industrial relations, was created with the objective of providing information needed for decision-making in labor policies. The group initiated the first and (as of 1982) the only surveys of employees in the Brazilian automotive industry. Referred to as worker-satisfaction surveys, these annual studies interviewed Volkswagen personnel for feedback on benefits, wages, and working conditions.

Mercedes Benz do Brasil, however, was concerned with the analysis of labor policies themselves and what changes would be most desirable given the inevitability of political liberalization. As a result of information received from personal government contacts, in 1974 the managing director of Mercedes Benz do Brasil attempted to prepare for a changing labor environment. He made contact with directors of national firms, local labor leaders, and government officials, and exchanged ideas on changes in labor practices, laws, and worker organization. Within one year, the managing director hired a lawyer to study labor issues ranging from developments in political parties and types of strikes to worker needs. The lawyer was to work directly under his supervision. In 1977 the managing director sent the lawyer to the Office of Personnel and Overseas Staff for Industrial Relations at the parent company in Germany for a year of training, followed by a course in England. After the lawyer returned, a second lawyer was hired as an assistant, with both responsible for briefing the managing director on labor developments.

Ford do Brasil, on the other hand, took no action until prodded by its parent staff. In 1975 the parent's Vice-President for Labor Relations, headquartered in Detroit, visited the Brazilian subsidiary and discussed the changing labor environment. This was reported as the first visit from parent staff in labor relations. As one Ford executive explained: ". . . before there were no subsidiary labor decisions. They were outside the firm in the domain of the Brazilian government, so parent intervention was not necessary."[2] The Ford parent reportedly wanted to convince subsidiary management of the importance of changing its labor policies in Brazil. The parent labor-relations staff drafted a proposal to change subsidiary labor policies, but it was not fully approved due to unspecified political reasons. However, this parent initiative did contribute to orga-

[2] Author interview with a senior executive of Ford do Brasil.

nizational change at the subsidiary the following year. According to the local Brazilian labor-relations staff, by 1976 the parent's influence led to a shifting of the responsibilities of the labor-relations staff from legal and security to labor issues within the plants. The change was formalized in 1977.

The management of *Saab-Scania do Brasil* also changed labor policies at the request of the parent; subsidiary management, however, successfully resisted the adoption of the original policy and, as a result, antagonized the local union. In 1976 labor representatives of the parent Board of Directors visited the Brazilian subsidiary. The visit was formally requested by the parent Board itself because criticism in Sweden of the Brazilian Saab subsidiary was widespread; Swedish newspapers had carried numerous stories claiming Saab-Scania do Brasil mistreated its Brazilian workers. The Board's hope was that reports from Saab-Scania do Brasil's labor leaders would disclaim such criticisms.

Upon visiting the Brazilian subsidiary themselves, however, Swedish labor leaders insisited on the establishment of worker committees, an almost nonexistent occurrence in Brazilian labor relations since the military takeover in 1964.[3] The scheme was revolutionary: it institutionalized union-firm dialogue, thereby recognizing the union as the representative of the workers. This notion of a worker-representative system was transferred directly from the parent company. The same proposed structure, based on the *Foretagsnmid* organization of committees, had already been established in the Saab plants in Sweden.[4]

According to Brazilian labor leaders, the Saab parent's proposal for work committees was applauded by the local union and the Saab-Scania do Brasil employees. By legitimizing and broadening union involvement with the firm, this proposal would result in a dramatic change in Brazilian labor relations. A Swedish labor representative remained in Brazil approximately one month to develop the worker-committee proposal.

However, after his departure, the management of Saab-Scania do Brasil discussed this revolutionary proposal with the other automotive subisidiaries at meetings with employers' representatives at ANFAVEA, the organization for the automotive industry. Other automotive subsidiaries were against encouraging union-firm dialogue. Furthermore, the Swedish director of labor relations at the Saab subsidiary was himself fundamentally opposed to this proposal as well as to any other significant changes imposed by Swedish labor leaders, whom he considered to be

[3] According to interviewees, only one worker committee (now defunct) was established after the 1964 military takeover of the Brazilian government.

[4] This is reflected in the written agreement (Sverige 1973) between the Swedish Employers Confederation and the Central Organization of Salaried Employees, to which the Saab parent is a party.

overly progressive. In his mind, labor dominated business in Sweden, and this had to be avoided if at all possible in Brazil.[5]

Accordingly, pressure from ANFAVEA and from the Saab subsidiary's Swedish director of labor relations resulted in significant modifications to the proposal that were totally unacceptable to the local Brazilian union. For example, the union was no longer to participate in the new worker-committee.[6] Interestingly enough, however, this singular measure, initiated solely by parent labor, was the only major change in labor-relations policy reported by Saab-Scania do Brasil.

In contrast to the other four subsidiaries, *General Motors do Brasil* reported no early response to the changing labor environment. Its plants were located in São Caetano, outside the territory of the strongest union, São Bernardo. Labor demands were not perceived as escalating by either subsidiary or parent, and no preparatory measures were reported by its management.

Therefore, the Brazilian case study demonstrates significant variety in how the five automotive subsidiaries detected a changing environment; notable differences were in timing, the loci of initiative, and the measures taken. (1) *Internal management policies* distinguished the *Volkswagen* and *Mercedes Benz* subsidiaries from the other subsidiaries. The management of both subsidiaries set up in-company units before the advent of crisis to study the changing labor environment. (2) *Relationships with key LDC actors* also differentiated the *Mercedes Benz* and *Volkswagen* subsidiaries: they attributed their closeness with host-country nationals as enabling them to better foresee the changes. Mercedes Benz's managing director claimed to benefit from his contacts with labor leaders and national business leaders, while Volkswagen's managing director relied on his close personal relationships with Brazilian government officials. (3) *Parent intervention and influence* explained the pre-crisis responses of the *Ford* and *Saab* subsidiaries. A visit from Ford's head-office labor staff resulted in a recommendation to enlarge the subsidiary's labor function, to prepare for change on the labor front. In the case of Saab, parent labor leaders visited the subsidiary and demanded the establishment of a worker-representation committee.

It is clear, then, that even before the eruption of crisis, and despite

[5] These viewpoints were expressed by the Swedish director of labor relations at Saab-Scania do Brasil.

[6] As a key Brazilian labor leader stated: "After the Swedish union representative left, Saab-Scania do Brasil completely changed the plan. We [the Sao Bernardo Union] called the Swedish union and they said the subsidiary had some independence of the parent. Because of these changes, we [the São Bernardo Union] don't recognize the Committee. And only 20 percent or so of the Saab-Scania do Brasil workers even recognize the Committee." Author interview with labor union leader.

shared products and close collaboration, the five automotive subsidiaries behaved very differently. The next sections examine whether this diversity in subsidiary behavior was also evident in later developments as to the degree of conflict between labor and subsidiaries, and subsidiary response.

Degree of Conflict: Labor versus Subsidiary

Throughout the mid-1970s, labor demands in Brazil escalated. Despite the indisputable targeting of the automotive industry, were all five automotive subsidiaries uniformly subject to the same level of pressure or were there inherently different levels of conflict between individual subsidiaries and labor? On labor's side, did the union deliberately discriminate betwteen the subsidiaries? And on the subsidiary side, did individual subsidiaries differ in their vulnerability to pressure?

In this section, the case study shows there were inherently different degrees of conflict between labor and individual subsidiaries. Key variables that differentiated the degree of conflict were: (1) *the pressuring group's perception of the subsidiaries and bargaining power*, (2) *historical policies*, and (3) *the parents' interests*. A review of specific factors cited as contributing to the degree of conflict between subsidiaries and labor illustrates the primacy of these key variables in explaining differences between individual subsidiaries.

First, the five automotive subsidiaries were definitely not pressured to the same degree by labor. Four of the five subsidiaries were lcoated in São Bernardo; *General Motors* alone was located a few kilometers away in São Caetano, outside the territory of the more powerful São Bernardo Union. As a direct result, the GM subsidiary suffered a total of only eleven strike days during the three years of strikes from 1978 to 1980, compared to a total of at least fifty-nine strike days for each of the other four subsidiaries. Therefore, a determining difference proved to be location.

Beyond the historical accident of location, there were inherently different levels of conflict between individual subsidiaries and labor. The reasons were a function of both the individual subsidiary's labor policies as well as differing subsidiary vulnerabilities to pressure. In some cases, pressure was not just a function of labor; pressure also originated from within the subsidiary itself.

From the very beginning, the *Ford* subsidiary was hit with relatively strong labor demands. First, it had inherited a more organized work force. The Ford subsidiary had formerly belonged to Willy's Overland do Brasil, S.A., and American manufacturer of jeeps. In 1963, Willy's managing director had established a labor-relations committee that included workers for handling worker grievances.[7] Despite Ford's termination of the committee, according to numerous labor leaders and company executives, the worker tradition of organizing survived through remaining workers and resulted in a more effective organization for worker demands.

Labor also perceived important distinctions between subsidiary labor policies. The previous labor policies of the Ford subsidiary were reported by its own staff as well as by other companies and labor as increasing labor pressure. Its previous policies were characterized as "erratic," sometimes relatively "liberal," with incidents of "insensitivity" that contributed to the politicization of its employees.[8] As one Ford labor-relations executive explained: At Ford, "in order to save money we must do anything, even if such an action leads workers to unify against the company."[9] Several specific policies were seen as leading to the increased politicization of Ford's workers. In 1974, Ford stopped providing free transportation for its employees to and from their homes; also, it charged a significantly greater amount for such transportation from its employees than was charged by the other automotive subsidiaries. Furthermore, until 1975, Ford, like the other automotive subsidiaries, fully reimbursed employees' medical expenses; however, that year Ford required employees to pay a special discounted price. Then, in April 1977, Ford attempted to implement a shorter work week accompanied by a salary cut. The union fought the proposal, with the result that Ford dismissed five hundred employees.

By 1978 it was clear that Ford, compared to the other four subsidiaries, had the most politicized and well-organized work force. During the first strike, Ford workers were the most successful in unifying their company's work force. For five full workdays, all of Ford's operations were at a complete standstill. In contrast, only two other subsidiaries were completely halted, and for shorter time periods—Mercedes Benz, for four days; and Saab-Scania do Brasil, two days. A small portion of Volkswagen's employees (twelve hundred) stopped work for three and a half days.[10]

[7] The committee at Willy's Overland do Brasil was begun at the company's initiative, but did not include the participation of the union; the committee's primary purpose was to formally handle worker grievances. See "Employee Representation Systems in Brazilian Auto Companies," *Business Latin America* (2 Feb. 1983): 38.

[8] Sources were labor union officials and the management of the subsidiaries in the study, including those of Ford do Brasil.

[9] Author interview with a labor-relations executive at Ford do Brasil. Information on Ford's labor policies provided by Ford's labor-relations staff.

[10] Information provided by subsidiaries. Also, see John Humphrey, *Capitalist Control and Worker's Struggle in the Brazilian Auto Industry* (Princeton: Princeton University Press, 1982), p. 173.

The other subsidiaries also incurred different levels of pressure. For the first strike of 1978, *Saab-Scania do Brasil* was the first target. Union strategists explained the choice as deliberate. Union relations had been particularly bad after the modification of the Saab parent's worker-committee proposal, as discussed in the previous section. Except for Volkswagen, the Saab subsidiary's relations with the union were reportedly worse than those of the other subsidiaries. As the smallest plant, the Saab subsidiary would also be the easiest for workers to influence and control. In addition, the employees knew that the parent's labor leaders would support their efforts; as noted, public opinion in Sweden was important, and the labor matters of the Brazilian Saab subsidiary had already stirred considerable public debate.

Over time, however, the key labor target increasingly became the *Volkswagen* subsidiary. A major reason was simply its visibility as the largest private-sector employer in the country and because of its potential role as a model for the rest of the industry and country. Its managing director, Wolfgang Sauer, agreed that the Volkswagen subsidiary bore additional risk due to its enormous size.[11] However, both union leaders and subsidiary labor-relations executives felt that Volkswagen was also targeted because its treatment of workers was perceived as being the most repressive in the automotive industry. Volkswagen, known in the industry as being a "tough" employer, was noted as adopting a more resistant anti-union position than the other subsidiaries. After the 1978 strike, four of the six union directors employed by the company were persuaded by Volkswagen management to abandon their union activities. Later that year in September, Volkswagen fired twelve of twenty workers attending the Third Metalworkers Congress.

Because Volkswagen worked within the government's guidelines (that is, not to negotiate with the union) and took additional antiunion actions, it was increasingly targeted by the union. Humphrey writes: "[I]t was clear that Volkswagen was the key plant. After the May 1978 strike, it was the symbol of management intransigence and also the most difficult factory to stop."[12] Many observers felt that Volkswagen was the govern-

[11] The managing director of Volkswagen do Brazil stated: "Volkswagen [do Brasil] is a vulnerable company from a standpoint of unionism in that a shutdown (by strike) is an attractive political achievement for union leaders, by virtue of the sheer number of workers that a walkout entails." Wolfgang Sauer, in response to author's questionnaire.

[12] Humprey, *Capitalist Control*, p. 181; also, see p. 165. Indeed, Volkswagen's labor policies may well have hurt overall productivity. Using one measure of productivity—dividing the average annual number of employees by the annual number of vehicles produced—Volkswagen's productivity declined 32.6 percent from 1976 to 1980. The next largest decline was Saab-Scania's (24.6 percent), followed by Mercedes Benz (17.1 percent) and Ford (16.2 percent). GM, probably due to its location outside of the main striking union, had a 13.3 percent *increase* in productivity.

ment's agent in taking on the union, and that its managing director, Sauer, was in a direct confrontation with the union's acclaimed leader, Lula. Thus, the Volkswagen subsidiary's close government relationship and antiunion positions contributed to its designation by the union as the key target.

The Volkswagen subsidiary was also pressured from within, namely from its parent. Under the German management structure, its parent Board of Directors included German union representatives and they were on the side of Brazilian labor. These Volkswagen union board members made periodic visits to Brazil, contributing funds to support auto strikes and lobbying the other parent board members. In effect, the Volkswagen subsidiary was in a bind, receiving conflicting pressures from both its parent union and the Brazilian government.

In contrast, the *Mercedes Benz* subsidiary was noted as incurring less pressure. Unlike Volkswagen, it parent ownership was entirely private and parent labor leaders were not concerned with the affairs of the Brazilian subsidiary. In terms of internal pressure, the managing director of Mercedes claimed pressure was not as great because of its superior labor-relations policies: given the more advanced training required to manufacture its buses and trucks, the company sought to keep turnover at a minimum. As a consequence, special efforts were made to keep workers satisfied. The other subsidiaries, excluding Saab-Scania do Brasil, mostly manufactured cars, which required less worker training and where high turnover did not present a problem. Labor leaders confirmed this notion, adding that overall the labor policies of the Mercedes Benz subsidiary were not "erratic" as in the case of Ford, "repressive" as at Volkswagen, or "antiunion" like those of Saab-Scania.[13]

Therefore, even precluding subsidiary response to the strikes, each automotive subsidiary was affected differently due to varying individual characteristics and how these related to the union's demands. (1) *Labor's perceptions and bargaining power* varied. The *General Motors* subsidiary was pressured least due to its location. *Ford* was perceived as being "more liberal"; and given the high level of worker organization, it was also seen as more vulnerable. *Saab-Scania* do Brasil was perceived as being easy to shut down and as having a supportive home union. *Volkswagen* was considered a valuable target because of its high visibility as the nation's largest employer. (2) *Past policy performance* of the subsidiary also affected the degree of conflict, with the union discriminating between subsidiaries. In the case of *Saab-Scania*, the nonunion worker committee actually soured its relations with the union. The *Ford* and

[13] Quoted from interviews with labor union officials.

Volkswagen subsidiaries had particular labor policies that conflicted with labor's demands, thereby earning them labor's ill will. Conversely, the *Mercedes Benz* subsidiary reportedly had superior employment and training policies. (3) *Parent interests* affected the degree of conflict between the subsidiary and labor: both *Saab-Scania* and *Volkswagen* were subject to the scrutiny of their home unions and parent board of directors. Saab-Scania do Brasil also reported pressure originating from Swedish public opinion. Therefore, although the automotive industry was uniformly caught in the midst of a changing labor environment, each automotive subsidiary was faced with distinctly different pressures based on a wide range of subsidiary-specific characteristics, many related to previous policies and decisions.

Subsidiary Response to Conflict

The degree of conflict between individual subsidiaries and labor varied; when confronted with labor demands, did subsidiaries react uniformly? Despite the commonality of industry and threat, the individual characteristics of subsidiaries resulted in differing types of responses. Why did Ford become the ultimate "response leader," leading the rest of the industry and the country into a new era of employee-employer relations? Key variables that differentiated subsidiary response were: (1) *parent preferences*, (2) *relationships with key LDC groups*, and (3) the *first policy responses* set forth by subsidiaries. A brief review of the factors cited as shaping subsidiary response illustrates how these variables accounted for differences between subsidiaries.

Subsidiary behavior in crisis—even for a policy domain normally considered the most autonomous on a day-to-day basis—was decisively influenced by the parent, with the relationship providing a conduit for differing home-country and parent policies, ideas, and resources. During the strikes, all subsidiaries reported increased contact with the parent. In fact, the managing directors of two subsidiaries, *Mercedes Benz* and *Volkswagen*, who claimed to have the most autonomy from their parents in formulating labor-relations policies, during the strikes reported the greatest personal contact with the parent. The *Saab* subsidiary, while also claiming a great deal of autonomy, reported increased contact with its parent. While the *General Motors* and *Ford* subsidiaries also reported increased contact with their parents, it was mainly through the clearly established functional channels between the parent and the subsidiary's industrial-relations department, and not through the managing directors. Therefore, in crisis all parents intervened in their subsidiaries' labor policies, regardless of the degree of centralization or day-to-day subsidiary autonomy.

The degree and type of parent intervention in subsidiary response to the strikes was related to the nature of the relationship with the parent. The more centralized subsidiaries, *General Motors* and *Ford*, reported more direct and immediate intervention by their parents in their local subsidiary labor policies; the parent labor staffs were involved in the development of policy responses. The more autonomous subisidiares—*Volkswagen*, *Mercedes Benz*, and *Saab-Scania*—responded more on the initiative of the subsidiary managing directors; the managing directors would personally present recommendations to their head offices for approval. However, both the *Volkswagen* and *Saab-Scania* subsidiaries identified home-labor influences from their parents and home unions as a significant factor affecting their behavior. Therefore, for the more centralized American subsidiaries, parent intervention was formalized while that of the European subsidiaries was indirect and, to a large extent, unintended and unavoidable.

In the case of the American companies, the parent labor-relations staff was immediately involved after the 1978 strike. In July 1978, two months after the first significant automotive strike in over a decade, *General Motors do Brasil* reorganized its Department of Industrial Relations. Industrial-relations staff from the parent visited the Brazilian subsidiary and offered supportive guidance in the labor-relations area. The military colonel in charge of employee services was transferred out of industrial relations to public relations and given the precise responsibility of "collecting, analyzing, and interpretating data, information, and documents that might lessen or prevent the continuity of the production program of General Motors do Brasil."[14] With parent support, the labor-relations area was transformed from its emphasis on security and legal matters to developing broader labor policies (the security function performed by the ex-Colonel being transferred to a less visible area in the subsidiary). Shortly thereafter, the parent's "Quality of Work Life" program was officially transferred to the Brazilian subsidiary.

Likewise, *Ford's* parent immediately responded to the crisis by restaffing the subsidiary's senior labor-relations position. In 1978 an American labor expert, employed by Ford for twenty-three years, was transferred to Brazil to assume the position of director of industrial relations. The American director indicated that his assignment as a seasoned Ford labor specialist was due to the parent staff's belief that Brazilian labor relations would be going through a period of significant change. The parent company wanted control until a national could take over the position. The American director had an extensive record in industrial relations at Ford, with experience in the United States and Europe, and could trans-

[14] Description provided by General Motors do Brasil.

fer American ideas to the changing labor environment while developing a staff that could later become self-sufficient.

When asked how Ford had responded to the strikes, the American director answered that it had done so mainly in terms of production employee assignments, scheduling, and capacity planning. The "erratic" labor management policies earlier discussed as contributing to labor difficulties at Ford were thereby recognized as being counterproductive. In the case of production employee assignments, Ford deliberately minimized production changes that might irritate workers. As for scheduling and capacity planning, management at Ford reevaluated total capacity requirements and work assignments in the event of work slowdowns. No further change of organization occurred because, in the opinion of the industrial-relations director, the existing organization was effective and sufficient.

Volkswagen, however, actively promoted government-endorsed labor policies while internally exploring the possibilities of adopting a European type of worker-representation system. The managing director continued his much-publicizied close relationship with the military government and actively supported government stands on labor policies. Meanwhile, internally, the company began secretly in 1978 to investigate the formulation of a worker-representative committee. The influence of parent philosophy was clear. According to the director of industrial relations, the impetus for researching a system for worker representation came directly from its German managing director, Wolfgang Sauer. In 1978, Sauer had evaluated the growing demand for worker-representation systems and decided that Volkswagen, as the country's largest employer, should play a major role in establishing a Brazilian model of worker representatives. Sauer decided to form a secret company group to discuss just how to define a worker-representation system and whether to negotiate directly with the union. For one year this small group secretly studied the labor systems of other countries, traveling throughout England, Belgium, Japan, and Germany. In England the group took a collective-bargaining course. A year later the group expanded to twenty and included the directors of production, quality control, and public relations. After meeting full time for two weeks, the group expanded again to include the managers of all departments. This was described as a "process of evolution with responsibility" by the Volkswagen director of public relations.[15]

It was only later in 1979 and 1980 that the *Volkswagen*, *Saab*, and *Mercedes Benz* subsidiaries formally reorganized their Departments of Industrial Relations. At the Volkswagen subsidiary, the Economist Group established in 1972 became the Social Planning Department, employing

[15] Author interview with the director of public relations for Volkswagen do Brasil.

some thirty researchers with backgrounds in sociology, law, and communications. At both the *Saab-Scania* and *Volkswagen* subsidiaries, Departments of Labor Relations were established. In 1980 the military general in charge of labor relations at *Mercedes Benz* was shifted to a different position. His former department was reorganized officially, renamed the Department of Labor Relations, and headed by a Brazilian lawyer who had been trained specifically for that position over a period of five years.

The 1980 strike was clearly a confrontation between the government and labor. As discussed in the previous chapter, in a closed meeting the Minister of labor prohibited the firms in the affected area from negotiating with the union. The *Volkswagen* subsidiary was central in coordinating information on the striking workers and providing it to the Brazilian government. As one executive director of labor relations stated, "Volkswagen has more information than the Minister [of Labor]."[16]

All the firms affected, including the automotive subsidiaries, complied with the government mandate throughout the forty-one days of the 1980 strike. Of the automotive subsidiaries, however, *Volkswagen* claimed to be hurt most by the strike, losing market share to competitors.[17] Volkswagen's alliance with the Brazilian government clearly became a liability, for as the instrument of government policy Volkswagen became the target of labor pressure. Labor's effectiveness and success cost the government and, especially, the Volkswagen subsidiary.

The Brazilian government also told the automotive subsidiaries to fire the strike leaders. Breaking with the government and the other automotive subsidiaries, *Ford do Brasil* did not fire its four strike leaders. The subsidiary explicitly stated that this independent and rebellious decision was very deliberate; it was Ford's philosophy at the parent that all employees, in any country, had the "right" to strike and could not be fired just for striking.[18]

The Volkswagen Worker-Representation System

In September 1980, Volkswagen do Brasil demonstrated again its close working relationship with the military government by taking the leadership role in its announcement of a new worker-representation system.

[16] Author interview with the director of labor relations for one of the subsidiaries in the study.

[17] The 1980 Annual Report of Volkswagen do Brasil stated: "As a result of the labor problems at the beginning of the year, which affected especially Volkswagen do Brasil . . . sales of 488,155 units were 6.5% lower than prior year (522,177 units). Volkswagen's car and light commercial market share decreased from 50.2% in 1979 to 46.8% in favor of competitors who were not drastically hit by the strike." Volkswagen do Brasil, "1980 Annual Report," p. 10.

[18] Author interviews with the director of labor relations and staff of Ford do Brasil.

The Volkswagen announcement brought chaotic responses from the other automotive subsidiaries, the union, as well as national firms and political groups throughout the country.[19] This was the first time an automotive subsidiary had initiated a significant change in labor policy without the tacit agreement of the rest of the automotive industry. The other automotive subsidiaries and the local union had not been consulted or included in the process. Interested parties simply received a closed envelope hand-delivered by a Volkswagen do Brasil chauffeur twenty-four hours before the press release.

Management executives of other firms suggested that Volkswagen do Brasil had been under heavy pressure from its employee representatives on the parent Board of Directors as well as from the Brazilian government, and was forced into its secretive policy. Irrespective of the wishes of the other subsidiaries, Volkswagen became a "response leader," its new policy resulting in a follow-the-leader effect, with the automotive industry being the first sector to adopt worker-representation systems in Brazil. The result was that each of the automotive subsidiaries was forced to quickly develop proposals for worker-representative systems.

The local union did not support Volkswagen's new worker-representation system. Before announcing the new system, the Volkswagen subsidiary had fired all strike leaders who would have been eligible to be worker representatives. Union leaders responded by publicly attacking Volkswagen's new policy as an effort to weaken the labor movement. The employee-representation system was perceived as an unofficial company union intended to replace the existing union and as a direct challenge to the traditional major function of the local union to provide for social needs. While the scheme did not interfere with the legal role of unions in wage negotiations, it preempted the issues surrounding work conditions; characteristic union demands for higher wages and job security could be voiced by the employees' new representatives in the Volkswagen scheme. Also, union delegates in the plants would be undercut by granting these rights to employee representatives outside the official union.

Some executives at other automotive subsidiaries and national firms felt that Volkswagen's policy stand was inappropriate for the industry and

[19] The scheme was based on a network of elected employee representatives who would collaborate in identifying and correcting problems within their respective work areas. Their responsibilities were strictly defined as encompassing only internal plant grievances having to do with issues such as working conditions, medical assistance, group insurance, food, transportation, and leisure activities. Delegates were not to participate in wage negotiations, which traditionally fell in the domain of the union. See "Volkswagen Introduces Scheme to Ward Off Labor Tensions in Brazil," *Business Latin America* (17 Sept. 1980): 297.

the political situation in Brazil as a whole. Volkswagen's system would be a failure because its employees would not actually participate meaningfully in such a system. Some of those interviewed suggested that the disenchantment of employees and the local union with Volkswagen's new policy harmed the efforts of the other automotive subsidiaries in jointly developing a true worker-representation system with the local union. The entire automobile industry suffered repercussions from Volkswagen's scheme. Others felt the move destabilized labor relations. National firms in particular were apprehensive of increased labor costs, which they felt they could not afford.

While developing this worker-representation system, Volkswagen do Brasil was in contact with both its parent and the Brazilian government. The subsidiary staff involved in initial proposals visited the parent company in Germany and consulted Brazilian government officials. The approval of both parties was evident from public statements. The Brazilian Minister of Labor called the Volkswagen initiative "an excellent idea."[20] Likewise, the approval of Volkswagen's parent employee-representatives can be inferred from the public statements made by representatives of the International Metalworkers Federation (IMF), the president of which was Volkswagen's labor representative. At an IMF meeting two months after Volkswagen's announcement in 1980, the General Secretary praised the establishment of Volkswagen do Brasil's new worker-representation system as a positive advance in Brazilian employer-employee relations, and claimed partial credit for its establishment.[21] Clearly the new labor policy of the Volkswagen subsidiary was greatly influenced by exchanges with its German parent and international labor organizations as well as with the Brazilian government.

However, just four months after the Volkswagen subsidiary had introduced the government-endorsed representation system, the working alliance with the Brazilian government, which had lasted more than a quarter of a century, suddenly broke. Due to a dramatic drop in auto sales, Volkswagen attempted to reduce its work force and obtain concessions from the Brazilian government. In response, the Brazilian government allied itself with Brazilian labor. The president of Brazil told journalists specifically that his aim was to force the Volkswagen subsidiary to bring in fresh parent-company funds to alleviate its troubles: "They've made a

[20] "Volkswagen Introduces Scheme," *Business Latin America*, p. 297.

[21] "The IMF Volkswagen workers meeting last year in Wolfsburg were able to stand solidly behind Volkswagen unions in these two countries [Brazil and South Africa]. As a result, strikes in both places have resulted in major changes at the plant level, including the recognition of elected shop stewards." Remarks made by Herman Rebhan, General Secretary of the International Metalworkers Federation (IMF), at the IMF Ford World Auto Council in Valencia, Spain (17–19 Nov. 1980, Mimeographed).

lot of money here. Now, let them take care of their own problems."[22] When asked by reporters if the economic slowdown would hurt his government-supported political party in state and congressional elections, the Brazilian president replied that he hoped voters would not cast ballots against him, but against Volkswagen, "which is a multinational company." During this public confrontation between Volkswagen and the Brazilian government, the subsidiary's executive in charge of government relations, the well-known Brazilian Mario Garnero, after more than two decades of representing Volkswagen, resigned in protest over Volkswagen's layoffs. The crisis revealed a critical change, with the Brazilian government suddenly breaking its traditional alliance with Volkswagen in favor of labor. In assessing responsibility for the development, many observers assigned much of it to Volkswagen itself.[23]

The Ford Worker-Representation System

In contrast, less than one year later the Ford subsidiary took the lead as "response leader," announcing a new policy that earned it the favor of labor and opposition groups throughout Brazil. In July 1981, Ford made a change in labor policy with far greater repercussions for Brazil than the innovation initiated by Volkswagen: the first worker-representation system in recent Brazilian history that was acceptable to Brazilian unions. Signed by the Brazilian president of the São Bernardo Union and the American managing director of Ford do Brasil, the legal agreement declared that the union and the Ford subsidiary had agreed on five common objectives for the Ford Plant Committee, the first being the establishment of an effective channel of communication between the company and its workers, and to improve the relationship between the company and the union.[24] Lula, the labor leader, declared: "We broke the historic re-

[22] "Volkswagen's Labor Dispute Underscores the Problems Surging Up in Brazil," *Business Latin America* (17 Sept. 1980): 137–38.

[23] For example, as a leading international business newsletter stated at the time, international investors in Brazil were "facing a rising tide of nationalist sentiment, labor militancy and the government's growing unwillingness to support them in disputes with labor and critics of foreign capital. . . . Volkswagen's labor troubles in Brazil and the government's unfriendly reaction to them have dismayed executives of other foreign-owned firms there. . . . *The government is now out to curry favor with labor, which it antagonized last year* by cracking down on striking São Paulo–area metalworkers." Emphasis added. Most notably, the report blamed Volkswagen for being singled out by the government. "Volkswagen's Labor Dispute," pp. 137–38. Also, see "How to Develop Worker Participation Schemes to Ward Off Tensions in Brazil" and "Labor Relations Plan Garners Good Results for MNC in Brazil," both in *Solving Latin American Business Problems: Case Studies of Over 100 Companies* (New York: Business International Corporation, Oct. 1982): 96–98.

[24] Two members, the coordinator and vice-coordinator, were to be named by the union. The functions of the committee would be to discuss grievances, suggestions, and proposals with the company's industrial-relations staff. See "Comissão de Fabrica," pamphlet pub-

sistance of the companies. . . . The plant committees are in practice our union delegates!"[25] The union hailed Ford's system as the defeat of the government's alleged plan to divide the powerful labor movement (the government's weapon being Volkswagen's nonunion worker-representation system).

Ironically, the breakthrough occurred when the Ford subsidiary again pursued what some labor experts termed "its old-style labor management policy," and it backfired. In response to a sales slump, Ford had dismissed 720 employees (3.5 percent of its total work force). In retaliation, eight thousand of Ford's workers went on a sitdown strike and demanded the rehiring of the dismissed employees, job stability, and an immediate halt to the dismissals. Later demands included the recognition of a group of fourteen employees formed to negotiate the strikers' demands. Under pressure, Ford accepted the demand for a union-based worker-representation system despite the absence of the Brazilian government's approval.[26]

While Ford's labor-relations staff agreed that labor pressure was instrumental in arriving at the landmark agreement, they emphasized the readiness of Ford's senior management to accept a union-based worker-representation system. Ever since the Volkswagen subsidiary had implemented its system in December 1980, various counterproposals had been sent to Ford's parent in Detroit. As one Ford executive explained: "We had to have the timing. There was little change from our proposal sent months before. . . . You have to take into account the parent's approach. . . . In fact, some staff members believe that our managing director and production manager were not really influenced by our local industrial-relations staff proposal but by their own previous conception that plant committees are natural."[27] During Ford's negotiations with the union, a member of the parent's labor-relations staff visited the Ford subsidiary and developed recommendations concerning the strategy, legal agreement, and sundry controversial issues. Fearing disapproval from the parent, the subsidiary made no radical changes from the proposal previously mapped out with the parent. The subsidiary staff believed the new system would benefit Ford in Brazil.[28]

---

lished by Ford do Brasil, Industrial Relations Staff, January 1982; and "Worker Representation Is Good for Management, Says Ford Brazil," *Business Latin America* (2 Feb. 1983): 40.

[25] "Operários conseguem comissão na Ford e voltam ao trabalho," *Journal do Brasil* (15 July 1981): 2.

[26] Author interviews with labor relations management of Ford do Brasil. See "Operários param Ford pela demissão de 700," *Folha de São Paulo* (7 July 1981): 1; and "Operários conseguem comissão na Ford e voltam ao trabalho," *Jornal do Brasil* (15 July 1981): 2.

[27] Author interview with a labor-relations executive at Ford do Brasil.

[28] Author interviews with labor-relations management of Ford do Brasil. Also, see Osmar

The new union-based worker-representation system, formally established in August 1982, was perceived as revolutionary and undesirable by many companies.[29] Indeed, the breakthrough resulted in immediate pressure on the other automotive subsidiaries. According to union representatives, clandestine committees were immediately established in the *Volkswagen*, *Mercedes Benz*, and *Saab* subsidiaries. Soon after, the São Bernardo Union began negotiations with each of the subsidiaries.

The local union's first priority was to change the much-despised *Volkswagen* representation system. Negotiations were difficult, however, breaking off in August. Soon thereafter, German union leaders from the Volkswagen parent came to Brazil. According to Brazilian labor leaders, their presence provided the necessary impetus for the Volkswagen subsidiary. The São Bernardo Union gave the German leaders a presentation on the existing labor relations in the Brazilian Volkswagen subsidiary, including the workers' demands for a union-based worker-representation system. Fifteen days later an agreement was reached. In the announcement of the new Volkswagen worker-representation system to its members, the São Bernardo Union declared the breakthrough as "an historic conquest."[30] The Volkswagen subsidiary, despite much resistance, but given a strong push from its parent labor leaders, finally succumbed to the Brazilian union's demand for a union-based worker-representation system.

Volkswagen's capitulation brought considerable new pressure on the remaining three subsidiaries. The two subsidiaries in the union's jurisdiction—*Mercedes Benz* and *Saab-Scania*—entered into negotiations with union leaders: when would they also join Ford and Volkswagen in establishing worker-representation systems? Again, Saab-Scania do Brasil's parent was reported as intervening, with its Swedish labor unions joining forces with the Brazilian labor union in pressuring the Saab subsidiary.

Valentin, director of labor relations for Ford do Brazil, "Comissão de Fabrica: interesse tambem das empresas," in *Analíses Econômicas* 17) (31 May 1982): 4–5.

[29] For example, as *Business Latin America* reports: "Ford's move was met with skepticism and criticism on the part of traditional Brazilian industrialists who charged the firm with undue liberality." "Worker Representation Is Good for Management, Says Ford Brazil," p. 40.

[30] The São Bernardo Metalworkers Union stated in its newsletter: "Our employers have succumbed to our most important demand, and now we can elect a true Plant Committee. . . . *Volkswagen, which in principle did not want to accept any of the statutes in Ford's Plant Committee, finally yielded*. . . . It is necessary, however, comrades, to never forget one thing: the capacity of the worker's struggle is only in its unity and basic organization. It is the Plant Committee that will strengthen the mobility and organization of workers. . . . Now let's organize to elect our most combative comrades for our Plant Committee." "Comissão de Fabrica na Volks: Uma arma a mais dos trabalhadores," *Tribuna Metalúrgica* (Edição Especial, Oct. 1982): 1. Emphasis added.

The capitulation of the remaining three subsidiaries was only a matter of time. Indeed, by year's end in 1984, the remaining subsidiaries had adopted union-based worker-representation systems, along with numerous other companies nationwide.

As shown, the five automotive subsidiaries responded very differently to labor demands. (1) *Parent preferences*, despite routinized autonomy in labor relations policies, had a sizable impact on how subsidiaries responded. These preferences were manifested through parent-approved options (*General Motors*, *Ford*, and *Volkswagen* parents reviewed labor proposals); parent practices (*General Motors* and *Saab-Scania* imported parent labor practices); parent philosophy (*Ford* refused to fire striking workers and accepted union-based committee); and home-country pressures (*Volkswagen* and *Saab-Scania*'s home unions and parent boards pushed for worker committees). (2) *The subsidiary's relationships with key LDC groups* also shaped the responses of *Volkswagen* and *Ford*. Volkswagen's close relationship with the Brazilian government made it an ally in the struggle against labor and limited its policy responses. In contrast, Ford disobeyed the explicit demands of the Brazilian government by not firing striking workers, and gave in to union demands for a union-based worker-committee—demands that the Brazilian government, in concert with Volkswagen, had aggressively been combating. (3) *The first subsidiary responses* set forth affected all the other subsidiaries. As "response leaders," Volkswagen with its worker-representation scheme, and later Ford with its union-based system, created a snowball effect, not only making it imperative for the other subsidiaries to respond but also setting the parameters of that response.

In summary, if we take into account the behavior of the five subsidiaries from the early 1970s to 1982, the differences are striking: *Mercedes Benz* and *Volkswagen* reported early attempts to study the changing labor environment. *General Motors* and *Ford* were the only subsidiaries to confer regularly about labor policy with international industrial-relations staffs at the parent companies and to utilize their parents' industrial-relations staffs for support, guidance, and training. *Mercedes Benz*, *Saab-Scania*, and *Volkswagen* had a wider range of direct influences from both the host-country environment and the parent, such as newly hired local personnel and labor representatives on the parent Board of Directors. *General Motors* and *Ford* generally had a limited range of direct influences, most originating from the parent company, such as the parent philosophy, parent programs, and visits from parent staff. The industry leader, *Volkswagen*, was the first "response leader," establishing new policies and programs to which the other automotive subsidiaries had to respond. It was *Ford* that finally succumbed to labor demands for a union-based worker-representation system, however, bringing considerable new pressure on the other subsidiaries, eventually even causing Volkswagen also to adopt the new labor scheme. In general, the European subsidiaries—*Mercedes Benz, Saab-Scania*, and *Volkswagen*—shared similar patterns in that they responded to labor earlier and in a more diversified way, while the American companies—*Ford* and *General Motors*—innovated later and were largely influenced by parent practices.

The case study suggests that, in LDCs, subsidiaries faced with a changing environment encounter very different risks. The five automotive subsidiaries, despite their common environment, did not share the same level or type of risks: organized Brazilian labor pressured *Ford* and *Volkswagen* significantly more than *General Motors*, *Mercedes Benz*, or *Saab-Scania*. However, the policies of *Volkswagen* and *Saab-Scania* were also complicated by their respective home unions. *Mercedes Benz* and especially *Volkswagen* operated within their close relationships with the Brazilian government. Each subsidiary had different factors affecting its options and its ability to respond.

Likewise, from the point of view of the Brazilian union, the subsidiaries did not all present the same benefits to their demands. The *Ford* subsidiary was clearly seen as heralding a breakthrough in Brazilian employer-employee relations, and by doing so forced other companies to follow suit. Likewise, Ford's subsidiary management claimed that this improvement in communication also benefited the company and gave it an edge over the other competing subsidiaries. In stark contrast, the *Volkswagen* subsidiary continued to bear the burden of a poor relationship with the union, even after the severing of its historically close relationship with the Brazilian government. Again, the explanation for the differing benefits represented by the subsidiaries is related to a multitude of distinguishing subsidiary characteristics. The next chapter will further analyze the factors determining subsidiary behavior.

CHAPTER 4

Determinants of Differing Subsidiary Behavior: Relationships within the Changing Labor Environment

THE CHRONOLOGICAL ANALYSIS in the last chapter showed that the five Brazilian automotive subsidiaries—even though they were in the same industry and faced the same changing labor environment—behaved very differently. Each subsidiary had its own distinctive characteristics which shaped its behavior. Crisis magnified the effect of these individual characteristics on subsidiary response. However, in that analysis many questions were left unanswered. Now we must put the five subsidiaries into a comparative framework: *how can their relationships further illuminate those variables that account for their differing behavior*?

This chapter continues to examine the five automotive subsidiaries, but in terms of each's relationship with key actors in the changing labor environment. These relationships provide a general basis for an additional understanding of the specific constraints and options available to each subsidiary in preparing and responding to crisis. Within this framework, the variables determining subsidiary behavior become clearer. First, the focus will be on pinpointing differences within the internal organization of the subsidiary, including its relationship with the local union. Next, the relationship of each subsidiary with key actors outside of Brazil, especially the parent company and the home union, is discussed. Then we will explore how each subsidiary related to the key actors in Brazil, the Brazilian government, and to the other automotive subsidiaries.[1]

THE INTERNAL ORGANIZATION: RELATIONSHIPS WITHIN THE SUBSIDIARY

Distinguishing characteristics of the subsidiaries' internal organization included (1) *size*, (2) *the subsidiary's posture toward the union*, and (3) *the mix of expatriates to Brazilians in management positions*.

[1] Unless stated otherwise, the information on subsidiary behavior in this chapter was obtained from extensive interviews with subsidiary management and labor leaders and from answers to detailed questionnaires given by the managing directors of each of the five subsidiaries. (See Appendix for a list of interviewees.)

Size

As shown by table 4–1, the size and worker characteristics of the automotive subsidiaries varied considerably. *Volkswagen do Brasil*, as the largest employer in Brazil, had a total of 46,025 employees while the *Saab-Scania* subsidiary had a total of 3,001 employees. The other three subsidiaries were in a comparative size range—*Ford* (with 21,733), *General Motors* (21,279), and *Mercedes Benz* (24,000). *Volkswagen*, even though it was the subsidiary with the largest number of employees, had the lowest level of unionization of its work force, at 29 percent. The other four subsidiaries had significantly higher levels of unionization, ranging from 32 percent for *Saab-Scania* and Ford to 39 percent for *General Motors*.

Subsidiary Posture toward the Union

While the subsidiaries' structures for labor relations were fairly standard, there were important differences in the way they interacted with the union. Even before the strikes, according to labor leaders, the nature of the subsidiaries' relations with the union differed considerably, with the worst union relations at the *Volkswagen* and *Saab* subsidiaries, and the

TABLE 4–1
Worker Characteristics of the Brazilian Automotive Subsidiaries (1980)

	Ford	*GM*	*MB*	*SS*	*VW*
Total number of employees	21,733	21,279	24,000	3,001	46,025
Union of major plant	São Bernardo	São Caetano	São Bernardo	São Bernardo	São Bernardo
Numbers of workers in major plant	9,473	8,749	13,627	1,758	30,319
Level of unionization	32.3	38.8	34.7	32.6	28.8

Source: Compiled by the author on the basis on information obtained in interviews and from company documents and ANFAVEA.

best at the *Mercedes Benz* subsidiary.[2] As discussed in the previous chapter, management at the Volkswagen subsidiary was perceived as being explicitly an ally of the miltiary government in its antiunion stance, and as being exceptionally "harsh" with union members. To a lesser degree, Saab-Scania was also perceived as antiunion, given the modification of

[2] Author interviews with labor leaders of the São Bernardo Metalworkers Union. Further discussion of the differing postures of the subsidiaries toward the union is covered in the later section on *Parent-Union Relationships*.

the worker-representation system proposed by its parent union. In contrast, the management of Mercedes Benz was perceived as open to the union.

In addition, while all subsidiaries delegated one person to be the official contact for informal communications with the union, subsidiary management in general differed in their willingness to sit down with labor leaders. Except for formal negotiating sessions, the only managing director reported to have had meetings directly with local union leaders was the German managing director of the Mercedes Benz subsidiary. After *Ford* introduced its union-based worker-representation system, however, it was considered to have far superior union relations relative to the other subsidiaries.[3]

Furthermore, union conflict varied considerably among subsidiaries. As noted in the previous chapter, a major reason was location: four subsidiaries were located within the jurisdiction of the São Bernardo Union and only one subsidiary, *General Motors*, was located within the jurisdiction of the adjacent São Caetano Union. Also, two subsidiaries—*Volkswagen* and *Ford*—were much more politicized than the others. As discussed in the previous chapter, reasons cited for *Volkswagen*'s politicization were management's harsh treatment of union employees and its antagonism toward the union, as well as the union's deliberate targeting, given Volkswagen's visibility as Brazil's largest private-sector employer. Differing explanations for *Ford*'s politicization included its more organized work force, several unpopular management decisions the union fought, and the fact that the union simply had more leeway under Ford's relatively liberal posture.

Expatriate / National Mix

The most distinctive contrast between subsidiary internal structures was the mix of expatriates to Brazilians in management positions. In accordance with studies on expatriate policy in MNCs, the American subsidiaries *General Motors* and *Ford* differed markedly from the European, *Volkswagen*, *Mercedes Benz*, and *Saab-Scania*.[4] The European subsidiaries generally had fewer expatriates but these remained in Brazil for many years, while the American subsidiaries had relatively more expatriates

[3] Author interviews with labor leaders of the São Bernardo Metalworkers Union, the managing director of Mercedes do Brasil, and labor-relations management at Ford do Brasil.

[4] Studies have indicated a general tendency of Europeans MNCs to have fewer expatriates in subsidiary management positions than American firms. For example, see Lawrence Franko, "Who Manages Multinational Enterprise?" *Columbia Journal of World Business* 9 (Summer 1973): 38–39.

and these rotated frequently between subsidiaries and the parent. For example, at the Mercedes Benz, Saab, and Volkswagen subsidiaries, the managing directors were expatriates who had worked in Brazil for thirteen, eighteen, and twelve years, respectively. The *Saab* and *Mercedes Benz* subsidiaries even went farther, with figurehead Brazilian "presidents" who were not active in the daily management of the firms nor did they even have their own offices at the subsidiaries. In contrast, the managing directors of the *General Motors* and *Ford* subsidiaries were only in Brazil for five years and one year respectively, but continuity at each American subsidiary seemed to be assured by a Brazilian executive vice-president, each of whom had been employed for over twenty years.

The pattern was also generally true in the subsidiaries' management of labor relations. At the *Volkswagen* and *Mercedes Benz* subsidiaries, Brazilians occupied the position of industrial-relations director. In contrast, at the *Ford* and *Saab* subsidiaries the position was held by expatriates and at *General Motors* by a naturalized Austrian.

In the overall picture, compared to the U.S. subsidiaries the European subsidiaries—*Volkswagen* and *Mercedes Benz* in particular—had more Brazilians in top management and advisory positions, and their expatriates had much longer tenures in Brazil. In summary, significant differences did exist in the organization of the five automotive subsidiaries, particularly in regard to size, posture toward the union, and the mix of expatriates to nationals at the management level.

Parent-Subsidiary Relationships

The case study illustrates how, despite the subsidiaries' various levels of autonomy from their parents, in a changing environment the behavior of each of the five was directly affected by its relationships with the parent and other key actors outside Brazil. The subsidiaries acted as channels of influence, importing new ideas and practices as well as resources from their respective countries into Brazil. Each varied considerably in terms of which influences were transmitted from the parent, as well as to the degree and means of influence. The different effects of parent-subsidiary relationships primarily depended upon these individual parent characteristics: (1) the *parent-defined role in subsidiary labor policy*, (2) the *parent philosophy*, and (3) the *parent-union relationship*.

Parent-defined Role in Subsidiary Labor Policy

With regard to the relationships between parents and subsidiaries, the *European subsidiaries* were distinctly more autonomous in industrial relations than the *U.S. subsidiaries.*[5] The European subsidiaries had markedly less regular contact with their respective parents on local labor policies than their American counterparts. The greater degree of structural autonomy in decision-making is illustrated by the fact that the managing directors and expatriate staff of the European subsidiaries were generally employed for periods longer than a decade, while American expatriates were rotated more frequently.[6] Despite this structural autonomy, two European subsidiaries, *Volkswagen* and *Saab-Scania*, reported the parent company union as an external factor directly affecting the timing and type of new local labor policies. In both cases, parent labor representatives had visited Brazil and had had contact with both subsidiaries' management. The resulting changes affected the organization of both subsidiaries as well as their labor policies.

Unlike the European subsidiaries, the *U.S. subsidiaries* maintained formal relationships with their parents' labor-relations staffs. Because they were more centralized, each American subsidiary received considerable international labor expertise from parent headquarters to support the subsidiary's own industrial-relations staff. Local Brazilians were even trained in industrial relations at the parent, and parent labor-relations staffs periodically visited both Brazilian subsidiaries.

Moreover, the American firms acknowledged that the parent had an approval function in the formulation of labor policy. Both subsidiaries were managed under strict performance guidelines established by their parents. These guidelines limited their ability to alter staffing or production arrangements. Changes usually required the petitioning of the parent. Furthermore, the U.S. subsidiaries claimed U.S. legislation such as the Foreign Corrupt Practices Act resulted in close parent scrutiny and reinforced the general tendency to oversee local relations and policies.

General Motors do Brasil had the most employees in industrial relations who reported regularly to the corporate office, the greatest number

[5] *Autonomy* is defined in terms of an institutionalized decision-making structure: the formal, official, and routinized relationship between the subsidiary and the parent. Incidences outside this structural relationship, in which the parent exercises decisive influence on the subsidiary, are treated separately. The autonomy of each subsidiary is measured by: (1) the amount of contact reported between subsidiary and parent staff on labor-relations policy, (2) the reported role of the parent in regard to formulating subsidiary labor policy, and (3) the managing director's length of employment at the subsidiary. Author interviews with subsidiary management as well as questionnaires submitted to the managing directors are the sources of information for this comparison.

[6] For an interesting discussion of transfer policies in this regard, see Anders Edstrom and Jay R. Galbraith, "Transfer of Managers as a Coordination and Control Strategy in Multinational Organizations," *Administrative Science Quarterly* 22 (June 1977): 248–63. Also, see Duane Kujawa, ed., *International Labor Relations Management* (New York: Praeger, 1971), pp. 65–120 (for Ford) and 123–77 (for General Motors).

who were trained at the parent, as well as the most visits from the parent to the subsidiary. General Motors do Brasil was the only subsidiary that reported compiling a Brazilian labor manual in the language of the home country and according to a format specified by the parent. The role of parent industrial-relations staff was described as largely supportive; yet the parent industrial-relations staff was integrated with the domestic staff to the extent that information on subsidiary policies and local labor development was regularly exchanged and discussed. Significantly, the General Motors subsidiary claimed to have imported its "Quality of Work Life" program even before the crisis of strikes, as a matter of global company policy.

As a general policy, General Motors considered itself a global company, with its subsidiaries integrated with the parent in areas which included certain aspects of labor relations. General Motors had a stated policy of providing "a maximum of opportunity for the employment and advancement of the citizens of each country in which General Motors operates."[7] Dating from 1945, General Motors had sent certain employees from overseas to its General Motors Institute (GMI) for two-year cooperative-study programs in conjunction with various assignments to U.S. operating divisions. The former chairman of the board, Frederick Donner, explained the objective of such training: "to achieve the goal of employing local citizens, General Motors had developed, on a continuing basis, an intensive program of overseas manpower development through education and on-the-job training."[8] In the specific area of labor relations, General Motors do Brasil had trained Brazilian staff at the parent since 1966. Despite these interchanges, however, General Motors do Brasil was one of the last subsidiaries to respond to Brazilian labor demands.

At *Ford do Brasil* there was less contact with the parent on matters relating to labor relations.[9] Reports to the parent were generally centralized through the American director of industrial relations. The parent industrial-relations staff was reported as being "helpful" in providing guidelines; yet policies and procedures had to be "obviously" different for Brazil. As a matter of routine, information on turnover, absenteeism, salaries, and organizational changes were sent to the parent. In the case of negotiations, approval had to be received from the parent after first being reviewed by the subsidiary managing director and the department

[7] Frederick G. Donner, *The Worldwide Industrial Enterprise* (New York: McGraw-Hill, 1967), p. 73.

[8] Donner, *The Worldwide Industrial Enterprise*, p. 84.

[9] There has been a great deal of discussion and literature on the relationship between the Ford parent company and its subsidiaries. For example, see *Bargaining without Boundaries: The Multinational Corporation and International Labor Relations*, ed. Robert J. Flanagan, and Arnold R. Weber (Chicago: University of Chicago Press, 1974), pp. 92, 135–45, 172–73, 204, 212.

heads of manufacturing, finance, and legal affairs. Training of Brazilian staff at the parent as well as visits from the parent were limited. While Ford did have a worldwide employee-relations manual, the Brazilian employees' manual was in Portuguese, and no English manual was sent to the parent as in the case of General Motors.

As a matter of company policy, Ford emphasized autonomy for its subsidiaries in labor relations. Ford's subsidiaries were responsible for developing and administering "an industrial-relations program appropriate to the national setting."[10] However, there was consultation between the subsidiary and the parent labor-relations staff, and in some cases approval by the parent. The vice-president of industrial relations at the Ford parent characterized the role of parent support as providing new ideas and approaches as well as providing information on international labor developments.[11] While Ford had a centralized staff, its training and supportive role, at least in the Brazilian case, was notably less than that between General Motors' parent industrial-relations staff and its Brazilian subsidiary.

According to Ford's own management, however, the Brazilian subsidiary was very limited in its ability to alter staffing and production arrangements. Parent guidelines were strictly enforced and were partly responsible for the subsidiary's "erratic" labor policies. A key factor, according to subsidiary management was the concern of senior expatriate employees with meeting the parent's performance criteria and their hesitancy to raise potential problems outside parent guidelines.

The centralization of labor-relations policies for the American subsidiaries was further demonstrated by collaboration between the U.S. parent companies themselves over their own Brazilian subsidiaries' labor policies. One of the American subsidiaries reportedly gave information on a new policy to its parent industrial-relations staff, which then conferred with the industrial-relations staff of the competitor's parent; the competitor's parent in turn communicated at least some of this information to its subsidiary in Brazil. This interaction was reported as having had a direct influence on the timing and type of response in both subsidiaries because of the parents' acknowledged approval function.

The *European subsidiaries* were distinctly more autonomous than the

[10] Robert Copp, "Locus of Industrial Relations Decision-Making in Multinationals," in *Multinational Unions and Labor Relations in Industrialized Countries*, Robert R. Banks and Jack Stieber, eds. (Ithaca: Cornell University Press, 1977), p. 44. Robert Copp held the position of overseas liàison manager, Labor Relations Staff, Ford Motor Company.

[11] "The importance of obtaining comprehensive information on union activities has been growing rapidly in recent years as the unions have established mechanisms for the interchange of information and experience, and for mutual consultation." See Malcolm L. Denise, "Industrial Relations and the Multinational Corporation: The Ford Experience," in *Bargaining without Boundaries*, Flanagan and Weber, eds., p. 140.

U.S. subsidiaries in areas related to industrial relations. At all three—*Mercedes Benz, Saab*, and *Volkswagen*—the industrial-relations staffs of the parents did not visit the subsidiaries. Communication with the parent was usually limited to information on subsidiary policies and statistical reports on employment. Unlike the U.S. subsidiaries, only in crisis did the parents perform an approval function.

For all five subsidiaries, the degree of autonomy from the parent also affected the restaffing of each subsidiary's labor-relations area. The *European subsidiaries* hired Brazilians from other Brazilian companies who assumed central positions in the development of the subsidiaries' new policies. In contrast, the U.S. *subsidiaries* either transferred expatriate staff from the parent (Ford) or transferred local staff to new management positions (General Motors).

For example, at *Volkswagen do Brasil*, the former Brazilian director of personnel for the largest Brazilian bank was hired as director of industrial relations. It was also the only subsidiary that reported hiring sociologists to conduct surveys on worker satisfaction. At *Mercedes Benz do Brasil*, the Brazilian director of labor relations assumed his position after being recruited for that job six years before. In the case of *Saab-Scania do Brasil*, a Brazilian, hired as director of labor relations, brought in management ideas and techniques acquired from his previous experience working in labor relations for American MNCs in Portugal. A new Brazilian director of information with journalistic experience was also hired at the Saab-Scania subsidiary to work on the improvement of employee-employer communication through company magazines and bulletins. The more autonomous European companies, therefore, hired new Brazilian employees from different backgrounds with the objective of using those experiences to formulate new company policies and procedures.

The U.S. subsidiaries, however, did not hire new employees for the first or second top management positions in industrial relations. In 1978 an American labor expert, employed by *Ford* for twenty-three years, was transferred to Brazil to assume the position of director of industrial relations. The American director indicated that his assignment as a seasoned Ford labor specialist was due to the parent staff's belief that Brazilian labor relations was going through a period of change. The parent company wanted control until a national could take the position of industrial-relations director. The American director had an extensive record in industrial relations at Ford with experience in the United States and Europe, and could transfer American ideas to the changing labor environment and develop a staff that could later be self-sufficient. The second position in industrial relations at Ford was given to a Brazilian employee of nineteen years who most recently had held the position of personnel plant manager. *General Motors* transferred long-term Brazilian employees in its reoganization, from positions as personnel plant managers and personnel staff.

Indeed, the difference between the European and U.S. subsidiaries in restaffing can be interpreted as only an exaggeration of preceding staffing trends. General Motors and Ford were the only subsidiaries that reported the training of local staff in industrial relations at parent headquarters before the beginning of the 1970s. This reflects the difference in autonomy between the European and American subsidiaries and their parents. The more centralized MNCs developed local employees in accordance with standards established for training at the parent headquarters. The subsidiaries that were more autonomous from the parent hired locally from other firms or trained locals for positions as the need arose. In crisis, the type of parent-subsidiary relationship would make all the difference: more dependent subsidiaries with expatriate staffing would be more likely to innovate with imported schemes from the parents, more autonomous subsidiaries with local staff more likely to rely on existing or government-endorsed practices.

Parent Philosophy

In most cases, the influence of parent philosophy on the subsidiary's policy innovation was tenuous. The relationship was clearest in the case of the *Ford* subsidiary with its refusal to fire strike leaders and its acceptance of the first union-based worker-representative system in Brazil explicitly drawn from parent philosophy. In response to a question as to which company characteristics determined labor policy, Ford do Brasil's managing director felt parent philosophy was second only to "practical policy" and its relationship with the union.

The managing directors of the other subsidiaries, excluding Volkswagen, also identified parent philosophy as a key factor. The *General Motors* subsidiary said parent philosophy was the most important, followed by its relationships with the government and the local union. The managing director of *Mercedes Benz* felt four company characteristics—parent philosophy, the company's status as an MNC, the domestic market size, and the number of employees—were equally the most important in determining labor policy. For the managing director of *Saab-Scania*, parent philosophy was less important than five other factors: the company's status as an MNC, domestic market size, the relationship with the government, the number of employees, and the relationship with the union. *Volkswagen*'s managing director differed the most—for him, the most important factors were the number of employees and production strategy; parent philosophy was not an influence.

However, three of the four subsidiaries that reported parent philosophy as an important factor in labor policy also considered it a constraint. For *Ford* it was second in importance as a constraint only to the bargaining structure. For *General Motors* it was third, after the constraints proposed by both government rejection and the bargaining structure. Both U.S. subsidiaries reported that their parent philosophy included the U.S. cultural "emphasis on honesty." They felt obligated, at least to each other, to "tell the truth." *Saab-Scania* also felt its parent philosophy was a constraint, but less than that of industry approval, in addition to those factors identified by General Motors. In contrast, *Mercedes Benz*, like *Volkswagen*, did not feel its parent philosophy was a constraint.

Parent-Union Relationships

Differing parent-union relationships also had a visible impact on subsidiary behavior. Again, the differences were especially wide between the European and the U.S. subsidiaries. Despite their official policy of autonomy in labor relations, the *European subsidiaries*—excluding Mercedes Benz—were greatly affected by their parents' unions. The home-country unions of the *Saab* and *Volkswagen* subsidiaries even joined forces with the Brazilian unions and entered into negotiations directly with their respective subsidiaries. In contrast, neither of the managing directors of the *U.S. subsidiaries* cited home-country labor leaders as direct influences on subsidiary labor policies.

As one of the highest-paid labor forces in the world, U.S. labor groups such as the UAW have had significant incentives to increase the bargaining power of labor unions in other areas of the world. Accordingly, the UAW, as the American union for General Motors and Ford, has had a local office in Brazil since the beginning of the 1950s. The Brazilian UAW office, however, was completely independent from the American subsidiaries.[12] While the UAW in the United States directly lobbied the U.S. parents to change their subsidiaries' labor policies and pressure the Brazilian government, neither subsidiary felt these activities affected its policies. The parent positions were not a function of the home union.

Historically, the UAW's influence on the parents had differed. In the case of *Ford do Brasil*, the managing director stressed that the parent company over the years had already incorporated many of the UAW's demands into the company corporate philosophy. After all, the parent had had a long history of conflicts with and capitulations to UAW demands not significantly different from the current demands of the Brazil-

[12] The UAW, however, did give financial support to the Brazilian union of the U.S. subsidiaries. Of particular note, they sent observers to the trial of the union leader Lula and sponsored two trips to the U.S. and Canada. See "Brazilians Watch Worker Candidate," *Wall Street Journal*, 29 Sept. 1982.

ian union. In fact, during the U.S. labor movement of the 1930s and 1940s, Henry Ford was characterized as putting "up a stiffer fight against organized labor than anyone else on the industrial horizon."[13] However, just as later in Brazil, the parent made a complete reversal in policy: in 1941, in response to a strike, Ford gave in to the UAW and officially recognized it as the company union. Ford accepted demands for wage increases, the abolition of Ford Service (a seniority system governing lay-offs and rehiring), the reinstatement of employees fired for union activity, overtime pay, a shop steward system, and other features of standard UAW contracts.[14] Ford's capitulation was acclaimed as "a historic victory for the American working class."[15] Therefore, over the years the Ford company had developed its own distinctive relationship with the UAW, as reflected in its labor policies and philosophy, and later reflected in its response to similar Brazilian demands.

Likewise, the *General Motors*—UAW relationship has evolved its own particular history, also mirrored in its Brazilian subsidiary policies. In the United States, the UAW has been cited as the most active union in launching "new approaches to problems of social and political concern."[16] For example, when the UAW submitted proposals in 1973 to Chrysler, Ford, and General Motors to establish union-management committees for the purpose of improving the quality of worklife, the only agreement for the establishment of these committees was with General Motors.[17] The parent's emphasis on its "Quality of Work Life" programs made it a ready-made response to the Brazilian labor crisis. Therefore, while General Motors and Ford as American companies both had centralized staffs in industrial relations, the influence of the parents was distinctive, reflecting the particular evolution of the parent's own union relationship.

Despite the increased degree of autonomy for the *European subsidiaries*, there was significant noninstitutionalized and informal contact between the parents and the subsidiaries that reflected unique parent-union relations. For example, at both *Volkswagen* and *Saab*, the labor representatives on the parent Board of Directors visited the Brazilian subsidiaries. All three European subsidiaries were regularly visited by the press from their countries, and they sometimes collaborated with the

[13] David L. Lewis, *The Public Image of Henry Ford* (Detroit: Wayne State University Press, 1976), p. 247.

[14] Lewis, *The Public Image of Henry Ford*, p. 266.

[15] *The Nation*, as quoted in Lewis, *The Public Image of Henry Ford*, pp. 265, 267.

[16] John Logue, "On the Road toward Worker-Run Companies: The Employees Participation Act in Practice," *Working Life in Sweden* 9 (Dec. 1978): 73.

[17] See, for example, Stephen H. Fuller, "How Quality-of-Worklife Projects Work for GM," Conference Papers in *Monthly Labor Review* (July 1980): 37–43. The well-known "Quality of Work Life" project at a General Motors plant in North Tarrytown, New York, is discussed in Beatrice Walfish, "Q.W.L. Project at General Motors Plant Cited as Key to Labor-Management Accord," *World of Work Report* 2, no. 17 (Dec. 1977): 133–40.

parent office of public relations in the preparation of statistical documents or brochures explaining practices toward employees, all written in the language of the home country. However, despite its official policy of subsidiary autonomy, Volkswagen reported the most parent intervention, followed by Saab; in contrast *Mercedes Benz* reported no intervention from employee representatives on the parent Board of Directors.

Volkswagen do Brasil, as the largest MNC subsidiary in all of Latin America, was extremely visible not only in Brazil but also in Germany. The managing director emphasized the subsidiary's complete autonomy in labor policy from its parent. The principle is "parent company acceptance of policy set by the subsidiary, as suitable to the prevailing legislation in the country where located."[18] However, despite this principle, Volkswagen was the only one of the three European subsidiaries that acknowledged the parent's approval function of subsidiary labor policies.

Volkswagen's relationship with its parent was very different from that of Mercedes Benz do Brasil and its parent. Thirty-six percent of Volkswagen was government-owned (20 percent by the German Federal Government). Traditionally, government and labor representatives on Volkswagen's Supervisory Board (*Aufsichat*) were politically aligned in contested decisions.[19] Since the Supervisory Board was comprised of ten members representing the stockholders and ten members representing labor, any political alliance between labor and government stockholder representatives was decisive.

The government and labor representatives on the Volkswagen Supervisory Board were public figures with high visibility throughout the country and, to a lesser degree, Europe. As of 1980, the two representatives of the government of Lower Saxony were the Minister of Economic Affairs and Transport and the Minister of Finance; the two representatives of the Federal Government were the Under-Secretary of State in the Federal Ministry of Finance and the Under-Secretary of State in the Federal Ministry of Economics. Meanwhile, the labor representatives on the Volkswagen Board of Directors included the strongest labor leaders in Germany and Europe: the chairman of the Board of Management of the company's union, Metallgesellschaft AG, and the president of the International Metalworkers Federation (IMF). Indeed, Brazilian labor leaders cited the IMF as the overseas organization most helpful during the automotive strikes.

In crisis, this unique management structure overrode the official sub-

[18] Response of the managing director of Volkswagen do Brasil to questionnaire.

[19] In German companies, under "codeterminism," the Supervisory Board has the responsibility of approving annual accounts and major financial decisions (such as investment in new plants or closures) as well as those members elected to the Management Board. One member of the Board of Management must be a Labor Director who is responsible for all matters relating to social and personnel policy.

sidiary autonomy in formulating labor policy, with the Volkswagen parent and its union leaders shaping subsidiary labor policies. Therefore, the significant difference between *Volkswagen* and *Mercedes Benz* parent involvement in the labor relations of their Brazilian subsidiaries would seem to be a function of larger, overall company characteristics.

In the case of the *Saab* subsidiary, according to both labor-relations executives and Brazilian labor leaders, the antiunion position of its industrial-relations director was directly linked to his personal disenchantment with the Swedish labor system. The Swedish director wanted to keep Brazil from committing the "mistakes" his country had made. One international labor authority noted that the "primary political fact of life in Sweden [is that] the country is dominated politically by the labor movement: even employer compliance represents recognition that the pressure for change is . . . irresistible, and that managerial absolutism is a thing of the past."[20] Unable to reverse the labor movement's domination of Swedish business, the Swedish director of industrial relations felt strongly committed to another path for Brazil and his subsidiary.

While Saab-Scania do Brasil's management claimed to transfer superior parent practices, local labor leaders claimed that the policies of Saab-Scania do Brasil were expressly directed against their union and felt that Saab, like Volkswagen, was decisively antiunion. In fact, one labor leader claimed that Saab's treatment of workers was worse than that of all other subsidiaries. Specific problems included Saab's treatment of the two union directors employed there. Saab was cited as the only subsidiary prohibiting directors from entering the plant with union bulletins, and the only one not providing them with free time to resolve worker problems. Another Saab action considered very important was the firing of one of the leaders of the 1980 strike without any supplemental payment. A labor court later resolved the case in the worker's favor. Labor leaders also cited the case of a former president of their union, who was allegedly fired by the Saab subsidiary for participating in the arrangement of union elections.

A second factor explaining the role of the Saab parent in regard to the labor policies of its Brazilian subsidiary was the extraordinary emphasis given to it by the Swedish press. Both Saab-Scania do Brasil and the local union underlined the importance of Swedish journalists in Brazil and their articles on labor problems in Brazil published in Sweden. This publicity ensured that the Swedish parent's agenda included Brazil's labor problems.

The response of the Swedish union and its collaboration with the Swedish parent in promoting progressive policies at the Saab subsidiary can be explained by the Swedish industrial-relations system. In Sweden

[20] Logue, "On the Road toward Worker-Run Companies," p. 10.

there is a close identification between union and firm management, with emphasis on cooperation and coordination. Much of the literature affirms the evolution of a union-management link to the point that "unions are being integrated into management."[21]

However, the ineffectiveness of the Swedish union's efforts in Brazil was also very much related to the relations between unions and companies in Sweden. Unlike Germany, the focus is not on worker influence in the boardroom but instead on collective bargaining. Wage negotiations are highly centralized, resulting in minimal overt confrontations at the plant or company level and between the union and management. Likewise, in accordance with the Swedish company-employee partnership, Saab's union leaders, as representatives of parent management, had involved themselves in the Brazilian subsidiaries' labor relations. Most significantly, this labor policy involvement was limited by the cooperative stance with Saab-Scania do Brasil's management, as well demonstrated by the 1977 worker-representation system: a product solely of Swedish labor initiative that was altered by subsidiary management and as a result completely rejected by local labor.

In summary, the relationships between the subsidiaries and the parents were significant in industrial relations for each of the subsidiaries in the study. In terms of autonomy, the *European subsidiaries* had significantly less regular contact with the parent in industrial relations than the *U.S. subsidiaries*. Regardless of autonomy, however, other factors, such as the home-country industrial-relations system and labor representatives on the parent Board of Directors, affected the local labor policies of the European subsidiaries. The study indicated that, despite structural or official autonomy, the subsidiary was likely to be directly affected by a multitude of factors related to the parent and the home country. The parent's policies, including its relationship to its home union, defined the conduit to the subsidiary in regard to how and to what degree the subsidiary would be influenced. Parent policies and philosophy could be deliberately transferred, or resisted. The home-country's industrial-relations system affected the subsidiary to differing degrees depending on the home union's relationship with the parent and its strategy for dealing with the parent's overseas operations. Other home-country factors emerged: legislation, press, public opinion, and public parent ownership. The case study illustrates the complexity of subsidiary behavior in response to pressure in LDCs, including the role of each subsidiary's origins, the diverse range of actors and interests outside the LDC that

[21] Logue, "On The Road toward Worker-Run Companies," p. 10. Also, see G. D. Garson, "The Codetermination Model of Workers' Participation: Where Is It Leading?" *Sloan Management Review* 18, no. 3 (Spring 1977): 63–78.

are an integral part of that origin, and the overall importance of understanding the uniqueness of each parent-subsidiary relationship.

Subsidiary Relationships with the Host Government

All the subsidiaries felt the Brazilian government was the key constraint in formulating their labor policies. Labor leaders agreed: the subsidiaries by virtue of their international origins understood labor demands much more clearly; like the Brazilian government, Brazilian national companies were fearful, and would resist. However, as noted in previous discussions, the automotive industry had been closely aligned with the Brazilian military government. The nature of each subsidiary's relationship with the government varied, and as a consequence so did the implications for subsidiary behavior.

The differences between subsidiary–host government relationships mainly revolved around (1) *the importance of the subsidiary to the government* as well as (2) the subsidiary's management structure for *government relations* and (3) its management structures for *industrial relations*.

Subsidiary Importance to Government

The reason both the *Mercedes Benz* and *Volkswagen* subsidiaries were characterized by close government contact may be related to the fact that each was a market leader. A market leader position resulted in a high level of visibility—*Volkswagen* was the nation's largest manufacturer, exporter, and employer; *Mercedes Benz* had what its managing director called a "political product" since the ultimate users of the buses were the public.[22]

Government-Relations Structure

Even before the strikes, subsidiaries differed in how closely they interrelated with the Brazilian military government. For example, all the subsidiaries—except for *Saab-Scania* and *Ford*—had labor management staff who had previously been with the Brazilian military. These ex-military officers were considered very valuable: they enabled effective communication with government intelligence units and facilitated the maintenance of plant security. Before the strikes, these ex-military officers were

[22] The managing director of Mercedes Benz do Brasil stated: "Our product has a very sensitive problem because we have 96 percent of the bus market and the bus is the main transport. This is a highly political product because every price increase is an increase in fares and the moment the public of bus clients goes against us, because they see us as earning too much money, that is quite something. . . . So you must be careful about the monopoly you exert." Author interview with managing director of Mecedes Benz do Brasil.

in "employee services" areas; after the strikes, *Mercedes Benz*, *Volkswagen*, and *General Motors* transferred their former military officers to public relations areas within the company. Management at the *Ford* and *Saab* subsidiaries, however, felt that hiring from the military was not "appropriate." Therefore, despite a similar approach in industry relationship with the government, the companies differed in their use of former military officers.

Furthermore, throughout the period of labor unrest, the depth of government contact differed greatly between subsidiaries. The managing directors of the German subsidiaries, *Mercedes Benz* and *especially Volkswagen*, had developed strong personal relationships with government officials. Both also had Brazilians on their Board of Directors. The Volkswagen subsidiary had the closest and the widest range of contact with the government: the managing director, the legal director, the director of industrial relations, and the manager of industrial relations all claimed direct access to the Minister of Labor. In the case of the *Mercedes Benz* subsidiary, the managing director claimed to have established important personal relationships with several ministers and other government officials during his tenure of thirteen years.

While the *U.S. subsidiaries* had been in Brazil over forty years longer than the other subsidiaries, their managing directors did not have personal relationships of the same intensity with government officials. This was due primarily to an expatriate rotation system, wherein top management usually shifted positions between the parent and various subsidiaries every few years. Over the years, American top management was at a special disadvantage in developing important contacts: most could not speak the country's language and were also limited in their knowledge of the country's sociopolitical, cultural, and economic dimensions.

While *Ford* generally rotated its expatriate management in Brazil more often then *General Motors*, the subsidiaries had similar structures supporting government relations. At both subsidiaries, government relations were usually performed by the Brazilian executive government adviser or by the expatriate managing director accompanied by an adviser. At *Ford* the government adviser had been employed for twenty years; he was on the Subsidiary Board and acted as legal director of the subsidiary. Likewise, the executive government adviser at *General Motors* had been employed for thirty years; he was the executive vice-president and the only Brazilian on the Subsidiary Board. Therefore, the relationships of the American subsidiaries with the Brazilian government fell predominantly into the domain of each respective Brazilian adviser, while the government relationships for the German subsidiaries directly involved the expatriate managing directors.

Saab-Scania had had both a long-term expatriate managing director and a series of government advisers. Contact between the managing director and the Minister of Labor, however, was reported as being less than the other subsidiaries, except for Ford. Also, the military was not a noted source of information. Instead, the Subsidiary Board was used for information, along with the Swedish-Brazilian Chamber of Commerce. Politics was avoided, reportedly due to a Swedish orientation that disapproved of business relationships in the political arena. The absence of military presence at Ford as well suggested that Saab-Scania do Brasil and Ford shared more extreme nonpolitical orientations than the other automotive subsidiaries.

At the *U.S. subsidiaries*, public statements were often made by the Brazilian director of public relations or the Brazilian executive vice-president, while the managing directors of the European subsidiaries were generally more dominant in playing the spokesman role. The general explanation given was that the managing directors of the American subsidiaries were not as well acquainted with Brazilian aspects of public relations or government relations as the other European managing directors, all of whom had lived in Brazil for over a decade. One top management executive interpreted the roles of the Brazilian public-relations directors and executive vice-presidents as providing "buffer systems" for the American managing directors. The managing directors had their seasoned Brazilian experts deal directly with problems, and always had a second chance to change their companies' official position with personal statements if necessary. In addition, these "buffer systems" could insulate the American managing directors from pressure to give donations (or bribes), as such actions are constrained by legislation in the United States. The European subsidiaries, on the other hand, due to their personal relationships with government officials, were sometimes under pressure to make personal public statements or donations to various causes.

Industrial-Relations Management

At subsidiaries where the director of industrial relations was not Brazilian, contact with high government officials such as the Minister of Labor was relatively limited. This was particularly true in the case of *Ford do Brasil* where the director of industrial relations was an American who could not speak Portuguese. His labor-relations staff felt his inability to have direct access to the Brazilian Minister of Labor was significantly disadvantageous in communicating company points of view and influencing government policy. Furthermore, expatriate staff was reported as resulting in less autonomy for the subsidiary, as they would tend to contact the parent before making decisions.

Therefore, as shown in figure 4–1, the structure of the individual subsidiaries indicated that the *European subsidiaries* were more integrated with the Brazilian government than the *U.S. subsidiaries*. The managing directors of the European subsidiaries, in particular Volkswagen and *Mercedes Benz*, had developed extensive personal relationships with government officials over the years. Second, the *European subsidiaries* had other Brazilians inside their company as well as on their boards who were influential with the Brazilian government. Third, contact between the government and the European subsidiaries involved more staff members than that of the American companies. The relationships between the

FIGURE 4–1
Comparative Avenues of Government Relations: Subsidiary Management and the Brazilian Government

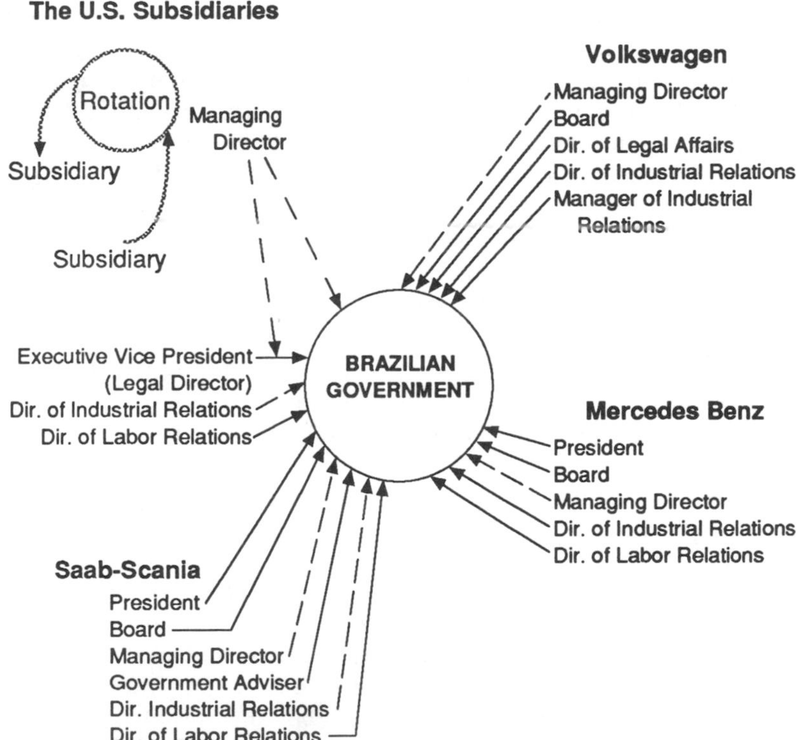

Source: Compiled by the author on the basis of information obtained in company interviews.

Note: *Dotted lines* drawn between a management position and the government indicate that the position is held by an expatriate. *Solid lines* drawn between a management postiion and the government indicate that the position is held by a Brazilian.

U.S. subsidiaries and the Brazilian government were more focused and limited, relying heavily on their respective Brazilian executive vice-presidents. Therefore, there were significant differences between the subsidiaries in their government relations due to differing competitive positions and products as well as management policies. As a result, the European subsidiaries claimed to have more information on the changing labor environment than their American competitors.

Subsidiary Interrelationships

The five automotive subsidiaries jointly dominated the Brazilian automotive terminal industry and collaborated on multiple fronts from government lobbying to labor policies. As a general rule, the automotive subsidiaries kept in very close contact with each other. However, in the case of the changing labor environment, a closer examination revealed distinctive differences in the functional usefulness of industry collaboration—with interesting implications as to what these differences mean. Differences in subsidiary interrelationships were largely related to the subsidiary's *ability to get information*, or conversely, its *reliance on other companies*.

Ability to Get Information

The *Volkswagen* subsidiary was cited as the key information source on labor developments. Volkswagen reportedly had more information than the Brazilian government: reports had it that Volkswagen had developed a staff with extensive information on the labor movement and would, on occasion, share it with the government and other subsidiaries. The U.S. subsidiaries relied on Volkswagen for information rather than each other, while the two German subsidiaries exchanged exclusive information in some areas.

The reasons give for the *U.S. subsidiaries'* reliance on Volkswagen do Brasil for information were related. American culture stressed competitive and honest business behavior, as reflected in legislation such as the Foreign Corrupt Practices Act and the laws on antitrust. The U.S. subsidiaries were reported as being especially careful to abide by these restrictions. However, these laws had no equivalent in Germany. Therefore a U.S. subsidiary could exchange information more freely and to greater advantage with a German subsidiary than with another American company. Second, Volkswagen in particular had better contacts with the host government. For example, expatriate staff of a U.S. subsidiary had reportedly been unable to develop superior government contacts, due in part to the lack of language ability, and had to ask Volkswagen staff to communicate certain points to government officials. In contrast to the relationship between the U.S. subsidiaries, the German subsidiaries—*Mercedes Benz* and *Volkswagen*—often collaborated on issues and shared information.

Reliance on Other Companies

Those subsidiaries that reported close government contact also reported little reliance on other subsidiaries. *Mercedes Benz*, as the subsidiary whose managing director spent the most time lobbying government officials, claimed to be less influenced by the individual positions of other firms. On the other hand, those subsidiaries with the least government contact—*Ford, General Motors*, and particularly *Saab-Scania*—reported other subsidiaries and the industry association as key reference points in the formation of subsidiary policy on labor. These claims were evidenced by the subsidiaries' memberships in industry labor-relations groups. The *General Motors, Ford*, and *Saab-Scania* subsidiaries reported extensive participation, with at least three staff members each participating in four industrial-relations groups. In contrast, *Mercedes Benz* had only one staff member participate and *Volkswagen* had a total of two memberships.

Therefore, distinctions between subsidiary interrelationships can be drawn on the basis of each subsidiary's ability to get information independently and its reliance on other companies for information. The subsidiaries more closely integrated with the government—*Volkswagen* and *Mercedes Benz*—had more access to information. The other subsidiaries—*Saab-Scania, Ford*, and *General Motors*—tended to rely on the industry and other firms for information as a reference point. The *Mercedes Benz* and *Volkswagen* subsidiaries were more independent of the employers' association and industry policies than the other subsidiaries. This development was intrinsically related to the integration of these subsidiaries with the host government. As a result, both subsidiaries, to varying degrees, had priority access to information on government actions and labor developments. However, this priority access could also be accompanied by government pressures to support or initiate government policies.

Conclusion

The Brazilian case study illustrates the argument: *when MNC subsidiaries are faced with host-country pressures on a particular policy, their responses differ according to individual subsidiary characteristics*. By examining subsidiary relationships, summarized in figure 4–2, we have identified a wide array of factors that help to shape subsidiary response to labor demands.

The entire subsidiary organization was brought into play—structures, strategies, policies, practices, individuals, relationships, philosophies, products, production requirements, and market positions. Crisis magnified the differences among the five subsidiaries. Only by enlarging the picture to include this multitude of subsidiary characteristics can the differing responses of the five automotive subsidiaries truly be explained. Only by considering the entire subsidiary organization can we begin to

FIGURE 4–2
Key Subsidiary Relationships: Reported Factors Shaping Response to Labor Demands

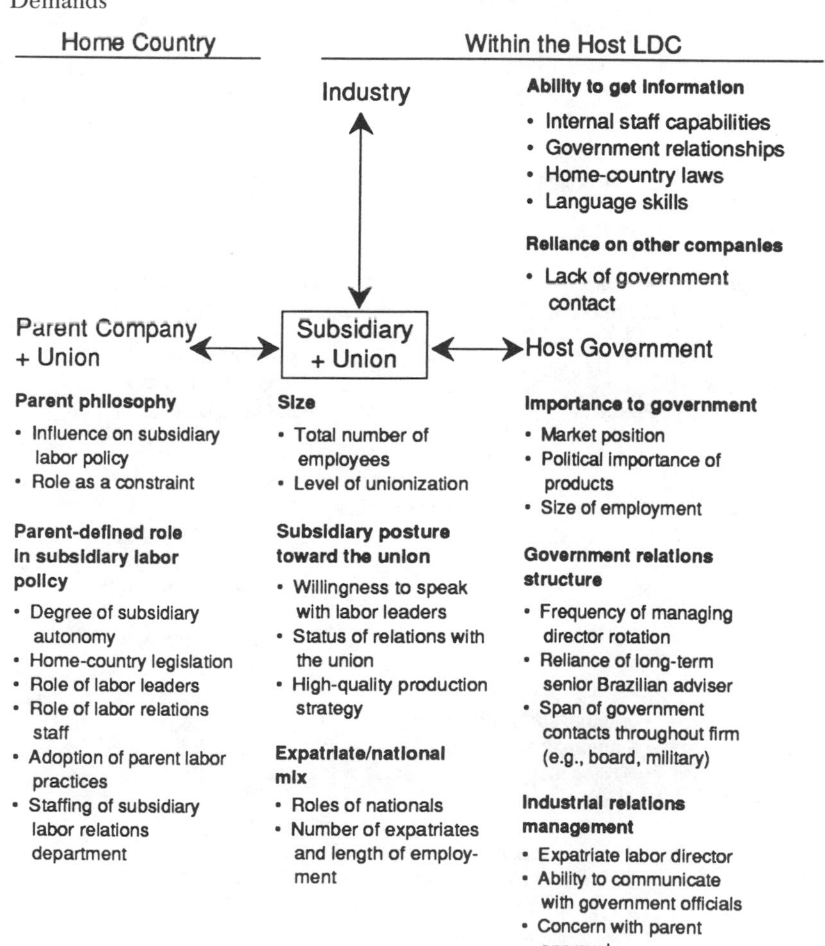

understand the complexity of subsidiary–host country interaction or MNC response to host-country demands. (See figure 4–3.)

Within this complexity, more specific variables emerge. Differences in subsidiary internal organization and relationships resulted in differing abilities and willingness to respond. Of the multitude of differing characteristics, certain ones shaped the subsidiaries' relationships with key

FIGURE 4–3
The Overall MNC Organization: Key Factors Shaping Response to Labor Demands

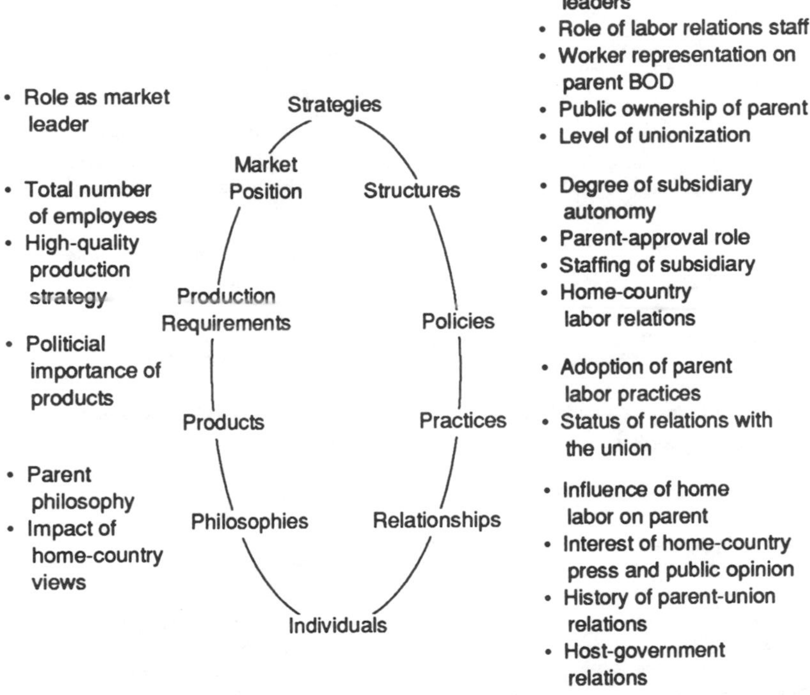

actors. Certain subsidiary characteristics determined a high degree of integration between the parent and the subsidiary: for example, regular rotation of expatriate management, expatriates in top management reporting positions, government relationships conducted mainly by Brazilian management, and restrictive home-country legislation on industry collusion and business practices. A different set of subsidiary characteristics reinforced a high degree of government-subsidiary integration: for example, a large number of employees, a market leader position, politically important products, extensive personal contact between a long-tenured managing director and government officials, and Brazilians in top management positions and on the subsidiary Board of Directors. Likewise, a set of complementary subsidiary characteristics were associated with a subsidiary's reliance on the industry or the employers' association for information and guidance: for example, a small to medium-sized company within the local economy, and a nonpolitical management orientation. (See figure 4–4.)

Furthermore, the degree of autonomy between a subsidiary and its parent seemed to be conversely related to the degree of integration between a subsidiary and the host government. The European subsidiaries were more autonomous from their parents in the formation of subsidiary labor policy and more closely integrated with the Brazilian government. The U.S. subsidiaries, in contrast, tended to rely on the parent company and the automotive industry for information and feedback on subsidiary policies. Saab-Scania do Brasil, despite its autonomy, was also generally more dependent on the industry because of its nonpolitical orientation and small size.

Therefore, the study shows that each subsidiary's labor policies were affected by a complex range of very different subsidiary characteristics. As the subsidiaries developed individual labor policies during this period, the specific relationships between each subsidiary and the parent, the host government, and the industry became visible determinants of subsidiary labor policy.

The Policy Reformulation Process

If we examine our proposition on the variables that differentiate subsidiary behavior, the answers are now clearer. The preceding examination of key subsidiary relationships helps to differentiate common key variables that explain subsidiary behavior.

PRE-CRISIS IDENTIFICATION OF LDC DEMANDS

The reasons why certain subsidiaries were able to identify a changing environment are now more evident. (See table 4–2.) We now see that

FIGURE 4–4
Management Characteristics and the Relationships of the Subsidiary to the Parent, Host Government, and Industry

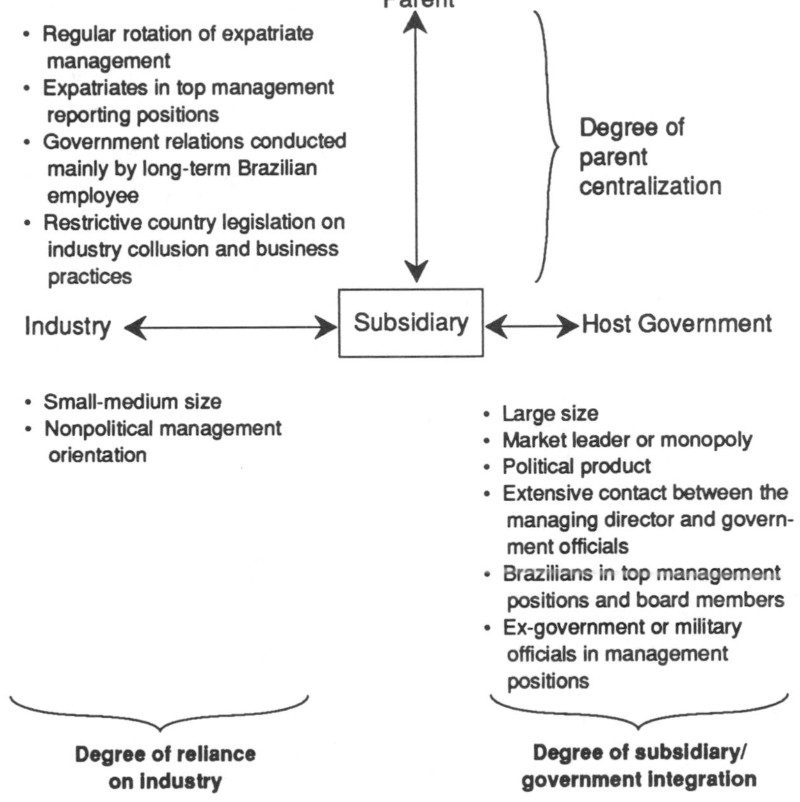

(1) *internal management policies* did make a difference. There was a clear distinction in how well each subsidiary management could read the environment. The managing directors of the *Volkswagen* and *Mercedes Benz* subsidiaries had lived in Brazil for decades; they knew its history and politics, and they spoke the language. In sharp contrast, the managing directors of the *Ford* and *General Motors* subsidiaries, while familiar with Brazil, were at a disadvantage in reading the environment compared to their Volkswagen and Mercedes Benz counterparts. Frequent rotations as a function of their parent's personnel policies lessened their ability to personally diagnose environmental changes.

Furthermore, internal managment policies differed in terms of resource availability and subsidiary latitude to adjust policies. Again, the managing directors of the *Mercedes Benz* and *Volkswagen* subsidiaries

TABLE 4–2
Brazilian Case Conclusions at Pre-Crisis: The Ability of the Subsidiary to Identify and Respond to LDC Demands

Internal subsidiary management policies		
• Knowledge of country by senior subsidiary management	+	*VW, MB*: Long-tenured expatriate management, speaks language
	–	*Ford, GM*: Expatriate rotation policy
• Resource availability and latitude to adjust policies	+	*MB*: Internal policy studies
	+	*VW*: Gathering information on employees
	–	*Ford, GM*: Limited funds and personnel
Relationships with key LDC actors	+/–	*VW, MB*: Managing director's close friendships with Brazilian government officials
	+	*MB*: Managing director communicates with labor leaders, national firm management
Parent intervention and influence		
• Day-to-day policies	–	*GM, Ford*: Subsidiary labor policies approved by parent
	–	*Ford*: Parent role in subsidiary organization and personnel
	–	*SS*: Rejection of Swedish labor model
• Participation in policy changes	–	*SS*: Parent union proposal
	+	*Ford*: Head-office labor-relations staff proposal

Note: + = reported as increasing ability; – = reported as decreasing ability.

claimed to have freedom to follow through on their initiatives. They had the resources and decision authority to respond pre-crisis. Without petitioning their parents, they began to study the labor environment, reorganize their companies, and prepare for the onset of crisis. In contrast, labor-relations staffs at *General Motors* and *Ford* emphasized constraints on resources and policymaking. Funds for additional personnel and studies were available only if the subsidiary wanted to take the risk of lobbying the parent, and then the parent would have been convinced.

(2) The second differentiating variable, *relationships with key LDC actors*, also explains varying subsidiary ability to identify change. Subsid-

iaries that had close relationships had the advantage of "insider" information on labor developments. The *Volkswagen* and *Mercedes Benz* subsidiaries benefited from the advance knowledge derived from their managing directors' relationships with government officials. Of particular assistance was the Mercedes Benz managing director's dialogues with labor leaders and national business leaders. The long-term commitment of these expatriates was critical. Sensitivity to the environment could only be developed through long-term relationships with the environment.

However, for exactly the same reasons, the Volkswagen and Mercedes Benz subsidiaries also had less latitude (and perhaps desire) to comply with labor demands. Close relationships with government officials made them allies. Even Mercedes Benz, while able to counter labor hostility through direct meetings with labor leaders, was like Volkswagen constrained in its policy options.

(3) The third differentiating variable, *parent intervention and influence*, also explains varying ability to identify change. Certain day-to-day parent policies and influences interfered with pre-crisis subsidiary response. In the case of *General Motors* and *Ford*, a key reason for their inability to adjust policies was related to their parents' role in approving policy changes. The subsidiaries operated under strict performance guidelines; requests to change labor policies had to be well-argued and supported by tangible reasons. Ford, in particular, reported strict parent rules in organization and personnel devoted to subsidiary labor relations. There was a fundamental organizational bias against petitioning head-office staff for modifications. Only post-crisis did visits from the head office occur. In addition, in the case of *Saab-Scania*, the parent influence was transmitted via the Swedish labor-relations director: in reaction against Sweden's liberal labor policies, he was personally determined to resist the Brazilian workers' demands.

Beyond day-to-tday policies and influences, parent intervention also occurred in terms of reported participation in policy changes. In the case of Saab-Scania, the parent's role in introducing worker committees was negative, the end result being the distancing of the subsidiary from its union. However, the proposal from *Ford*'s head office for enlarging its labor-relations area was, after initial resistance, finally adopted. While this parent initiative did spur subsidiary response before crisis, the effect was limited to organization change and not reflected in day-to-day policies. Ford's "erratic" labor management policy remained intact.

Therefore, common variables differentiated the ability of the five subsidiaries to identify and respond to their changing labor environment before crisis. Critical response variables included flexible subsidiary policies formulated by knowledgeable senior management with resource availability and the latitude to adjust policies, develop close relationships with LDC actors, and coordinate effective parent intervention.

DEGREE OF CONFLICT

The preceding review of subsidiary organization and relationships also clarifies the reasons for differing levels of pressure on subsidiary policies. (See table 4–3.) *Historical subsidiary policies* did make a difference. *Saab*'s poor union relationships were largely due to the antiunion stance of its labor management. The explanation for *Ford*'s "erratic" labor policies was at least in part reportedly due to strict parent performance guidelines. *Volkswagen*'s "repressive" labor policies grew largely out of

TABLE 4–3
Brazilian Case Conclusions at Conflict: The Level of Pressure on Subsidiary Policies

Past subsidiary policy performance		
• Pre-crisis response	+	*SS*: Poor union relations (subsidiary management bias)
• Innate conflict	+	*Ford*: "Erratic" labor policies (parent performance guidelines)
	+	*VW*: "Repressive" labor policies (host-government relations)
	–	*MB*: Less turnover (need for more highly trained workers for truck/bus manufacture)
Pressuring-group perception		
• Ability/willingness	+	*SS*: Easy to shut down, supportive home union
	+	*Ford*: History of more "liberal" policies; previous worker committees
• Overall subsidiary value	+	*VW*: Visibility as nation's largest employer; market leader
Parent interests		
• Home country pressures	+	*SS, VW*: Home union and parent board of directors
	+	*SS*: Home-country public opinion, influence of labor
	+	*VW*: Public ownership of parent, influential labor leaders

Note: + = reported as increasing pressure; – = reported as decreasing pressure.

its close alliance with the Brazilian military government, and out of its role as the country's largest employer in enforcing its antiunion stance. *Mercedes Benz*'s relatively superior labor relations was related to its particular production needs: the manufacturing of trucks and buses required highly trained workers.

Identifying the union's *differing perception* of each subsidiary also helps clarify why certain subsidiaries were under more pressure. *Saab-Scania* was perceived as being easy to shut down, its home union supportive of labor activities. Similarly, *Ford* had a history of more liberal labor policy, including worker committees. *Volkswagen*, on the other hand, was seen by the union as a very valuable challenge—as the nation's largest employer and the automotive market leader, any labor progress would be guaranteed high visibility.

The structural examination of the subsidiaries fleshed out the reasons for differing *parent interests*. In the case of the *Saab* subsidiary, the unique development of the Swedish industrial-relations system was key: labor had a great deal of influence on public opinion and company policy. For the *Volkswagen* subsidiary, the critical variable was not the German codetermination labor system, but the public ownership of the company and the influential labor leaders on its Board of Directors. In contrast, the other German subsidiary, Mercedes Benz, was not affected by home-country pressures.

TYPE OF SUBSIDIARY RESPONSE

With this microstructural examination of the five subsidiaries, the explanations for differing subsidiary responses are also more complete. (See table 4–4.) In terms of *parent preferences*, the higher degree of subsidiary-parent integration differentiated the *U.S. subsidiaries* from the European subsidiaries. The U.S. parents expected to play a role in shaping their subsidiaries' responses. Both American subsidiaries were affected by their parents' historical relationships with the UAW. The General Motors subsidiary official adopted its "Quality of Work Life" program from its U.S. operation. The Ford subsidiary followed the parent philosophy that had evolved over years of UAW conflicts: workers had the right to strike and have union-based worker committees. Expatriate labor management in concert with the parent labor staff transmitted U.S. labor views to Brazil.

The European subsidiaries were also affected by their parents, but in different ways and for different reasons. The subsidiaries served as conduits for advancing the respective agendas of home-country labor groups. Given the Swedish industrial-relations system, *Saab*'s parent labor leaders became directly involved with the Brazilian union in setting up worker committees. In contrast, *Volkswagen*'s parent labor leaders pro-

TABLE 4–4
Brazilian Case Conclusions by the Type of Subsidiary Response: Key Influences Reported

Past preferences	
• Parent-approved options	*GM, Ford*: Head-office labor review of proposals (parent policies)
• Parent practices	*GM*: "Quality of Work Life" program (historical parent-union relationship)
• Parent philosophy	*Ford*: Does not fire striking workers; accepts worker committees (historical parent-union relationship)
• Home-country pressures	*VW, SS*: Home union and parent board pressures for worker committees
Subsidiary relationships with key LDC groups	*VW*: Adopts Brazilian government preferred policy (alliance with government) *Ford*: Adopts labor-preferred policy (aloofness from government)
First subsidiary responses in changing policy	*Ford, MB, SS, GM*: Impacted by VW's new policy *VW, MB, SS, GM*: Impacted by Ford's new policy

vided direct funding and training for Brazilian labor and only secondarily became involved with subsidiary management in the establishment of worker committees.

Interestingly enough, European subsidiary management was aligned with the Brazilian labor model and resistant to changes, while U.S. subsidiary management's first impulse was to import the U.S. labor system. In part the answer lies in the nature of subsidiary relationships. The European subsidiaries were the most closely integrated into the Brazilian environment, with long-tenured expatriates, some of whom were considered "more Brazilian than the Brazilians." In particular, the Volkswagen subsidiary's close alliance with the Brazilian government made it captive to advancing the government's preferred labor scheme, which was basically antiunion.

In contrast, the U.S. subsidiaries were largely managed by short-tenured Americans who were more integrated with their parent and their corporate culture than with the Brazilian environment. In crisis, they turned to their respective parents—their corporate cultures, labor practices, and home-country viewpoints. The Ford response illustrates the point well: Unlike the Volkswagen subsidiary, Ford had not developed a close alliance with the Brazilian government. In crisis, the subsidiary's response was parent-approved through formal channels; the Brazilian government was not even consulted.

Implications: Risks for MNC Subsidiaries and Benefits for LDC Groups

The Brazilian case study illustrates how MNC subsidiaries vary systematically in their will and capacity to deal with a changing sociopolitical environment. Differing characteristics of the subsidiaries shaped their relationships with the parent, host government, and industry. The responsiveness of the subsidiaries could be related to their varying degrees of parent centralization, integration with the host government, and reliance on the industry.

Those subsidiaries with the highest integration with the host government and least reliance on the industry responded earliest. As demonstrated, the *Mercedes Benz* and *Volkswagen* subsidiaries reported the first attempts to analyze the changing labor environment as the result of directives from their managing directors. Independent of their parents, they hired local staff and redefined job responsibilities.

However, subsidiary integration with the host government also included potential risks. For example, while the Volkswagen subsidiary had the ability to respond early, its options were significantly constrained by its obligation to promote government-endorsed schemes. The Volkswagen subsidiary was seen as the government's principal ally against labor. The Mercedes Benz subsidiary was able to retain more independence due to its lower economic visibility and the managing director's policy of maintaining informal contacts with labor leaders. The *Saab* subsidiary, however, did not benefit from its day-to-day autonomy: no policy changes were made except those absolutely necessary to satisfy parent labor leaders. It is clear, however, that while the labor decisions of the three more autonomous subsidiaries were made by expatriates, their personal associations with the Brazilian government and integration into the local culture made them closer allies with the Brazilian elite. By living for many years in Brazil, their options had narrowed. By no means could they herald ideas and schemes unacceptable to their Brazilian business and government colleagues.

The less autonomous subsidiaries, *Ford* and *General Motors*, were less able to identify and respond to a changing labor environment. Parent approval was needed for any important policy changes; also important, however, was the short-term and limited orientation of subsidiary expatriate management. Ironically, the impetus for Ford's early and limited changes in 1976 came not from subsidiary management, but rather from parent staff in Detroit. On the other hand, the parent-dependent subsidiaries also had more options on how to respond to labor demands. The functional support from the parent provided great resources and a channel for a distinctly American, and relatively liberal, viewpoint on acceptable proposals. Ford's role of heralding the first union-based worker-representation system was not chance: the parent decision-makers had as their context the American labor experience, and shop delegates were perceived as only a natural and inevitable development.

In summary, we have seen how subsidiary relationships shape subsidiary behavior. The labor policies of *General Motors* and especially *Ford* proved to be more innovative in the Brazilian context as they represented a more direct transfer of labor practices from the parent company. *Mercedes Benz, Saab-Scania*, and particularly *Volkswagen*, on the other hand, were more responsive to host-government pressures. Notably, however, the intervention of their parent unions was decisive. Within this context of differing subsidiary capacity for response, Brazilian labor was successful in utilizing the MNC automotive subsidiaries as "levers for change"; with *Ford do Brasil* in the forefront, they led the rest of Brazil into a new era of employee-employer relations.

PART 2

Host-Government Demands and Subsidiary Response: The Case of the Mexican Automotive Industry

CHAPTER 5

MNCs within a Changing Regulatory Environment

THE BRAZILIAN case study illustrated the arguments on MNC behavior: *within a changing sociopolitical environment, MNC policies can serve as "levers for change," with individual subsidiaries differing significantly in their behavior.* However, by definition, MNCs not only operate in the fluid sociopolitical environments exemplified by the Brazilian case study, but also under the subjugation of national government regulations. The next three chapters concern MNC behavior within a changing regulatory environment. Applying these arguments to this second major type of MNC-LDC conflict will illustrate their wide applicability. Whether analyzing sociopolitical or regulatory environments, any assessment of the risks to the MNC or benefits to the host country must be interactive and dynamic, encompassing the role of the MNC itself within the particular country's development process, and allowing for significant differences based on individual subsidiary characteristics.

Again, the adequacy of the generalized country-risk approach is challenged by examining a specific case study of five MNC subsidiaries in the same industry facing the same threat—increased regulatory demands on their investment and sourcing policies. As in the Brazilian case, the analysis is divided into three parts. Chapter 5 examines the overall evolution of the Mexican government's demands as related to automotive investment and sourcing policies. Chapter 6 focuses on the individual behavior of each subsidiary: Were all uniformly prepared? Was the degree of conflict similar? The responses comparable? Chapter 7 seeks explanations for differing subsidiary behavior.

THE CASE

The MNC Subsidiaries

When the Mexican government cracked down on the investment and sourcing policies of the automotive industry in 1977, all five MNC subsidiaries had been operating in Mexico for over fifteen years. As in Brazil, the U.S. subsidiaries of *Ford* and *General Motors* had entered the country earliest, in 1925 and 1935 respectively. In 1937, *Chrysler* followed. Almost twenty years later, in 1954, the German MNC *Volkswagen* entered, followed in 1960 by the Japanese MNC *Nissan*. In 1978 these five

MNC subsidiaries accounted for over 85 percent of total vehicle production in the Mexican automotive industry.

The Host Country

From the outset the automotive industry in Mexico has been greatly affected by the intervention of the Mexican government, whose overall objective has been to broaden the country's industrialization. Notably, this intervention by the Mexican government has been specifically aimed at the investment and sourcing policies of the automotive subsidiaries. Since 1925, with its first automotive regulation, the Mexican government's objective has been to extract benefits from the automotive MNC subsidiaries. This objective over time has widened to encompass an increasing range of subsidiary policies: in 1925, the inducement of assembly operations through favorable import duties; in 1962 compulsory automotive production; in 1969 required automotive exports; and in 1977 increased investments, local content (locally manufactured auto parts), and exports in order to attain trade balances by 1982. Like many governments, the Mexican government perceived the automotive industry as contributing to the creation of the country's industrial base. The automotive industry was set forth as the country's model for import substitution and, later, for export promotion. Being part of enormous worldwide MNC networks, with the ability to enlist increased investments and export markets from their parents, the automotive subsidiaries were expected to formulate investment and sourcing policies compatible with Mexican national development goals.

However, despite these government policies, very large automotive trade deficits not only persisted but magnified over time. In 1967 the automotive trade deficit of U.S. $161.1 million represented 25 percent of the country's total deficit; by 1980 the automotive trade deficit had nearly grown by eight times to U.S. $1.5 billion, 47 percent of the country's total trade deficit. Particularly as a result of these deficits, the Mexican government applied pressure on the investment, export, and local-content policies of the automotive subsidiaries.

In 1977, with the new wealth and power of its oil discoveries, the Mexican government cracked down on the automotive industry. The newly issued 1977 Decree stated that within four years trade balances would be required of each automotive subsidiary; in other words, each subsidiary would have to fully compensate its imports with exports. Then, in 1981 when Mexico faced economic collapse, the elimination of chronic automotive trade deficits became an imperative. Confrontation ensued, with sharp conflicts between the Mexican government and the automotive MNCs. After extensive bargaining, the Mexican government kept to its trade balance demands, effectively forcing all parent companies to increase significantly their investments in Mexico as well as their auto-parts purchases from their Mexican subsidiaries and other Mexican auto-parts suppliers. The automotive industry was stunned: the Mexican government's flexibility was limited. Each MNC parent was effectively induced to comply to a host-country's demands in regard to one of its subsidiaries. Mexican automotive subsidiaries would have to attain trade balances or close shop.

As a result of this conflict, the automotive subsidiaries finally complied with the Mexican government's demands; moreover, acting as "levers for change" within Mexico, they led the country into a new era of export promotion. As a major sourcing location within the global strategies of the automotive MNCs, Mexico would have the much-coveted access to international markets. Ten years after the 1977 government crackdown, automotive exports surged from U.S. $253 million to U.S. $3.3 billion. Automotive exports, second only to oil, would lead the way for other manufacturing exports.[1]

The Changing Regulatory Environment

The purpose of this chapter, as the first of three on the Mexican case study, is to map the evolution of the host-government demands that would eventually require radical changes in the investment and sourcing policies of the automotive subsidiaries. Again, as in the Brazilian case, to illustrate the first main argument it will be shown that conflict was not sudden or unexplainable. A long gestation of Mexican government demands can be traced, in which recognizable themes become pronounced in the advancement of larger governmental developmental objectives. It will also be seen that the MNC subsidiaries themselves inadvertently created the conditions for increased government demands. The host-government's targeting of the automotive industry was not chance, but a logical outcome of specific subsidiary behavior and characteristics within the context of Mexico's development process.

Host-Government Objectives and MNC Strategies

While labor policies usually are the most decentralized of all MNC policies and are formulated in the context of the local labor environment, investment and sourcing policies usually are the most centralized, based

[1] In 1987, Mexican exports totalled U.S. $20.7 billion—oil accounting for U.S. $8.7 billion and nonoil exports U.S. $12.0 billion. Automotive exports, as the largest nonoil export category, amounted to U.S. $3.3 billion. For an excellent comprehensive portrayal of the development of Mexico's automotive policy, see Douglas C. Bennett and Kenneth E. Sharpe, *Transnational Corporations Versus the State: The Political Economy of the Mexican Auto Industry* (Princeton: Princeton University Press, 1985).

on the parent's overall global strategies, and are of key importance to the host country. Therefore, while the Brazilian subsidiaries' labor policies were reviewed in terms of their adaptation to the Brazilian labor environment, Mexican subsidiary investment and sourcing policies will be reviewed in terms of their relation to the Mexican government's objectives and MNC strategies.

From its inception the development of the Mexican automotive industry can be categorized into four main eras according to the policies of the Mexican government and their relationship to the interests and strategies of the automotive MNCs: (1) From 1925 to 1947 the interests of the Mexican government complemented those of the automotive MNCs dominating the Mexican market. (2) From 1947 to 1962, however, the Mexican government introduced new policies, guided by developmental objectives that were, to varying degrees, incompatible with the interests or strategies of the automotive MNCs. (3) Then, in 1962 the Mexican government followed the moves of other Latin American governments and established by decree a full-scale national automotive industry, forcing the MNCs to construct manufacturing plants. From this date to 1977, the conflict between the development objectives of the Mexican government and the strategies of the automotive MNCs became more acute, with the 1969 Resolution for export promotion and the 1972 Decree. (4) In 1977 this conflict accelerated with the passing of a new government decree furiously lobbied against by the automotive MNCs. Despite widespread initial resistance, however, each subsidiary was forced to comply, increasing investments, local content, and exports in order to retain its share of the Mexican market.

Complementary MNC and Host-Government Interests

The first Mexican government regulation specifically addressed to the automotive sector founded the Mexican automotive assembly industry. The [14 October] 1925 Decree gave special fiscal treatment to *Ford* when the company was looking to overseas markets. Assured that import duties on components for vehicle assembly were to be reduced 50 percent, Ford in 1925 established Mexico's first assembly plant. Later, in 1935, *General Motors* terminated a study of the Mexican market which concluded that the "[Mexican] automotive market is developing rapidly as the result of programs to expand the network of roads throughout the country; the increase in agriculture, and above all the interest of the government is encouraging the industrialization of the country."[2] Based on these conclu-

[2] "Bienvenido a General Motors de México!" Edición de Departmento de Relaciones Públicas de General Motors de México, n.d.

sions, General Motors decided the same year to build a plant to assemble trucks in Mexico City, adding an assembly line for cars to the plant in 1937. Shortly thereafter, in 1939, *Chrysler* joined its American competitors in the race for the Mexican car market by entering into a licensing agreement with a Mexican company, Fabricas Automex, wholly owned by the Azcárraga family. By 1940, Mexico had six assembly plants, which met 60 percent of the total national demand.

New Rules for Market Expansion: Government Protection and Control

After World War II, governments worldwide, faced with trade balance deficits, set up trade barriers. In 1947 the Mexican government followed suit and enacted the "Regulation for the Automotive Assembly Plants," with the stated objectives of protecting assembly plants and their employees from a great diversity of cheaper car imports as well as of reducing the automotive trade deficit.

During World War II, CKDs (completely-knocked-down car kits for assembly) and parts had been unavailable, creating a basis for the establishment of a Mexican national auto-parts industry. However, the postwar demand for cars surged "to such a magnitude that the Mexican government was obligated to prohibit imports [and] openly support the assembly plants established to strengthen national supply."[3] The 1947 Regulation advanced this objective, with the Mexican government assuming two new roles in the automotive sector—to protect the Mexican assembly industry with limits on the importation of finished vehicles and to control individual assembly production. While the first role meant unilateral protection of the assembly companies, the second was applied on the basis of each company's differing ability to meet the government's development objectives.

The new law ruled that imports were subject to permission. A quota system was to be used as a mechanism to control imports: the production of each assembly firm would be limited by the Mexican government via an "import quota." The law established a committee, "Comisión Nacional de Control de Importaciones" (consisting of the Ministries of Economy, Treasury, and Foreign Affairs as well as the Director of the Bank of Mexico), to establish importation guidelines and restrictions. The quota system became one of the most important instruments applied by the government to regulate the development of the automobile industry.[4]

[3] Alfred Jaime Blanco, "Evaluación Económica de la Industria Automotriz en México" (Mexico, D.F.: Tesis Profesional, Escuela Nacional de Economía, UNAM 1971), p. 12.

[4] See, for example, Organization for Economic Cooperation and Development, C. Sán-

Each company was also granted an assembly quota representing the maximum number of vehicles of specified makes and models that could be manufactured during a six-month period. Government officials were to decide on the total amount of foreign exchange to be allocated to the importation of auto parts by the assembly industry. The industry's allocation of foreign exchange was divided among the automotive firms based on secret calculations. This process of setting individual company quotas became one of intense bargaining, particularly since quotas were often below the operating capacities of the firms.

The Mexican government was reluctant to increase the industry's overall quota due to the cost of automotive importing part: From 1955 to 1959 automotive imports accounted for 10 percent of the country's total imports, while there were no significant exports of automotive products made in Mexico. Furthermore, the number of assembling firms in Mexico had increased almost fourfold, from five before World War II to nineteen by 1958. A total of seventy-five different makes were being produced. As a result, the automotive firms had to compete among themselves for scarce foreign exchange to increase their individual quotas as a prerequisite for gaining market share. Because the method of quota allocation was vague and secretive, firms were encouraged to improve their government relations: "The best way to obtain a larger [quota] was to become a successful lobbyist."[5]

In 1958 another mechanism for increasing government control of the automotive firms was enacted. The "Law of Ministries and Government Agencies" gave the Ministry of Industry and Commerce the responsibility for identifying locally manufactured parts that the automotive industry would be obliged to substitute for imports. This new policy was the result of the government's wish to reduce the number of makes and models and to increase locally manufactured parts (local content), thus reducing the automotive trade deficit. Until this time, local content, estimated at less than 20 percent, was limited to certain material inputs such as lubricants, electricity, a very small number of parts and components, and the value added in the assembly process.[6] In granting this responsibility to the Ministry of Industry and Commerce, the Mexican government had taken its first step toward the local integration of the automotive industry. Immediately, the Ministry acted by adding the level of local content in each

chez Marco, "Introduction to the Mexican Automobile Industry" (Paris: Preliminary Draft prepared for the Industrialization and Trade Project, 1968), p. 18.

[5] Guillermo S. Edelberg, "The Procurement Practices of the Mexican Affiliates of Selected United States Automobile Firms" (Ph.D. diss., Harvard Graduate School of Business, 1963), p. 16.

[6] Sánchez, "Introduction to the Mexican Automobile Industry," p. 7.

company's vehicles to the criteria for its quota: a firm's level of local content would henceforth affect how many vehicles it would be allowed to produce.

On 10 November 1960 the Ministry of Industry and Commerce further extended its local-content domain with a policy that is still in place today: a list of parts was identified that the automotive companies had to buy locally instead of importing. Published periodically in the government publication *Diario oficial*, this list is absolutely mandatory; noncompliance can result in "the imposition of fines or . . . the definite closing of assembly plants that may be found offering such resistance."[7] With the establishment of the mandatory local-content list, the Mexican government also declared its official policy against the vertical integration of assemblers.

These local-content policies of the Mexican government changed the orientation of the assembly plants and produced uncertainty: to what degree would automotive subsidiaries have to alter their operations to meet government demands? The automotive MNCs were caught in a bind. Greater profits were to be made from continuing to import cheaper parts from the large-scale and efficient (and in the case of the U.S. companies, relatively close) production centers of the parent.[8] But more imports meant conflict with the Mexican government's request to increase local content.

Furthermore, some government officials were proposing to eliminate all but two makes and models for the entire Mexican market. However, for the government to implement such a proposal would have meant "abandoning completely the past policy of giving the consumer a wide choice of makes and models, a traditional tenet in Mexico where the U.S. demonstration effect plays an important role."[9] The Mexican automotive market was structured similarly to that of the U.S., with a major market segment demanding American-style cars with annual changes—and American manufacturers eager to expand the market for American products.

[7] *Diario oficial*, 28 April 1961, pp. 7–8.

[8] For example, one industry observer noted: "The [American] assembly plants . . . had not been designed originally to purchase locally, but rather to import components from the different United States corporations with which they were affiliated. Consequently, when the purchases of increasing amounts of local components was imposed on Mexican assembly plants' management, the managers found themselves having to purchase locally with an organization that was better suited to the importation of components. As a result, more functions have to be added to the management organization. The existence of the mandatory list added a new uncertainty . . . [as to] which components were to be added . . . and when." Edelberg, "The Procurement Practices of the Mexican Affiliates," pp. 20–22.

[9] Sánchez, "Introduction to the Mexican Automobile Industry," pp. 7–8.

The Escalation of Government Demands

By the early 1960s the conflict between the objectives of the automotive MNCs and the Mexican government had considerably sharpened. From the point of view of the MNCs, Mexico was a growing and profitable market. A study by the Organization for Economic Cooperation and Development (OECD) estimated that total assembly-plant profits in 1960 were U.S. $211 million, over 10 percent of total sales, with assembly operations enjoying an effective protection rate of 4,100 percent. From the Mexican government's point of view, the automotive industry—in 1960 contributing 3.2 percent (2,357 million pesos) of the country's national output—was paving the way for Mexico's emergence as a developed industrialized nation.[10] Between the two camps, as was evidence by defeated government proposals, came a third party of government technocrats and outside observers who advocated significant changes in government policy.

THE ESTABLISHMENT OF MANUFACTURING OPERATIONS

Government regulation was the impetus for the establishment of vehicle production in Mexico; as in other LDCs, automotive MNCs invested in production facilities only as a direct result of compulsory government decree. Unlike government regulations concerned with import tariffs, compulsory in-country automobile manufacturing was in direct conflict with the corporate strategies and interests of the MNC automotive companies. Shipment of parts in CKD kits allowed the longer production runs in home plants and economies in transportation costs that were required to meet increasing international competition. The U.S. automotive MNCs in particular had an enormous home market which provided large economies of scale for competitive exports, especially to nearby countries such as Mexico.[11] Baranson pointed out in his World Bank study (1969) that while manufacturing subsidiaries in LDCs may only account for a small percentage of total earnings, they represent a "sizeable customer for components and parts. . . . Their investments in overseas manufacturing facilities are in a sense an investment in future demand for components and parts."[12] For example, approximately half of

[10] Sánchez, "Introduction to the Mexican Automobile Industry," pp. 7–8.

[11] See Rhys Owen Jenkins, *Industrialization in Latin America: the Automotive Industry in Argentina, Chile, and Mexico* (New York: Praeger, 1977) pp. 34–40; Sánchez, "Introduction to the Mexican Automobile Industry," p. 1; and Frederick G. Donner, *The Worldwide Industrial Enterprise* (New York: McGraw-Hill, 1967), p. 14.

[12] Jack Baranson, "Automotive-Industries in Developing Countries," World Bank Staff Occasional Papers, no. 8 (Baltimore: Johns Hopkins University Press, 1969), pp. 13, 19.

U.S. automotive exports in 1967 (U.S. $15 billion) were auto parts sold by U.S. automotive companies to overseas subsidiaries.[13]

As Knickerbocker has shown, manufacturing oligopolies tend to conform to a follow-the-leader pattern of defensive investment, resulting in a "trump card for the LDCs."[14] This oligopolist pattern was especially pronounced in the establishment of Latin American automotive industries due to the simultaneous shift from geographic market divisions—with the U.S. concentrating on Latin America and the Europeans on their respective colonies—to the internationalization of competition. With the maturing of European markets and the drive for new export markets, U.S. hegemony in Latin America was seriously threatened; the area became the competitive battleground of the major European and U.S. automotive companies.[15] The MNCs' competitive struggle for Latin American automotive markets was for maintaining both profitable in-country sales as well as profitable exports from the parent. The defensive investment response of automotive MNCs coupled with the national development objectives of Latin American governments set the basic dynamics for future automotive MNC-LDC government bargaining.

Sharing development objectives similar to other Latin American governments, the Mexican government was concerned with increasing its economic growth and broadening industrialization. On 25 August 1962, with the announcement of the 1962 Decree, the Mexican government formally stipulated the country's automotive policy, "considering the general interest in accelerating the program of national integration of the industry . . . and stimulating the establishment of new industries."[16] As

[13] Judd Polk, "U.S. Exports and U.S. Production Abroad" (Staff memo prepared for the United States Council of the International Chamber of Commerce, 11 Aug. 1967), as quoted in Baranson, "Automotive-Industries in Developing Countries," p. 13.

[14] Frederick T. Knickerbocker, *Oligopolistic Reaction and Multinational Enterprise* (Boston: Harvard University School of Business, 1973), pp. 178–79.

[15] See Jenkins, *Industrialization in Latin America*, p. 49.

[16] "Decreto que prohibe la importación de motores para automóbiles y camiones, asi como de conjuntos mecánicos armados para su uso o ensamble, a partir del lo. de septiembre de 1964," *Diario oficial*, 25 Aug. 1962, 4.

The principal government official responsible for the decree, the Minister of Commerce and Industry, classified four key reasons for it: (1) The driving goal of development: "There has never been one country that has developed without having its own mechanical industry. The automotive industry is only an element—[but] the most important without a doubt—of a complete and indispensible mechanical industry." (2) Mexican officials had studied the newly established automotive industries in Mexico's rapidly developing Latin American neighbors, Brazil and Argentina, and had concluded that each had "overcome numerous obstacles . . . and developed very quickly." (3) All three countries had followed the popular economic doctrine of import substitution as the major policy guiding economic development. By 1959, as the result of continuous heavy current-account deficits, the Mexican government focused on local integration as a means of accelerating industrialization. The

of September 1964 the importation of motors and power trains for assembly in cars and trucks would be prohibited (Article 2), and local content measured by direct cost of production would have to be a minimum of 60 percent (Article 4). Any automotive company that wished to remain in the Mexican market would have to submit a program to the Mexican government for official approval of its proposed investments, import schedule, and timetable (Article 3). The previous system of production quotas, used to limit the total volume of automotive imports, was to be extended with the stated purpose of ensuring Mexican-owned automotive suppliers a market. In addition, the decree allowed companies that exported finished vehicles, parts, or tooling the right to import items up to the value of total exports (Article 12).[17]

---

automotive industry, as one of the largest contributors to total imports, was to be the first of several industries that the government would subject to a formal requirement of local integration. (4) "An objective of great importance to the Mexican government was the creation of new sources of employment." Statements by Raúl Salinas Lozano in "1962–1972 Una Década de Progresso en la Industrialización de México," *Auto Industria* (15 Aug. 1972): 3.

[17] However, as the direct result of intensive bargaining by automotive MNCs, the *actual* policy measures established in the 1962 Decree were very different from those contained in the original government proposal. The specific interests of the automotive MNCs are illustrated by three main recommendations of the government proposal that were excluded from the official final draft of the 1962 Decree. The first major recommendation was to limit the number of automotive manufacturers to "five for cars and two for mid-sized trucks . . . to avoid the industry growing into an onerous burden for the national economy." Instead of the number of firms being limited, all the companies that "qualified" (ten) were given permission to begin manufacturing operations. Each automotive MNC did not want to take the chance that it would be excluded from the Mexican market, so the Mexican government decided to endorse the MNC view, assuming incorrectly that keen competition would almost immediately result in fewer firms and lower prices.

A key objective of two other excluded recommendations dealt with increasing local content. The first recommendation was to limit the number of makes each company could have to five, with a five-year freeze on model changes. The government proposal read: "In order to attain a rational development of the industry, that it will not become onerous for the country's economy, *it is absolutely necessary to dispense with the frequent changes of models that the U.S. manufacturers are used to imposing in Mexico.*" However, after intensive lobbying by the U.S. automotive firms, no restrictions were applied on the numbers of makes or on the annual change of models. The U.S. firms, unlike the European or Japanese, were threatened because their centralized strategies were based on product differentiation achieved through annual change.

The other key issue was the proposed centralization of the production and standardization of key manufacturing activities, including stamping. The proposal also elaborated, in depth, different parts that should be made by both car and truck manufacturers. The 1962 Decree, however, ignored this point, leaving any centralization or standardization of production to the initiative of the companies. As in the standardization of makes and the freezing of the number of models, this proposal threatened the subsidiaries' abilities to follow their respective corporate strategies; it was successfully defeated by the MNCs. See Nacional Financiera, "Elementos para una política de desarrollo de la fabricación de vehículos auto-

The 1962 Decree forced the automotive MNCs to make a choice: they had to engage in local manufacturing or leave the country and forfeit the growing Mexican market to their competitors. Spurred by the importance of the Mexican market, the 1962 Decree caused eighteen companies to submit programs to the Mexican government for acceptance. Therefore, despite conflicting MNC interests, the Mexican government in its first major bargaining negotiation with the automotive industry was able to use its market potential to induce MNCs to establish manufacturing in the Mexican automotive industry.[18]

---

motrizes en México," NAFIN Dec. 1960): 50, 52–53, and 57; and Sánchez, "Introduction to the Mexican Automobile Industry," p. 12.

[18] Other factors cited in various studies as increasing the bargaining power of the automotive MNCs include: (1) the influence of both political and economic groups inside Mexico, (2) pressure from the MNCs' respective home countries on the Mexican government, and (3) financial and technological dependence.

Bennett and Sharpe identified the importance of the relationship between the Mexican state and its national bourgeoisie and emphasized the latter's centrality in the quest for economic growth: "These classes [national bourgeoisie and middle class] wanted what they had become accustomed to: modern, U.S.-style products. A Mexican car would not have been acceptable. The relationships of the Mexican state thus demanded that Mexico needed the sort of automobile industry only the transnational firms could provide." The influence of the Mexican consumer was economic. As the Mexican consumer had been accustomed to having such a large choice of vehicles, it would have been difficult to reduce that choice without affecting the demand and risking an increase in smuggling from the United States. Therefore, the very success of the U.S. firms in marketing their products to Mexican consumers provided them with added bargaining power.

Second, but perhaps most important, the home governments of the MNCs, particularly that of the United States, exerted considerable influence on the final shape and outcome of the Mexican government's 1962 Decree. As Bennett and Sharpe state: "[I]n its pursuit of industrial development by way of import substitution, Mexico had come to be dependent upon certain industrialized countries, particularly the United States, for trade and capital inflows. These relationships shaped a set of needs for continued flows of trade and capital in a number of sectors that limited the state's power in the automobile sector: a favorable investment climate had to be maintained if growth was to continue."

For example, in the case of the U.S. government, highly placed government officials communicated the American MNCs' views directly to the Mexican government. The U.S. Ambassador, Thomas Mann, personally informed the Minister of Industry and Commerce that the Department of State would look unfavorably on the exclusion of any one of the three U.S. firms. In the case of Japan, pressure applied by the Japanese government was reputedly responsible for the Mexican government's acceptance of Nissan's application two years after the legal deadline for approval. As Mexico's most important trade partner after the United states, Japan in 1963 bought approximately 70 percent of Mexico's cotton exports—the single most important source of foreign exchange—accounting for over 20 percent of Mexico's total foreign-exchange earnings. The Japanese government allegedly threatened to cut cotton imports if Nissan's application was not approved.

In addition, Wionczek underlined the financial and technological dependence of the Mexican automotive industry on the MNC parents, especially the American. As Tsunekawa pointed out, eight out of the ten firms whose programs were accepted planned to receive technical assistance and machinery from MNCs. In addition, the development of the sup-

In 1967 the automotive industry association, *Asociación Mexicana de la Industria Automotriz* (AMIA), presented its first major industry report that simultaneously acknowledged the importance of the government's new automotive policy and defended the automotive industry's contribution to Mexico's economic development. The 1962 Decree had in fact elicited an immediate and tremendous positive response from the automotive MNCs. Results were hailed unanimously by government technocrats, officials, and scholars. All agreed overwhelmingly that the Mexican government's 1962 Decree had been successful in establishing a Mexican automotive industry through import substitution, and that the results included increased investment, more employment, and growth for the supplier industry and for foreign exchange savings.

The automotive companies increased their total investment 171.0 percent in four years, from 1,952 million pesos in 1962 to 5,289 million pesos in 1966. Likewise, employment in the terminal sector jumped 148.2 percent from 9,021 employees in 1962 to 22,387 in 1966. Including the autoparts suppliers, total employment in the automotive industry by 1966 came to 70,000, with approximately 25,000 persons and 22,000 persons, respectively, employed in the supplier and distribution sectors. Wages and salaries nearly doubled in four years, increasing 196.2 percent from 238 million pesos in 1962 to 705 million pesos in 1966. The supplier industry surged: locally purchased parts skyrocketed 149 percent—from 1,468 million pesos in 1962 to 3,657 million pesos in 1966—replacing imported parts as the main source for Mexican automotive companies.

Nevertheless, despite the subsidiaries' compliance to the 1962 Decree by increasing investment, employment, and local content, the automotive trade deficit continued to contribute significantly to the country's overall trade deficit. While exports had increased 561.5 percent from 13 million pesos in 1962 to 86 million pesos in 1966, the amount relative to imports was still very small. Total automotive imports increased 14.7 percent between 1962 and 1966, from 1,870 million pesos to 2,144 million pesos. In those four years, exports only increased by 73 million pesos,

---

plier industry depended on the willingness of MNC suppliers to enter into joint ventures or licensing agreements.

For an excellent discussion of Mexican governmental factors that influenced its bargaining position, see the work of Douglas C. Bennett and Kenneth E. Sharpe, especially "Agenda-Setting and Bargaining Power: The Mexican State versus Transnational Automobile Corporations," in *World Politics* (Oct. 1979): 76–86, 77–78. Also, see Miguel S. Wionczek, Gerardo M. Bueno, and Jorge Eduardo Navarette, *la transferencia internacional de tecnología* (Mexico: Fondo de Cultura Economica, 1974), pp. 86–87; and Keiichi Tsunekawa, "Dependence and Labor Policy in Mexico: Interactions among the State, the Automotive Industry and Labor Unions during the Echeverria Administration (1970–1976)" (Ph.D. thesis, Cornell University, n.d.), Chap. III (draft), 14.

while imports shot up by 274 million pesos. In 1966 automotive exports only represented 4 percent of the cost of automotive imports. Yet, in terms of the entire country, automotive imports accounted for over 10 percent of the country's total imports.[19]

THE FORMALIZATION OF EXPORT PROMOTION: THE 1969 RESOLUTION

In 1969 the Mexican government again sought to realize its multiple objectives for the automotive industry with a new policy: export promotion. The automotive industry became the first industry the Mexican government would specifically require to export as a means of compensating for imports and alleviating the industry trade deficit.[20] The 1969 Resolution thus required the automotive subsidiaries to export, in order to retain and keep their market share.

Despite the earlier elaboration of the basic quota system encouraging companies to export, automotive exports were still relatively insignificant. Exports as a percentage of imports increased from 5 percent in 1967 to ten percent in 1969. However, the absolute increase in imports had far outpaced that of exports. In two years, imports had increased by almost 600 million pesos, while exports increased by less than 150 million pesos. As one industry observer commented, with the 1969 Resolution "the industry . . . has been in effect forced into an exports-for-imports program."[21]

[19] Since 1967, AMIA has periodically issued major studies on the automotive industry documenting items such as unit sales, employment, and the trade balance. See AMIA, *La industria fabricante de vehículos automotores en México: su participación en la economía nacional* (Mexico, D.F., 1967), pp. 1, 13, 23, 68.

[20] See AMIA, *La Industria Automotriz de México en Cifras 1972* (Mexico, D.F., 1972), p. 3. While the automotive industry was the focus of the first industry-specific regulation concerned with export promotion, other export policies for the manufacturing sector in general had been established more than a decade earlier. Mexico's first policy concerned with export promotion was the "Law for Promoting New and Necessary Industries" in 1955. Exports of manufactured goods with at least 60 percent local content received tax exemptions. In 1961 greater exemptions were given for products with more than 80 percent local content. In 1963 the government established the Fund for the Export Promotion of Manufactured Goods to finance export activities. See Nacional Financiera, *La política industrial en al desarrollo de México* (1971), pp. 187, 193–95, 311.

[21] John H. Christman, "The Automotive Industry," in *Business Mexico* (Mexico, D.F.: American Chamber of Commerce of Mexico, A.C., 1973), p. 127. Exports that qualified as earning the basic quota could either be automotive products of the automotive companies themselves or those of their Mexican parts suppliers. Direct exports from the automotive companies were principally vehicles sold to third markets or motors sold to the parent company and sister subsidiaries. Supplier exports were mainly sold to the subsidiary's parent, since national suppliers were largely unable to find export markets for their noncompetitive expensive products. Bennett and Sharpe provide a detailed account of the forces that brought this government resolution into being, showing how one automotive subsidiary

A 1968 OECD study summarized the government's rationale for the new exports policy as principally exploiting economies of scale for an excessive number of automotive firms. The creation of export markets was perceived largely as an acceptable means both to increase the efficiency of the domestic automotive industry and to reduce the trade deficit, thus generating benefits for both the companies and the government.

As in the 1962 Decree, the 1969 Resolution was prefaced in the official announcement with the objectives of improving the country's trade balance, increasing employment, and advancing overall economic development. The new regulation was based on the existing production quota system: in eight to ten years each automotive company would have to compensate 100 percent of its imports with the corresponding value of exports. The basic quotas would not be automatically granted as previously under the the 1962 Decree, but rather earned by compensating imports with exports under the following schedule: the value of 5 percent of imports would have to be exported in 1970, 15 percent in 1971, and so on, reaching 100 percent in 1979. If a company was unable to comply, the Ministry of Industry and Commerce would reduce that company's basic production quota in proportion to its satisfaction of the export requirement. The additional exportation quota would still be used as a reward, but only for those firms that exported more than the year's minimum requirement. Therefore, the Mexican government had further strengthened its use of the basic quota, for the first time controlling each company's access to the domestic market in order to force each company's exports.

Immediately exports began to surge, reaching 29 percent of the value of imports by 1972. The automotive industry as a whole was able to meet the escalating export requirements from 1970 to 1972, respectively, of 5, 15, and 25 percent the value of imports. Exports included motors, vehicles, transmissions, radiators, tooling, shatterproof glass for front windshields, and replacement parts.

THE 1972 DECREE: THE AUTOMOTIVE INDUSTRY AS EXPORTERS OF THE SUPPLIER INDUSTRY

In 1972, ten years after its first major automotive decree, the Mexican government issued its second. The underlying objective of the new decree was to strengthen the Mexican supplier industry.[22] The 1972 Decree

(Ford) provided the impetus. This illustrates the dynamics of this book's argument that, due to differences between subsidiaries, one may act as a "lever for change," its response creating policy imperatives for competitors. See Bennett and Sharpe, *Transnational Corporations Versus the State*, pp. 155–75.

[22] One key government official explained: "[T]he conditions are distantly different than a decade ago. Now the purpose is to integrate this industrial sector, not create the base for a

further limited the vertical integration of the terminal industry and reconfirmed the 1969 export promotion policy. Production of new automotive parts by the terminal industry was only permitted if, in the judgment of the Ministry of Industry and Commerce, all the production would be exported, thus contributing to the industrial development of the country (Article 10). Furthermore, the terminal firms were prohibited from producing any automotive part if that part could be produced by the Mexican supplier industry (Article 9).[23] The timetable of compensating imports for exports outlined in the 1969 Resolution was reconfirmed, with companies exceeding the required minimum being granted larger production quotas (Articles 11 and 12). In addition, beginning with the 1974 model year, 40 percent of each company's exports would have to consist of the products of suppliers with at least 60 percent Mexican capital (Article 23). In effect, the terminal companies were being requested to act as both supportive purchasers and salesmen for a new Mexican supplier industry.

Initially the decree was successful: supplier exports surged and export obligations for the industry (30 percent of imports) were met in 1973. With market share dependent on the volume of exports, the government had a powerful tool that initially affected the behavior of the automotive MNCs. However, this commitment on the part of the MNC subsidiaries to increase Mexican exports was short-lived. The accelerated export requirements set forth in the 1972 Decree for 1974 and 1975—that total automotive exports reach 40 and 50 percent of imports—were not met. In the face of a worldwide recession, the Mexican subsidiaries could not convince their parents to increase their purchases of parts or to increase sales of finished vehicles. The policy of export promotion had opened Mexico to two external factors—recession in export markets and the global sourcing strategy of each subsidiary's parent.

---

major development. . . . [The 1972 Decree] modifies aspects of the 1962 Decree and creates new policies that will help the development of the automotive industry and as a consequence that of our country." Statement by former minister Raúl Salinas Lozano, in "Reconocimiento a los Creadores de la Industria Nacional Automotriz," *Auto Industria* (15 Dec. 1972): 8.

[23] This requirement was qualified by the stipulation that the price of parts on the government's mandatory list for local purchase not exceed the price of equivalent imports by over 60 percent (Articles 4 and 5). For all other parts not included on this list, if the price was not more than 25 percent of the imported equivalent and reliability of delivery was satisfactory, local purchase was obligatory (Articles 2 and 3). The 1972 Decree also addressed the old issues of increasing local content and limiting the number of models. Similar to the local-content quota, the decree stipulated that companies that exceeded the minimum local content of 60 percent would be rewarded with the right to produce additional vehicles. Each percentage point above 70 percent resulted in the right to produce an additional one hundred cars. "Decreto que fija las bases para el desarrollo de la industria automotriz," *Diario oficial*, 24 Oct. 1972.

By year's end 1975 the failure of the export promotion policy contained in the 1969 Resolution and the 1972 Decree in correcting the automotive trade deficit was undeniable. Domestic sales had continued to boom, with the subsidiaries continuing to import a significant amount of parts for manufacture. With exports level, the automotive deficit almost tripled in five years, from U.S. $230 million in 1970 to U.S. $628 million in 1975.[24] Mexico's export promotion policy failed because it was intrinsically dependent upon decisions and factors external to both the automotive subsidiaries and the Mexican government: the MNCs' parents—at least for the time being—were not interested in significantly increasing the sales of their Mexican subsidiaries' products outside Mexico, and thereby failed to comply with Mexico's demand for an automotive trade balance.

The Government Crackdown: The 1977 Decree and the Cocoyoc Resolution

On 20 June 1977 the Mexican government enacted a new automotive decree that was to elicit opposition of unprecedented strength from the captive in-country automotive subsidiaries and their parents, as well as from several groups and individuals in the United States, including the Federal government, labor unions and politicians. The policymakers in the new administration of Mexican President Lopez Portillo had examined the reasons for the subsidiaries' noncompliance with previous investment and sourcing requirements and decided to alter the rules of the game: this time the aim was to convince the senior decision-makers in each MNC parent headquarters to modify the behavior of its Mexican subsidiary so that it would be brought into compliance with Mexican development objectives. Their instrument was to be yet another government decree, but this time more than ever their strategy was carefully mapped out and orchestrated.

The Mexican government knew that its advantage lay in controlling one of the most rapidly growing automotive markets in the world, and that its bargaining power was enhanced by the oil boom as well as by the revolutionary changes occurring in the global automotive industry. To keep their market share and profits, the parents of each of the automotive subsidiaries would again be forced to increase substantially their investments in order to meet specific export requirements. However, unlike the 1962 Decree the Mexican government, from the announcement of the 1977 Decree until its third year of implementation, held to its objective. In response, the subsidiaries reacted very differently this time,

[24] SEPAFIN, "La Industria Automotriz en México," p. 117.

but in line with the government's game plan, according to government officials.[25]

Endorsing the 1969 Resolution for export promotion and the 1972 Decree, the 1977 Decree was primarily concerned with broadening the country's industrialization. But the resolve to eliminate the chronic automotive deficits became more pronounced.[26] On an annual basis, the Ministry of National Property and Industrial Promotion would assign a foreign-exchange budget to each subsidiary. Armed with algebraic formulas, a new school of government technocrats with backgrounds in both economic planning and the automotive industry was determined to implement its policy directives. Each of the subsidiaries would have to move steadily toward a positive trade balance, so as to eliminate its deficit by 1982.

The 1977 Decree presented the subsidiaries with two choices—to increase either exports or local content. The degree to which each company was required to export would depend on the level of local content. If a subsidiary's models met only the minimum local-content level of 50 percent, then more exports would be required.[27] Higher levels of local content were recommended, climbing to 75 percent for vehicles and 85 percent for trucks by 1981. Compliance would mean a higher quota of foreign exchange and thus less required exports. The subsidiaries were captive: they either had to convince their parents to comply or else suffer the consequences locally in the Mexican market.

Immediately, the Mexican government was faced with a diverse set of

[25] In an excellent analysis of the 1977 Decree based on four years of extensive field work, Bennett and Sharpe provide many insights into the bargaining process between the automotive MNCs and the Mexican government, the involvement of the U.S. government, and the actual mechanics of the regulation. See Douglas C. Bennett and Kenneth E. Sharpe, "Transnational Corporations, Export-Promotion Policies, and U.S.-Mexican Automotive Trade" (Latin American Program of the Woodrow Wilson International Center for Scholars, Smithsonian Institution, Washington, D.C., Sept. 1981, Mimeographed); and *Transnational Corporations Versus the State*, pp. 201–26.

[26] The 1977 Decree stated: "Considering that during the last fifteen years a protection policy has been followed, stimulating and promoting the automotive industry and . . . it is mandatory that companies of the automotive industry rationalize the use of foreign exchange in accordance with the priorities of this industrial sector . . . it is necessary that this industry becomes in the medium term a source of net foreign-exchange generation in order to contribute towards an equilibrium in the country's balance of payments." "Decreto para el fomento de la industria automotriz," *Diario oficial*, 20 June 1977, 1–2.

[27] Minimum local-content requirements were 50 percent for passenger cars and 65 percent for commercial vehicles. Costs were to be measured by a material-cost formula instead of the direct-cost formula, which was based on the prices of auto parts in the countries of origin. With the new basis of computation, required local content was approximately 8 percent higher. In addition, the 1977 Decree calculated local content on a model-by-model basis rather than on an average company basis and only included the net Mexican content of parts produced in Mexico.

resistant foreign interests. From U.S. labor unions to politicians and automotive executives, cries were sounded against its further intervention into the automotive sector. The 1977 Decree was seen by many as a way to aid the LDC's development at the expense of the deindustrialization of the parent MNC country. The United Auto Workers and others strongly felt that the Mexican government was forcing automotive MNCs to shift their production sites from the U.S. to Mexico: the new requirements to invest in Mexico would lead to runaway plants from the U.S.

However, actual implementation of the 1977 Decree was slow. New factories had to be built. As shown in table 5–1, while the subsidiaries increased their imports, exports were relatively static. Between 1977 and 1980 imports increased threefold to U.S. $1.9 billion, while exports increased only 60 percent from U.S. $253 million to U.S. $404 million. By 1981 the automotive deficit had skyrocketed to U.S. $2.1 billion and was 58 percent of Mexico's total trade deficit.

In 1981 national crisis made the reduction of the automotive deficit extremely urgent. The objective to reach an automotive trade balance,

TABLE 5–1
The Mexican Automotive Sector's Trade Deficit (millions of U.S. $)

			Auto Trade Deficit	
Year	*Auto Imports*	*Auto Exports*	*$MM*	*% Mexican Deficit*
1950	55	—	(55)	88.8
1955	94	—	(94)	64.8
1960	147	—	(147)	32.8
1965	203	—	(203)	44.3
1970	257	26	(231)	22.2
1975	750	122	(628)	17.3
1976	719	192	(527)	19.9
1977	639	253	(386)	36.5
1978	893	334	(559)	30.1
1979	1,426	377	(1,049)	33.2
1980	1,903	404	(1,499)	47.2
1981	2,519	370	(2,149)	57.7

Source: Banco de México, S.A., as quoted in SEPAFIN, "La Industria Automotriz en México: Analisis y Expectativas" (Mexico, D.F.: Dirección General de Industrias, Subdirección de la Industria Automotriz y del Transporte, July 1982), pp. 117, 132.

underlying so many previous government regulations over the decades, had at last become imperative. Despite oil exports of U.S. $15 billion, the trade deficit was U.S. $10 billion. The Mexican government set out to reduce imports by U.S. $6 billion—U.S. $3 billion in the public sector and U.S. $3 billion in the private sector. As the largest single contributor to the trade deficit in the private sector, the auto industry was given a specific mandate to reduce imports. The fourth year of the 1977 Decree brought a distinct hardening in the government's behavior: the decree was henceforth to be strictly enforced and trade balance requirements accelerated.

In late July 1981, senior subsidiary management of the automotive industry joined Mexican government officials for a weekend oceanside seminar at Cocoyoc. On the first day, new restrictive measures were unexpectedly announced by the government in a resolution called "Measures for Rationalizing the Trade Balance Deficit in the Automotive Industry," commonly referred to as the Cocoyoc Resolution. In three months, on 31 October, the subsidiaries would be subject to production reductions depending on their trade balance, imports of any optional parts for luxury cars would be prohibited, and advance of foreign exchange would not be granted for the 1982 model year. The seminar came to an abrupt and premature end in this first overt confrontation ever between the Mexican government and automotive industry.

The Cocoyoc Resolution was considered by many to be the most significant government move against the automotive industry. The resolution would force companies to comply with the 1977 Decree, and revealed a new and uncharacteristic inflexibility in the Mexican government's attitude. As subsidiary executives explained: "Overnight it transformed the auto industry into a different ballgame." "We have a new regulation enforcing the old [the 1977 Decree]. The companies less affected are those practicing the government's philosophy." "If we had complied with the 1977 Decree, we wouldn't have a problem now. The government needed to push us to comply."[28] Despite its earlier flexibility, the Mexican government was now determined to implement policies that would for the first time compel the subsidiaries to change certain policies.

Several automotive executives claimed that the Cocoyoc Resolution marked the turning point for their MNCs: a company either had to comply with the government's overall trade balance objectives or withdraw its entire operation from Mexico. The 1977 Decree and the Cocoyoc Resolution demonstrated that the Mexican government's flexibility was lim-

[28] Representative statements of senior management from different companies in the Mexican automotive industry.

ited. The Mexican government had persuasively convinced senior management of the subsidiaries and their parents that the trade balance concerns underlying earlier regulations were now paramount and to be enforced.

The MNC Subsidiaries as "Levers for Change"

Just as in Brazil, the Mexican foreign-dominated automotive industry, irrespective of intent, acted as an agent of change. The MNC subsidiaries had led the country into import substitution, helping to generate a broad industrial base. Their success in building a large automotive market, however, also had a side product: substantial automotive trade deficits. In effect, by not complying with earlier regulations, the MNC subsidiaries created the conditions for a future run-in with the Mexican government. Moreover, given their multinational nature, it was natural for the host government to expect the subsidiaries to employ their distinctive multinational advantages, including the use of their parents' captive export markets. The MNC subsidiaries were equipped to remedy the situation—but voluntary submission to a reverse strategy of export promotion would be critical. The MNCs had not intended to include Mexico in their worldwide sourcing strategies, but the government utilized the special capacities of the MNC subsidiaries and successfully fulfilled its expectations. As in the Brazilian case study, however, the story goes further. In crisis, forces outside the country intervened—sometimes successfully, sometimes not—and helped to shape the roles of the MNC subsidiaries as agents of change.

Outside Intervention: Parent and Home-Country Opposition

During the crisis, one home-country government engaged in an unsuccessful attempt to change the Mexican government's demands—the U.S. government fought the 1977 Decree. In November of that year, representatives of the U.S. Departments of State, Treasury, Commerce, and Labor met with representatives of the Mexican government. Both sides presented their viewpoints, but Mexican officials later walked out, considering the discussion ended.

Shortly after this meeting, the MNCs were persuaded to dissociate themselves from U.S. government pressure. The Mexican government had made it clear that U.S. intervention, by government or business, was not welcome. A complete reversal had taken place, with the Mexican subsidiaries of American MNCs convinced that pressure from the United States no longer constituted effective bargaining power, but rather had become a disadvantage. Furthermore, the Mexican subsidiaries successfully persuaded their parents in Detroit to this opinion.[29]

Change from within the MNCs

However, the MNCs themselves were soon to become voluntary "levers for change." That same November of 1977, the Mexican government's plan—to have one opportunity-seeking subsidiary initiate defensive investments—was put into action. *General Motors* broke the automotive subsidiaries' resistance, dissolving their collective bargaining power with a startling announcement: to comply with the 1977 Decree, General Motors would begin to meet the required export volume with an in-bond assembly plant (*maquiladora*). Conductores y Componentes Eléctricos de Juarez, S.A. de C.V. would sell its total production of automotive rear-body wiring harnesses to General Motors in the United States.

Because of this reversal in the attitudes of the automotive MNCs, the united thrust of U.S. government pressure disappeared and a coordinated policy position could no longer be sustained. The Departments of Commerce and State wished to respond to the American MNCs' requests for noninvolvement, while the Bureau of Economic Affairs felt the issue should be pursued. The last pressure tactic was formulated by the Bureau of Economic Affairs. On 7 February 1978 the U.S. government through its Embassy in Mexico sent a Diplomatic Note to the Mexican government "respectfully" requesting it to "review" the decree. The significant increase in auto parts from Mexico contemplated by the decree was highlighted: "U.S. manufacturers of parts (and the workers involved), losing orders as a result of the U.S. automotive industry's sourcing in Mexico to meet their export requirements under the decree,

[29] Bennett and Sharpe described how the Mexican government communicated its message: "The U.S. subsidiaries in Mexico found themselves on the receiving end of stern admonitions from the Mexican government to discontinue efforts to mobilize U.S. government pressure. Such efforts would only be counterproductive. The decree is here to stay, SEPAFIN told Ford pointedly. This kind of reaction could lead to real conflict. We could go back to price controls. The message was clear: the firms needed smooth relations with the Mexican government in further negotiations over interpretation and implementation of the decree. Even if the government were unwilling to change the basic policy, there might be flexibility or leniency in meeting deadlines and targets. . . . As one executive put it: 'We here in Mexico have taken the position that because of the idiosyncrasies of the Mexican government it would be counterproductive to have the assistance of the U.S. government in settling our "difference" with the Mexican government. . . . They could create a nasty situation.' The message was relayed from Mexico to Detroit and from Detroit to Washington. The U.S.-based firms distanced themselves from the U.S. government's efforts to change the decree. The firms had discovered that in this matter, at least, their interests converged as much with those of the Mexican government as with those of the U.S. government." Bennett and Sharpe, "Transnational Corporations," p. 22.

would likely seek remedial U.S. Government action."[30] This final effort to pressure the Mexican government failed: the U.S. government lacked not only coordination but the support of the automotive MNCs as well.

The year following the Diplomatic Note was one of negotiations between the MNC subsidiaries and the Mexican government.[31] After government negotiations that were characterized as the most difficult of any in its corporate experience, *General Motors* again emerged in the forefront.[32] In February 1979, General Motors President Elliot Estes flew to Mexico to announce plans for a major new GM investment of U.S. $250 million, its largest one-time investment commitment ever in a single site. The Mexican government had succeeded: Four new plants were to be constructed. GM's exports would expand twentyfold, from approximately U.S. $10 million in 1977 to U.S. $150–200 million in 1983. The new plants would make the Mexican subsidiary the largest exporter of internal combustion engines in all of Latin America.[33] As a result, GM's Mexican subsidiary would be able to claim a much larger share of the Mexican market as well as supply engines to the U.S. domestic market.

Immediately GM's competitors rushed to protect their market share in the follow-the-leader pattern of defensive investment. Within one month, in March 1979, both *Ford* and *Volkswagen* announced plans to expand production capacity for export and the domestic market, but as Bennett and Sharpe have pointed out, "could only give sketchy details."[34] Ford only outlined an investment amount of 1 billion pesos, while Volkswagen stated more than 8 billion pesos.

One month later, in April 1979, specific investment programs for engine export plants began to be announced by GM's competitors. By the end of 1980, the new planned investments of the automotive subsidiaries

[30] The Diplomatic Note also stated: "The United States understands Mexico's desire to make its domestic motor vehicle industry more efficient. However, the United States Government believes that the degree and regulations could have a severe, adverse impact on U.S.-Mexican trade. Such a policy requires U.S. firms operating in Mexico to export Mexican products without regard to efficiency or cost advantages." Quoted in Bennett and Sharpe, "Transnational Corporations," appendix.

[31] Two announcements of minor import were made during this period. Chrysler's managing director announced in October 1978 that the company expected to invest 3 billion pesos in the next three years in order to comply with the new regulation. In early February 1979, Ford announced a joint venture with the Mexican company, Grupo Industrial Alfa, S.A., for manufacturing aluminum heads. Total production, estimated at one million units a year, would be for export to the United States and Canada.

[32] Author interviews with senior management of General Motors de México.

[33] William G. Slocum, Jr. (managing director of General Motors de México), "General Motors de México," *Memoria II: Segundo Simposium de la Industria Automotriz Mexicana* (Mexico, D.F.: Canacintra, 1980), p. 77.

[34] Bennett and Sharpe, "Transnational Corporations," p. 24. Also, see "Programa de expansión de Ford" and "V.W. inició su nueva inversión," *AMIA Boletín* 160 (April 1979): 1.

were projected as increasing capacity for engine production in Mexico by over 2 billion engines a year. An American automotive industry study estimated that exports of Mexican auto parts to the United States alone would increase from U.S. $89 million in 1976 to over U.S. $2 billion by 1985.[35]

By July 1980 new investments were valued at 48 billion pesos, with *General Motors* and *Volkswagen* representing 81 percent of the total. Between 1977 and 1980 employment in the terminal industry alone increased 45 percent, from 39,806 people to 57,573. The new investments were expected to further increase employment to 80,000 by 1985, an increase of 100 percent in only seven years.[36]

The trade deficit continued, however, and in 1981, with the Cocoyoc Resolution, one subsidiary again set the pace for industry performance. In line with the Cocoyoc Resolution, automotive imports were to be reduced by setting production reductions for each company. The maximum automobile volume to be produced for the domestic market in the 1982 model year was set to be equal to that produced in 1981. Exceptions were permitted only if the subsidiary's foreign-exchange budget was positive in 1982. The negotiations were portrayed as follows: The government asked each company for its export plans, stating that this would be the major factor in deciding how much the company would be allowed to import. Each company would supply its most optimistic export plan, and the government then specified how much the company could import. Based on this volume of imports, each company would thus determine its production reduction.[37] *Nissan Mexicana*, however, was the only subsidiary to meet its foreign-exchange requirement.

As a direct result of the Mexican government's 1977 Decree, Mexico has become one of the major sourcing countries for automobile engines in the world. By 1982 the other subsidiaries had substantially increased their investments: The automotive parents planned to manufacture a total of 3.5 million engines in Mexico, of which 3 million would be for export.[38]

[35] "Performance Requirements: A Study of the Incidence and Impact of Trade-Related Performance Requirements, and an Analysis of International Law" (The Labor-Industry Coalition for International Trade, Washington, D.C.: March 1981, Mimeographed), 29.

[36] Source of investment figures, "Programa de inversiónes de la industria automotriz terminal" (AMIA, 24 July 1980, Mimeographed). Employment figures were provided by AMIA.

[37] On 11 August 1982 a new resolution ("Resolución para Racionalizar el Déficit de la Balanza en Cuenta Corriente del Sector Automotriz en el Año Modelo 1983") imposed further restrictions on automobile production during the 1983 model year. Consistent with previous measures, the terminal companies had to balance their foreign exchange budgets. In addition, before the end of 1983 the companies had to pay back deficits incurred in 1982, advances granted before 1981, and interest due in 1983.

[38] See Jane Bussey, "Gearing Up to Export Three Million Engines to Auto Plants Abroad," *R & D Mexico* (Feb. 1982): 20–23.

By 1985 the five automotive subsidiaries would account for one-third of Mexico's total manufactured exports. Ten years after the 1977 Decree, the results were spectacular: automotive exports had skyrocketed 1,175 percent, from U.S. $253 million to U.S. $3.3 billion, transforming the automotive trade deficit into a significant surplus.

One subsidiary, *General Motors de México*, had led the rest of the industry and Mexico into a new era of export promotion, securing large international markets for the country's exports. Another subsidiary, *Nissan Mexicana*, set the standard for meeting the trade balance requirement. The success of the government's 1977 Decree in shaping MNC behavior rested on identifying the convergent interests of the MNCs and the Mexican government and then gauging the different abilities and willingness of each MNC to comply; with one company successfully targeted to comply, the others were forced to follow the leader with defensive investments and changes in sourcing strategies.

Therefore, as in Brazil, the Mexican automotive subsidiaries played a distinctive role in the host country as "levers for change."[39] Because of their MNC origins, the Mexican government expected certain special benefits from the automotive industry. Government regulations were especially targeted at the subsidiaries' investment and sourcing policies. As leaders in import substitution, the automotive subsidaries assumed a prominent role in generating employment and the creation of an industrial infrastructure. Their very success, however, laid the groundwork for a regulatory crackdown. The government's historic objective of achieving a trade balance was repeatedly hindered by a growing automotive market needing more imports of auto parts. The automotive subsidiaries—through no formulated intent—created the conditions for change with decades-long auto deficits, finally culminating in an inflexible government policy of export promotion and increased local content. Yet, the automotive subsidiaries also provided the solution: their MNC origins made them the natural means by which to lead the country into export promotion and a positive trade balance.

The Mexican case study, like the Brazilian one, illuminates the arguments. The government's demands were increasingly targeted at the investment and sourcing policies of the subsidiaries because these policies were seen as potentially advancing key government objectives. The Mexican government's specific priorities and tactics (and their import for the

[39] The Mexican case of government intervention in the automotive industry is not closed. The administration of President Miguel de la Madrid in September 1983 issued a major new decree that attempts to address the structural difficulties previously discussed by restricting the number of models each company can manufacture. "Decreto para la racionalización de la industria automotriz," *Diario oficial*, 15 Sept. 1983.

MNCs) changed as the country's industrial and economic development progressed. The buildup of demands on the automotive subsidiaries to achieve trade balance was not sudden or mysterious. As in Brazil, a historical analysis of these demands highlights the accelerating buildup of pressure, and the foreseeable role of the automotive MNC subsidiaries as "levers for change." But, as shown, the ability and willingness of individual subsidiaries to comply varied considerably. Why was *General Motors de México* willing and able to respond to the Mexican government's 1977 Decree? Why was *Nissan Mexicana* the first to achieve a trade balance? The next two chapters will delve into specific subsidiary behavior, first identifying, then explaining, the critical response variables.

CHAPTER 6

Individual Subsidiary Response: The Reformulation of Investment and Sourcing Policies

THE LAST CHAPTER showed how the Mexican subsidiaries became, as in the Brazilian case study, "levers for change": the subsidiaries inadvertently created the conditions for escalating host-country demands that would eventually require making use of parent resources outside the host country. The Mexican government succeeded in eliciting huge investments from the world's automotive MNCs, thus establishing Mexico as a major global source for automotive engines. Yet, the historical overview also indicated significant differences in subsidiary response to the 1977 Decree, with *General Motors* setting the pace, forcing competitors to follow. This chapter examines in detail *how* the MNC subsidiaries differed in their ability and willingness to comply. By showing the wide variance in subsidiary behavior, we can challenge generalizations on MNC risks and benefits to LDCs, while underlining the latitude for intervention available to MNC managers and LDC groups.

As in the Brazilian case study, the examination of each of the five Mexican subsidiaries is twofold. This chapter is devoted to a chronological portrayal of how each behaved over time, documenting in particular its trade balance policies before the government's regulatory crackdown, and afterwards, the subsidiary's policy response to government demands. Chapter 7 searches for further explanations, with a structural analysis of each subsidiary's internal organization and its relationships with key actors: If the MNCs' risks and the LDCs' benefits were not similar, what explanations resided within the subsidiaries themselves?

THE FRAMEWORK

This chapter will focus on subsidiary behavior from 1969 to 1982. As in the Brazilian case, a comparative framework is used to present the behavior of the five subsidiaries chronologically. Once again (see figure 1–2), three aspects of the policy reformulation process of each subsidiary are analyzed: (1) the identification of a changing regulatory environment and response before crisis, (2) the degree of conflict between the subsidiary and the government at crisis, and (3) the subsidiary's type of response.[1]

The first section, pre-crisis identification, shows how each subsidiary behaved before the Mexican government hardened its demands in the 1977 Decree: before the crackdown, were there differences between subsidiaries in the detection of a changing regulatory environment and in the measures taken? Then, the degree of conflict between the Mexican government and each subsidiary is considered: with the issuance of the government's 1977 Decree and, later, the Cocoyoc Resolution, were there significant differences in the government's pressures and in each subsidiary's vulnerability to pressure? The last section examines each subsidiary's type of response: how did subsidiaries vary in their ability and willingness to finally comply with the Mexican government's demands? Such an in-depth study reveals, as in the Brazilian case, the underlying dynamics of MNC-LDC conflict, and also exposes the importance of different subsidiary characteristics in determining MNC risks and LDC benefits.

Pre-Crisis: Detection of the Changing Regulatory Environment

The Mexican automotive subsidiaries, as was true in the Brazilian case, shared the same operating environment, participated in the same national market with similar products, and collaborated closely with their competitors in addressing issues related to the overall industry. Yet the firms differed to a significant degree in their ability to identify and respond before crisis. Before the outbreak of crisis in 1977, the subsidiaries varied considerably in their detection of the escalating demands of the Mexcian government and in the measures taken to ensure that subsidiary policies were in step. As in the Brazilian case, three key variables differentiated subsidiary ability to identify and respond before crisis: (1) *internal management policies*, (2) *relationships with key LDC actors*, and (3) *parent intervention and influence*. A brief chronological survey of subsidiary behavior before the 1977 Decree illustrates the primacy of these variables in explaining each subsidiary's ability to identify and prepare for a changing regulatory environment.

As discussed in the previous chapter, the 1969 Resolution and the 1972 Decree clearly stated the Mexican government's concern over the auto-

[1] The information in this chapter, except where noted, was obtained in extensive personal interviews with Mexican government officials and subsidiary management of the Mexican automotive industry, and from answers given by the managing directors of each of the five subsidiaries in a detailed questionnaire. A list of interviewees is included in the Appendix.

motive trade deficit and explicitly required the subsidiaries to increase exports. The subsidiaries, however, varied in their interpretation of these regulations. Management at two subsidiaries—*General Motors* and *Ford*—claimed that the government's objective of a trade balance became an issue only in 1981, and that early government regulations were not of major significance. Yet the other subsidiaries thought that while the Mexican government did have other priorities, such as increased industrialization, it had always been concerned about eliminating the automotive trade deficit. Subsidiary management at the three other subsidiaries—*Chrysler, Volkswagen,* and *Nissan*—stressed the importance of the Mexican government's 1969 and 1972 regulations to increase exports. These three subsidiaries maintained that company resources had been devoted to analyzing government regulations and in deciding how they could best comply. In fact, as will be seen, these subsidiaries claim to have changed their export and local-content policies in response to the 1969 and 1972 regulations.

These varying perceptions of subsidiary management were mirrored by differing subsidiary policies for local content and exports. From 1964 to 1977 the policies of two subsidiaries, *Nissan* and especially *Volkswagen,* were most in line with government objectives; the *U.S. subsidiaries,* for the vast majority of the time, however, maintained minimum local content, relying (unsuccessfully) on exports to compensate for a high import bill.

Volkswagen consciously set out early on to strengthen its relationship with the Mexican government, extending its bargaining power by aggressively increasing local content. According to Volkswagen management, the MNC's practice worldwide called for its subsidiaries to adapt their local operation to the particular characteristics of each host country. Building a strong bargaining position meant operating like a national company. Developing close relationships in-country was the key. In line with this company philosophy, a member of subsidiary management proposed a high local-content strategy, arguing that the parent's objective of adapting to the host country and increasing bargaining power would be enhanced: "In the 1960s I had to fight with groups at the [Volkswagen] parent. They finally understood that we had to put roots into the [Mexican] economy if we wanted the [Mexican] market. If the government attacked Volkswagen, it would have to attack all of its suppliers. . . . We had to be particularly sensitive to the Mexican government because the U.S. companies were influencing it, and we were newcomers."[2] The high local-content strategy was initiated by the Volkswagen subsidiary and,

[2] Author interview with a senior executive of Volkswagen de México responsible for developing local-content strategy.

after some resistance, endorsed by the parent. As hoped, this strategy did facilitate the overall objectives of close in-country relationships, adaptation, and increased bargaining power.

Furthermore, Volkswagen subsidiary management claimed their subsidiary had particularly difficult problems responding to the local-content requirements of the 1962 Decree. Local suppliers were not geared to manufacturing the car parts required by the Volkswagen subsidiary, and volume was not sufficient to justify local manufacturing. The three U.S. subsidiaries, on the other hand, enjoyed the advantage of sharing the same local suppliers; by jointly buying the same parts locally, they benefited from economies of scale, and hence lower costs. In addition, some key U.S. suppliers had established operations in Mexico. By 1964 there were approximately one hundred U.S.-affiliated suppliers.

Specific policies to increase local content were successfully enacted by Volkswagen's subsidiary management. First, the Volkswagen subsidiary successfully negotiated the government's 1962 Decree; as Volkswagen could not produce engines because there was no aluminum foundry, it received permission to have a stamping facility in lieu of producing engines. Years later, when it began to produce engines, this would enable Volkswagen to have the highest local content of the automotive companies. Second, at every possible point, the Volkswagen subsidiary aggressively fought rules prohibiting vertical integration, producing its own parts whenever possible. Third, in the 1960s, Volkswagen convinced German suppliers to come to Mexico and create a German supplier industry. By 1982 there were approximately twenty joint ventures between German and Mexican companies, as well as roughly forty to fifty Mexican suppliers operating with German licenses. Since the Nissan subsidiary was unable to convince its home suppliers to establish subsidiaries in Mexico, it became a customer of many Volkswagen suppliers.

On the export side, Volkswagen's subsidiary management also devised an early answer, enabling it later to comply more fully than its competitors with the Mexican government's trade balance requirement. The production of the Beetle model was no longer economical in Germany, and the local German market was small. All production would therefore be shifted to Mexico and Brazil. The mature German product—"The People's Car"—was appropriate for the growing popular segment of the Mexican market. Lower Mexican wages would make production less costly and export sales to Germany and other countries more profitable. As a senior executive of a competitor stated: "Volkswagen has played the game since 1972. It's been the strategy of the parent to export to Germany from Mexico."[3] Thereby, first by negotiating aggressively with the Mexican

[3] Author interview with senior management of automotive subsidiary.

government upfront, modifying regulations in line with company needs, then by successfully pursuing simultaneous high local-content and export policies, Volkswagen's subsidiary management ensured its policies were in sync with the overall objectives of the host government.

Management of the *Chrysler* and *Nissan* subsidiaries also made major changes that were in line with the government's demands. According to the managing director of *Chrysler*, subsidiary management began to be worried about a trade balance equilibrium in 1969. Subsidiary management attributed their ability to read early on the significance of Mexican government demands to their close relations with Mexican government officials. The former majority owner of the company, then chairman of the board, was very closely linked with high officials in the Mexican government. The Chrysler managing director claimed that the key period of adjustment for the subsidiary had come at the time just after the 1972 Decree. Changes in the subsidiary's policies were widespread, and many company objectives were modified, including management processes involving: the subsidiary's relationships with its parent, the U.S. government, and the Mexican government; local-content policies, including the subsidiary's relationship with home suppliers and parent component divisions; and export policies, including parent sourcing strategy.[4] Indeed, the export requirement was reported as the principal reason Chrysler increased its equity share of the Mexican subsidiary from 33 to 99 percent. As majority owner, the subsidiary's managing director explained, the Chrysler parent would thereby increase the subsidiary's "exporting potential and its capacity to . . . identify economic products the U.S. could buy in Mexico."[5]

Furthermore, after the takeover, the Chrysler subsidiary made major investments to increase its export capacity. First, in 1973 the Mexican subsidiary inaugurated a (75 million pesos) plant to manufacture exclusively for export air conditioner condensers valued at 100 million pesos annually. Second, in 1974, Chrysler invested another 65 million pesos to expand an engine plant for exports. The Chrysler subsidiary was also able to sell transmissions to its U.S. parent, thereby getting export credits from the exports of the supplier company TREMEX. By 1975 the Chrysler subsidiary's exports included engines, air conditioner condensers, transmissions, and trucks to more than twelve countries, the principal

[4] Author interview with managing director of Chrysler subsidiary.

[5] Statement made by T. J. Andersen, former managing director of the Chrysler subsidiary, quoted in *Expansión*, 16 May 1973, p. 30. Also, see Douglas C. Bennett and Kenneth E. Sharpe, *Transnational Corporations Versus the State: The Political Economy of the Mexican Auto Industry* (Princeton: Princeton University Press, 1985), p. 173; and John Christman, "The Automotive Industry," in *Business Mexico* (Mexico, D.F.: American Chamber of Commerce of Mexico, A.C., 1973), p. 127.

clients being the Chrysler parent in the U.S. and a sister subsidiary in Venezuela. The Chrysler subsidiary by that time had become the largest exporter in the Mexican automotive industry.

The *Nissan* subsidiary also had to make significant changes to align its policies with the objectives of the Mexican government. Its exports had been minimal and, like Chrysler's, had not been scheduled to increase within the overall strategy. In 1968 voluntary exports on a very small scale were begun, not owing to Mexico's requirements but because of Chile's. Under an interchange program with Nissan Motor of Chile, Nissan Mexicana exported engines, transmissions, and rear axles in order to meet the Chilean government's requirement for local content (exports of LAFTA countries such as Mexico were considered local content). However, by 1971 the value of Nissan exports were still minimal, only totaling U.S. $613 thousand.

The managing director of the Nissan subsidiary argued that the Mexican government had "always" been concerned with the automotive trade deficit. Nissan Mexicana had changed its export and local-content policies expressly to conform with the government's objectives. Nissan, like other Japanese companies, shared a strong philosophy of government compliance. The parent agreed with the subsidiary: exports were imperative. In 1971, worried about their company's poor export performance in light of the Mexican government's demands, Nissan Mexicana's management established an Export Committee composed of the managing director, vice-president, and director of commercial relations. Export policies were examined and changed. In March 1971 the subsidiary began to export auto parts to its parent in Japan.[6]

In 1972, as the result of the new Mexican decree, according to the director of exports, Nissan Mexicana "initiated export activities more systematically and deliberately, corresponding to the Mexican government policy that gradually required us to make the balance of trade."[7] Nissan Mexicana started exporting commercial vehicles to Central America. Specific markets were chosen by the parent and given exclusively to Nissan Mexicana; in other countries, the subsidiary had to compete with the parent and its lower prices. This price competition meant Nissan Mexicana had to sell at a loss. By 1976 exports increased to U.S. $15 million, and Nissan announced a new investment of 250 million pesos to increase

[6] Author interview with managing director of Nissan Mexicana, Summer 1982. Nissan Mexicana's exports to the parent included oil filters, rubber electronic components, and wheel covers. Information on export policies was obtained in multiple interviews with Nissan Mexicana management, including the managing director, the director of exports, and the deputy director of exports.

[7] From speech made by Nissan Mexicana's director of exports, June 1982.

exports. Like the Chrysler and Volkswagen subsidiaries, Nissan Mexicana had to enlist the aid of its parent to augment its export capacity.

In summary, despite the unilateral buildup of government pressure on their investment and sourcing policies, the automobile subsidiaries differed considerably in their ability to identify and respond pre-crisis, with wide variations in their perceptions of the importance of adjusting their policies. (1) *Internal management policies* differentiated the *Volkswagen, Chrysler,* and *Nissan* subsidiaries. Due to their perception of increasing regulatory demands, both the Volkswagen and Nissan subsidiaries deliberately increased local content, thereby reducing their respective trade deficits. Chrysler joined Volkswagen and Nissan in analyzing government regulations. When the Chrysler subsidiary could not meet the export requirement, subsidiary management convinced the parent to change its ownership structure, and the parent invested in products to increase subsidiary exports.

(2) *Relationships with key LDC actors* differentiated the pre-crisis responses of the *Volkswagen* and *Chrysler* subsidiaries, both of which deliberately established close relationships with the Mexican government. The Volkswagen subsidiary deliberately set out to strengthen its relationship with the Mexican government, using its high local-content strategy to augment its bargaining power. The Chrysler subsidiary credited its responsiveness in part to the close government relationships of its Mexican joint partner. To a lesser degree, because it perceived a need to strengthen its government relations, *Nissan Mexicana* deliberately set out to increase exports. In contrast, the other subsidiaries, *General Motors* and *Ford,* while they enjoyed close government relationships (and in some cases significantly influenced government policy), did not report government relations as increasing their ability to identify and respond pre-crisis.

(3) *Parent intervention and influence* also helped to explain the pre-crisis responses of *Nissan Mexicana, Volkswagen,* and *Chrysler.* Nissan Mexicana benefited from its parent's philosophy of government compliance. The parent increased its subsidiary's export capacity by assigning to it certain Central American markets. Volkswagen de México was able to respond in part due to its parent's practice of subsidiary adaptation. It was also given the production of the Beetle and its export markets. Chrysler de México's ability to export was also enlarged by parent intervention. In contrast, the same government demands were only peripheral to the strategies of the *General Motors* and *Ford* subsidiaries; they were dominated by their global strategies and no changes, no major conflicts had transpired. The following sections examine whether this diversity was also evidenced in later developments—at the point of crisis and in subsequent subsidiary responses.

Crisis and Degree of Conflict: Host Goverment versus Subsidiary

The automotive trade deficit continued to deepen, nearly tripling in five years from U.S. $230 million in 1970 to U.S. $628 million in 1975, almost one-fifth of the country's total trade deficit.[8] Government pressure on the automotive industry continued to escalate with extensive government-industry discussions during 1976 on the industry's local-content and export policies. In 1977 government pressure broke into overt conflict: the Mexican government crystallized its demands into law with the enactment of the 1977 Decree. The 1977 Decree set into place specific guidelines and requirements for each subsidiary: the trade balance of each subsidiary would be systematically measured. Each subsidiary had a foreign-exchange budget that had to be balanced by 1982. During the height of conflict—from the 1977 Decree to the aftermath of the Cocoyoc Resolution in 1981—were all five automotive subsidiaries uniformly subject to the same level of pressure? Or were there inherently different levels of conflict between individual subsidiaries and the Mexican government? On the government side, did officials deliberately discriminate between the subsidiaries? On the subsidiary side, did individual subsidiaries differ in their vulnerability to pressure?

Again, as in the Brazilian case, despite the commonality of the industry, the individual characteristics of the automotive subsidiaries accounted for significantly differing degrees of conflict. Moreover, the same three key variables differentiated the degree of conflict: (1) *historical policy performance*, (2) *the pressuring-group's perception of the subsidiaries and bargaining power*, and (3) *the parents' interests.*

First of all, despite the fact that these five subsidiaries shared many similarities, the degree of conflict between the subsidiaries and the Mexican government varied largely due to different historical trade balance policies. As one of the subsidiary's government-relations executives stated: "The companies least affected [by government regulations] are those practicing the government's philosophy."[9] As discussed, *Volkswagen*'s strategy best fit the government's specifications. *Chrysler* and *Nissan* management had already perceived the need to make significant changes to accommodate government trade balance objectives and, after in-depth discussions with parent management, had taken specific measures to better fulfill government objectives. In contrast, the strategies of *General Motors* and *Ford* had not been changed. In addition, parent

[8] SEPAFIN, "La Industria Automotriz en México," p. 117.

[9] Author interview with director of government relations at one of the automotive subsidiaries. This viewpoint was widely held throughout the industry.

resources had affected the subsidiaries' trade balances, especially that of *Chrysler*. Therefore, when the 1977 Decree was issued, it was the American subsidiaries that held the greatest responsibility for the trade deficit.

Why in the same industry were some subsidiaries innately out of sync with host-government objectives, while others were in greater conformity? The reasons were multiple, including: differing subsidiary strategies (local content, markets and their location, growth objectives, government relations); distinct corporate cultures (view of government regulation, parent-subsidiary philosophies, utilization and role of expatriates); and divergent products and production economies (suppliers, economies of scale, production requirements). External factors such as exchange rates also played a role.

In terms of local-content policies, the *General Motors*, *Ford*, and *Chrysler* subsidiaries had followed similar strategies—the purchases of auto parts from within Mexico were kept to a minimum while maximizing purchases from each parent company and their suppliers in the U.S. In contrast, the *Nissan* and *Volkswagen* subsidiaries had both adopted higher local-content strategies, thereby incurring lower trade deficits.

The reasons for the higher local content of the Nissan and Volkswagen subsidiaries were product- and strategy-specific. As discussed in the previous section, in the early 1960s the non-U.S. subsidiaries were newcomers to the Mexican automotive industry and were thus at a distinct disadvantage in developing suppliers compared to the "Big Three" U.S. subsidiaries. Ironically, however, they were to comply more, increasing local content more than the U.S. subsidiaries. For example, as discussed in the last section, there was no aluminum foundry—which Volkswagen required to produce engines—so Volkswagen was able to negotiate a stamping facility that proved to be invaluable as requirements for local content increased. And, given the products of Nissan and Volkswagen (unlike those of the U.S. subsidiaries), it was cost-effective to increase local content since model changes were infrequent and production of the standard parts had become more efficient over the years. Furthermore, they were far away from their home suppliers (again, unlike the U.S. subsidiaries), so importing parts was more costly, time-consuming, and hence less desirable.

Fast market growth also pressured the Volkswagen and Nissan subsidiaries to increase local content. In 1965 the U.S. subsidiaries had 70 percent of the market; only seven years later, in 1972, their share had dropped to 50 percent, and the share of the Volkswagen and Nissan subsidiaries had surged from 14 percent to 34 percent. In 1972, Volkswagen was number one in market share with 23 percent, up from fourth place with 13 percent in 1965. Likewise, Nissan's share was 9 percent, up from 1 percent of the market.

Volkswagen subsidiary management also claimed that two other factors contributed to a high local-content strategy: home-country exchange rates and Volkswagen's corporate culture. The revaluation of the deutsche mark increased the cost of German imports and spurred the incentive to augment local content with cheaper Mexican parts. These reasons reinforced what Volkswagen's management called part of their corporate culture. Volkswagen's management also had a strong preference to produce many parts itself: "We do not trust others."[10]

Nissan subsidiary management, however, stressed high local content for different reasons. Unlike Volkswagen, imports from the parent were cheaper than Mexican-made parts. However, given its few exports and its parent's reluctance to invest heavily in export-generating projects, the Nissan subsidiary had no alternative if it was to comply with government regulations but to increase local content.

In contrast, the *U.S. subsidiaries* followed a low local-content strategy, maximizing imports from the United States and exporting a significantly higher level of auto parts within their global MNC network. Yet exports within their networks could not offset their huge volume of imports. Their models were changed each year in sync with the U.S. market, their main products being American luxury cars. Faced with host-government demands, the GM and Ford subsidiaries did not make major changes; Mexico was viewed as an extension of the U.S. market, and the type of imports and exports were determined exclusively by parent sourcing considerations.

However, long before any export regulation, *Ford* became the first of the Mexican automotive subsidiaries to export. In 1963, Ford de México started an assembly tooling plant, with 90 percent of its production for export. Indeed, the Ford subsidiary was the industry leader in promoting the Mexican government's push for export promotion in 1969. Ford had a competitive advantage in its ability to export: it was the only subsidiary with a consistent export program already in place, a wide network of sister subsidiaries to enlarge exports, as well as close relationships with key Mexican subsidiaries of its U.S. suppliers that were anxious to export. By 1975 the export credits of Ford's Mexican subsidiary had increased to 40 million dollars, 72 percent of which were produced by its Mexican suppliers (mostly Mexican subsidiaries of its U.S. suppliers). Ford's export activity was an integral part of the strategic sourcing network of its U.S. parent, but it was mostly limited to its suppliers' exports and was not merely a concession to the Mexican government's pressures.

Likewise, in 1965, long before Mexican export demands, the *General*

[10] Author interview with Volkswagen de México's executive in charge of local-content strategy.

Motors subsidiary had started to export voluntarily within the sourcing network of the parent. An export office was established. Engines were exported to the U.S. and auto parts to subsidiaries in South America, South Africa, and the U.S. However, GM's exports did not surge with the enactment of the 1972 Decree. GM's sourcing network was far more limited than Ford's: sourcing was less developed and its U.S. suppliers—many within the GM divisions—did not relocate to Mexico. In 1972, GM's exports were valued at U.S. $14 million, half of Ford's. The GM divisions were expected to compete cost-effectively, and losses in intracompany sales were not tolerated. Therefore, from the mid-1960s into the 1970s, the Ford and GM subsidiaries exported within their global parent networks, but not in sufficient volume to offset imports.

From the mid-1970s on, however, the exports of the other three subsidiaries shot up. By 1975, the *Volkswagen* and *Nissan* subsidiaries nearly tripled their exports. The *Chrysler* subsidiary became the top exporter with U.S. $50 million, *Volkswagen* the second at U.S. $46 million. *Ford* fell from being the top exporter to third with U.S. $40 million of exports, followed by *General Motors* with U.S. $15 million of exports. While the *Nissan* subsidiary still exported the least (U.S. $8 million), this was up threefold from U.S. $2 million three years earlier.

Compared to General Motors and Ford, the *Volkswagen* subsidiary was better positioned within its established subsidiary network to export. Volkswagen decided that exports were good business due to low Mexican labor costs and increased economies of scale. In 1968, a senior subsidiary executive explained, Volkswagen began to export to increase economies of scale, since "one way to stop cost increases was to produce more."[11] The Mexican subsidiary would have a monopoly for providing spare Beetle parts to the U.S. market. In 1973 the Mexican subsidiary's role with the Volkswagen sourcing network was expanded: Safari jeeps would henceforth be exported to the U.S., Germany, and other export markets. Exports almost tripled from U.S. 419 million in 1972 to U.S. $74 million in 1974, with the U.S. and West German markets absorbing 90 percent. That year, with the production of the Beetle shifted from Germany to Mexico and Brazil, the Mexican subsidiary would have an international monopoly of important overseas markets.

Just as the inherent conflict between subsidiary policies and Mexican demands differed, so did the Mexican government's perceptions of the ability and willingness of each subsidiary to respond. Over the years, the Mexican government had accumulated extensive experience from negotiating with the automotive subsidiaries and eventually devised an explicit strategy for eliciting response. Policymakers had an increasingly so-

[11] Author interview with Volkswagen de México's executive in charge of exports.

phisticated knowledge of the automotive industry and, most importantly, of the dynamics in subsidiary-parent decision-making of the five subsidiaries in question. The Mexican government felt that success—the deriving of benefits from the pressuring demands of the 1977 Decree—had resulted from its ability not only to distinguish the differing capacities of the MNCs to respond but also to effectively target the underlying decision variables. The decree would read the same for all subsidiaries, but the individual responses were calculated to make all the difference.

Therefore, the Mexican government did not even intend to pressure the five subsidiaries unilaterally; rather it pursued a "divide and conquer" strategy even before orchestrating the crisis with the 1977 Decree. The Mexican government felt the industry was controlled by the "Big Three" U.S. companies. Over the years the government had experienced the collective strength of these three powerful American multinational companies, whose natural ally was of course the U.S. government. The Mexican government had had less bargaining power and influence with the U.S. companies; negotiating had been more direct, simple, and flexible with the *Volkswagen* and *Nissan* subsidiaries. In short, given these experiences the Mexican government now wanted to break the "Big Three."

The Mexican government prepared its battleground by specifically targeting the *General Motors* subsidiary. The government knew that General Motors wanted to increase Mexican sales, but that its manufacturing plants were capacity-constrained. To meet the objective of increasing Mexican sales, the plants would have to be significantly expanded, requiring substantial new investment. Furthermore, the GM parent was at that time in the grips of a U.S. automotive crisis and had a pressing need to downsize and decrease costs, but to increase investments, and so was debating alternative production sites worldwide. The time was clearly right for Mexico to bid for a significant role within General Motors' new global strategy. The Mexican government held high-level discussions with GM and felt assured that the MNC would invest in Mexico. Capitulation was almost guaranteed: GM's compliance would set off defensive counterinvestments by the other subsidiaries. With this game plan in mind, the Mexican government announced the 1977 Decree.[12]

The vulnerability of the two other American subsidiaries to Mexican demands was especially high. Both competed with GM in the luxury car market segment, and all imported many auto parts from their U.S. operations and had large trade deficits. Mexico and its government clearly did not need three automotive companies manufacturing luxury cars. The

[12] Author interviews with senior Mexican government officials responsible for the 1977 Decree.

Nissan and *Volkswagen* subsidiaries competed principally in the popular segment and imported less from their parents. Their products were more politically justifiable, especially given their relatively low trade deficits. However, from the point of view of the American MNCs, Mexico was a growing and profitable extension of the U.S. market.

The unique pressure on the *Ford* subsidiary was clearly illustrated by its parent's lead role in opposing the Mexican government. The Ford parent felt that its Mexican subsidiary was at a distinct disadvantage in complying with the 1977 Decree. Its automotive deficit was one of the largest. In order to comply by increasing exports, huge new investments would be required. But unlike General Motors, Ford had yet to define its product strategy and production sites, and was also in weak financial shape. The Mexican decree was in direct conflict with the current needs of the parent's overall strategy. Furthermore, U.S. labor was aggressively pressuring Ford *not* to invest in Mexico.

Likewise, the *Chrysler* subsidiary was hampered in its capacity to comply with the decree. Its auto trade deficits were the largest, and the subsidiary's parent, due to its financial weakness, was hardly eager or able to increase its investments in Mexico. Yet, the Mexican subsidiary was its only profitable subsidiary: as one of its financial executives explained, the parent needed to protect its lifeline to this "cash cow."[13]

Several government officials and company executives claimed that the Chrysler subsidiary was under less pressure than the Ford subsidiary because the government gave it special treatment—partly because of its parent's difficulties and its special ties with the Mexican government. Due to its origins as a Mexican company, Chrysler was cited as more integrated within the Mexican environment than its competitors. Contacts with high levels of the Mexican government were very close, and Chrysler was seen as benefiting from its limited Mexican capital of 1 percent.[14]

As the strategies of the *Nissan* and *Volkswagen* subsidiaries were more in agreement with overall government demands, they were less threatened by the 1977 Decree. Unlike the American subsidiaries, neither subsidiary contested the Mexican government's decree or resisted its implementation. As one of the country's largest employers, the *Volkswagen* subsidiary felt secure in its ability to negotiate any minor problems to the

[13] Author interview with senior financial management of Chrysler de México.

[14] Author interviews with Mexican government officials responsible for automotive industry and management of the automotive subsidiaries.

Other government officials pointed out, however, that Chrysler's huge trade deficit mattered more than its government relations; the regulations were increasingly clear, and obvious noncompliance was unacceptable in a situation where the subsidiary's large share of the trade deficit was hurting the country.

satisfaction of both parties. Its trade balance was better than the other subsidiaries', and it enjoyed a close and powerful relationship with the Mexican government. However, executives of *Nissan* claimed they were under more pressure than the other subsidiaries due to a lack of bargaining power, and the "Japanese way of thinking." Nissan Mexicana claimed to lack bargaining power because of its small size and weak Japanese-Mexican relations. Furthermore, as is consistent with studies on Japanese MNCs, the behavior of the Nissan subsidiary was affected by Japanese values—the level of pressure was increased by the Japanese view that the regulations must be seriously and correctly observed.[15]

Therefore, while the Mexican government's demands were uniform for an automotive trade balance, the actual degree of conflict varied for each subsidiary. (1) *Past policy performance* affected the level of pressure. Those subsidiaries—*Volkswagen* and *Nissan*—that had successfully aligned their policies with the host-government's demands before crisis were, as a consequence, under less pressure. The reverse was true for those subsidiaries—*Ford, General Motors*, and *Chrysler*—that continued to have surging trade deficits. The subsidiaries' trade balance policies had innately different levels of conflict with the Mexican government. Factors driving policies were multiple, including: global strategy, product, the locations of markets, and sourcing. (2) *Pressuring-group's perception and bargaining power* varied: the Mexican government discriminated in its pressure on the subsidiaries, negotiating separately with General Motors precisely because it felt the subsidiary would willingly respond, thus setting off defensive investments by its competitors. The *Chrysler* subsidiary was pressured less because the government was convinced it was temporarily unable to respond, and given its Mexican origins, it was perceived to be more a Mexican company and still maintained strong, special relations with the Mexican government. The government also discriminated between subsidiaries, depending on the particular products, market needs, national origins, and size. *Volkswagen* and *Nissan* were pressured less in part because they were the most important manufacturers of popular car models, and they were furthering the government's objective of diversifying foreign investment. In addition, given the size of their operations, the *Chrysler* and *Volkswagen* subsidiaries were perceived as important employers. Conversely, the *Ford* and *General Motors* (and, to some extent, *Chrysler*) subsidiaries were pressured more because they manufactured luxury cars in an oversupplied market and because they were American MNCs. (3) *Parent interests* also increased pressure on the subsidiary: home labor opinions in-

[15] Author interviews with senior management of Nissan Mexicana and the Mexican government officials responsible for automotive policy.

creased pressure on *Ford de México*, the parent philosophy of compliance increased pressure on *Nissan Mexicana*, and parent constraints increased pressure on the *Chrysler* and *Ford* subsidiaries. Only in the case of *General Motors* did parent interests serve to decrease pressure: given the coincidence between parent strategy and Mexican government demands, the subsidiary was interested in making a major commitment to new investment. Therefore, despite the apparent uniformity of the Mexican governments' demands, in actuality its degree of conflict with each of the automotive subsidiaries at the point of crisis differed significantly.

Subsidiary Responses to Conflict

Clearly, at crisis, there were important differences in the degree of conflict between individual subsidiaries and the Mexican government. Subsequently, when confronted by the Mexican government's demands, all five subsidiaries did not respond uniformly. Why was *General Motors* first in committing itself to large investments? Why was *Nissan* the first subsidiary to actually comply with the trade balance demand? The case shows, as did the Brazilian one, that despite any commonality of industry and threat, the responses of subsidiaries to national demands differ widely as the result of a multitude of factors. Again, key variables that differentiated subsidiary response included (1) *parent preferences*, (2) *relationship with key LDC groups*, and (3) the *first policy responses* set forth by subsidiaries.

Immediate Response

As in the Brazilian case, when faced with crisis the parents of the *U.S. subsidiaries* immediately became involved. The magnitude of involvement was much greater, with visits from high-level parent staff, and even reached the point of seeking intervention from the U.S. government. Again, however, the behavior of the three U.S. subsidiaries was not uniform. *Ford* led the fight, with Henry Ford II actively and aggressively arguing his case with high-level U.S. and Mexican government officials. The MNC fought for an extended period, even threatening to leave Mexico. *Chrysler* claimed it was a special case, needing exemption due to the financial difficulties of the parent. As discussed, *General Motors*, from the top down, was open to discussion: before the 1977 Decree was enacted, GM had already indicated its desire to increase significantly its Mexican investment.

The 1977 Decree was perceived as presenting major problems for the entire *Ford* operation worldwide. As the U.S. automotive MNC with the greatest overseas experience, Ford was moved to make an unusual statement in its 1977 Annual Report: "Increasing sophistication is required to deal with the complexities of doing business in international markets. [One] example is the action taken by the Mexican government in 1977 to increase exports and enlarge the local content of Mexican-built vehicles. Decisions of this kind are making it more difficult to achieve potential market gains in some parts of the world. . . . Ford of Mexico is searching for ways to cope with the impact of these new regulations."[16] The Ford parent took the lead in lobbying against the new decree. Immediately after the publication of the decree, Henry Ford II brought his company's case forward in a personal visit with the Mexican president. He lobbied Secretary of State Cyrus Vance and the U.S. Ambassador to Mexico Patrick Lucy. The Ford parent involved the Motor Vehicle Manufacturers Association (MVMA), which conferred with the U.S. Departments of Commerce, State, and Treasury. Ford's strategy was simple. The U.S. automotive MNCs had a powerful bargaining tool: their home country was the main source of direct foreign investment in Mexico, bought the majority of Mexico's exports, and supplied the majority of Mexico's imports.

In contrast, at no time did either the *Volkswagen* or *Nissan* subsidiaries fight the government's enactment of the 1977 Decree nor did their home governments intervene. Parent management involvement was also limited. On a company basis they did not question the validity of the 1977 Decree or the trade balance requirement. Indeed, just five months after the government's crackdown, the *Volkswagen* subsidiary staged an emotional ceremony attended by government officials, including the Mexican president. The first Mexican-made Beetles were ready to be exported to Germany and other European countries. A part of the speech by Volkswagen de México's managing director was aimed at the Mexican president and emphasized the role of the Volkswagen subsidiary: "Mr. President, as members of Mexico's productive infrastructure, your presence stimulates us to continue working with dedication and . . . commitment and vision in order to achieve one single objective, which is the well-being of all Mexicans."[17]

Soon thereafter, following suit, the managing director of the *Nissan* subsidiary stepped forth to announce that "To comply with the regulations of the new decree, it is necessary to increase exports," stressing the company's increase of capital and efforts to further increase local con-

[16] Ford 1977 Annual Report, p. 11.

[17] "Volkswagen exportará cuarenta mil unidades Sedan a Europa en 1978," *AMIA Boletín* 143 (Nov. 1977): 1.

tent.[18] The Volkswagen and Nissan subsidiaries both were publicly supporting the 1977 Decree, endorsing the government's objectives, and affirming their commitment to comply with them. As one senior government official stated, "Both Volkswagen and Nissan prefer others to make the complaints. After all, they still get the benefits."[19]

The General Motors Investment

However, it was General Motors that went beyond ceremony, committing itself to major investment in engine exports, thus becoming the "lever for change" that would lead the rest of the industry into making Mexico a global source of automotive engines. While GM was, in principle, against any further governmental regulation of its Mexican subsidiary, the new decree nevertheless gave its subsidiary a way to increase its market share while at the same time offering the parent a cheaper sourcing site for its global strategy.

The moment was opportune: the parent had secretly boycotted the Mexican subsidiary and now that boycott was ended. Since 1962 the GM subsidiary had been losing market share. During those years, the chairman of General Motors reportedly felt that the Mexican government had not lived up to some undisclosed commitment and during his tenure was unwilling to increase GM's investment in Mexico. By 1976, General Motors' share of the market had dropped 55 percent, from 27.1 percent in 1962 to 12.3 percent. However, with a new chairman in place at the parent, Mexico was back on the list as a possible site for new investments. GM could now compete for an increase in market share against weakened competitors such as Ford that were less able to meet the required investments. GM's decision was strictly competitive; the need to respond to the 1977 Decree reinforced its decision to be "a viable manufacturing subsidiary in an expanding market."[20]

Furthermore, General Motors' global strategy had changed. Senior GM management had already decided by 1977 to challenge Ford in its superior foreign operations. The parent had the resources to invest, and with demand decreasing in the industrialized countries, Latin America was recognized as a major growth area in the world automotive market.

Moreover, the entire automotive industry was beginning to face the challenge of global restructuring. The GM parent had started to formulate a new global sourcing strategy with new downsized products, and Mexico was placing a bid for its selection as a major low-cost production

[18] "Nissan Mexicana duplicó en 1977 sus exportaciones de Pick-up Datsun," *AMIA Boletín* 145 (Jan. 1978): 1.

[19] Author interview with senior government official responsible for automotive policies.

[20] Author interview with a senior executive of General Motors de México.

site. Mexico could now provide GM with a potentially cheaper sourcing location for auto parts to be used in its downsized models.

As part of the company restructuring, in January 1976 the Mexican subsidiary began to report to GM's domestic division, the North American Assembly Division. The support of the head of the domestic division was cited as decisive in persuading GM's parent management to meet the investment requirement of the Mexican government. Compliance to the Mexican government's demands was seen as reinforcing GM's global competitive advantage.

Less than five months after the decree, General Motors broke rank with the other U.S. subsidiaries and announced that it would comply with the 1977 Decree. Subsidiary management had gone to the parent corporation to argue for compliance by increasing exports; consequently, the parent requested its U.S. supplier division to invest in a Mexican in-bond assembly plant (*maquiladora*) that would sell its total production of automotive rear-body wiring harnesses to GM's operations in the United States. The interests of the parent and its subsidiary coincided—the subsidiary would receive needed export credits, and the parent divisions would benefit from the cheaper Mexican wages.

In February 1979, one year and eight months after the decree, the president of General Motors flew to Mexico to announce a major commitment—the largest investment ever by GM in a single place at a single time. The General Motors subsidiary had realigned its export strategy with an explosive expansion: it would invest U.S. $250 million in Mexican engine plants and would become a major source of engines for sister subsidiaries in Canada, Venezuela, Chile, South Africa, Australia, the United Kingdom, and Belgium as well as the U.S. parent operation. With the construction of four new engine plants, GM's Mexican subsidiary would become the "largest exporter of internal combustion engines in all of Latin America,"[21] and would also be able to claim a much larger share of the Mexican market.

The Volkswagen Investment

Due to their large trade deficits, Ford and Chrysler were under the most pressure to respond to GM's initiative. Yet it was Volkswagen that first leapt to General Motors' challenge. In April 1979, Volkswagen announced a detailed plan to invest 6 billion pesos for a new 4-cylinder-engine plant in Mexico, with 75 percent of its production to be exported to Volkswagen of America; Volkswagen management had decided to tie

[21] William G. Slocum, Jr. (managing director of General Motors de México), "General Motors de México," *Memoria II*, p. 77.

its Mexican subsidiary into its new American operation. Unlike the U.S. subsidiaries, Volkswagen did not have a problem meeting the decree's local-content specifications. Also, while the U.S. subsidiaries preferred to export, Volkswagen was uncertain as to the actual desirability of exports: compared to Germany, Mexican production costs were higher, the quality lower, and transportation costs to Germany were also expensive. However, Volkswagen realized compliance was necessary. As one of its top executives stated, "Only because of the Decree did we decide to construct the engine plant."[22] Volkswagen already had a U.S. strategy in place; now Volkswagen's Mexican subsidiary could provide many of the engines required by Volkswagen's American subsidiary. The time was right. Mexico had placed a compelling bid for its share of supplying parts to this new U.S. operation.

The Chrysler Investment

Five months later after the Volkswagen announcement, Chrysler revealed its plan to build a 4-cylinder-engine plant with an annual capacity of 400,000 engines in Ramos Arispe: 80 percent would be exported to the U.S. for Chrysler's own operations in the United States. How could the Chrysler subsidiary make such an investment commitment while its parent was struggling to retain its solvency? The Mexican operation was critical to the survival of the parent: its profits were subsidizing the U.S. operations. The subsidiary's requests were forwarded immediately for review and considered very seriously despite the overwhelming difficulties of the parent. The high profitability of Chrysler's subsidiary shaped the structure of the investment: not only was the investment to be funded locally, but it also was expected to be cost-effective like the existing operation. The Mexican market, and its profits, were to be retained.

Chrysler's parent was able to respond with a pledge of increased investment because, like General Motors, it had already completed a parent investment plan, complete with product and a strategy ready to implement. The Chrysler parent had made its decision on its product plan in 1977; the Mexican subsidiary would integrate the K car and export engines. The 1977 Decree, however, was the motivating force. As one Chrysler executive explained: "We would have made a different decision. The engine plant would have been one-third of its size. We would have made production more manual."[23] If Mexico had not used its 1977 Decree to gain a share in Chrysler's new production strategy, the planned operation in Mexico would have been significantly smaller.

[22] Author interview with senior management of the Volkswagen subsidiary.

[23] Author interview with senior management of the Chrysler subsidiary.

The Nissan Investment

Almost three years after the announcement of the 1977 Decree and over one year after GM's investment bombshell, Nissan revealed plans to build two 4-cylinder-engine plants with an annual capacity of 300,000 engines at a cost of approximately U.S. $300 million.[24] Sixty-seven percent would be exported, half to its American subsidiary and half to its parent in Japan.

Nissan's management explained the three-year delay in parent approval was largely the result of the parent's decision-making processes. Immediately after the 1977 Decree, Nissan Mexicana had given several investment proposals to the parent, but several export programs had to be studied and decided upon. They involved not only the Mexican subsidiary but also the parent and its competitors. While Nissan and Volkswagen both shared high local content, Nissan was at a distinct disadvantage in exporting. Volkswagen's exports were an integral part of the parent's strategy; Nissan Mexicana, however, had to compete with its parent for exports. As one Japanese executive of Nissan phrased it, "The question is whether the Mexican government can drive Nissan Mexicana to push the parent into global production exchange." The perception of country risk was cited as a major concern. The administrative area of the parent's Overseas Division was preoccupied with Mexican risk: "Selling the parent [on the Mexican investment] is very complicated. You have to sell everyone. Every day we send volumes of information, which complicates the task." Only three years later, in 1980, did the parent finally approve a proposal, and even that specified a gradual investment over five years.[25]

Unlike Volkswagen, the Nissan subsidiary's main export markets included not only the newly founded American subsidiary, but the parent as well. It was not simply a matter of dictating to the Nissan subsidiary in the United States: exports would have to be cost-competitive and of high quality. The consensual Ringi decision-making process was in full force. In December 1981, a special committee was established to investigate exports to the American operation. The amount and choice of exports from Mexico was to be negotiated. The Nissan parent had to commit itself to subsidizing the exports of its Mexican subsidiary. It would buy engines and give its Mexican subsidiary more Latin American vehicle markets. The 1977 Decree forced the Nissan parent to revise the role of the Mexican subsidiary within its global export markets.

[24] Nissan decided also to build an aluminum foundry at an approximate cost of U.S. $34 million.

[25] Author interviews with senior management of the Nissan subsidiary.

The Ford Investment

Finally the last automotive subsidiary, Ford de México, capitulated: in June 1980 the company responded to the 1977 Decree. A year and a half after General Motors' announcement of its engine investment, Ford committed itself to an eight-billion-pesos investment in 4-cylinder-engine plants with an annual capacity of 400,000 engines: 80 percent would be for export to the U.S. operation.

The Ford subsidiary delayed committing itself to the major investments required by the 1977 Decree for various related reasons. First, several executives of Ford's subsidiary felt they had mistakenly believed that they could change the Mexican government's stance. As one of its key Mexican executives explained, "We were waiting to see how serious the [Mexican] government was."[26] Second, unlike its other U.S. competitors the Ford parent had not yet determined how it would downsize: it did not have a product, a strategy, or resources. In lieu of a significant investment in an engine production plant, Ford committed to three insignificant joint ventures, compromises that revealed the parent's weakness. The delay was costly. As one senior Ford executive explained, "We lost time negotiating with the government when instead a strategy could have been developed."[27]

Ford subsidiary executives also attributed the subsidiary's delay to profit-driven politics at the parent. Ford de México was a part of the Latin American Automotive Operations (LAAO), which in turn reported to International Automotive Operations (IAO). Incentives for sourcing components for the U.S. operation, North American Operation (NAO), were very low. As one Ford executive explained, "Already IAO [International] makes all the profits, which pay the U.S. [operations] debt. The profit centers of the organization have very much affected investment decisions."[28] In short, the profitable international part of Ford had no interest in further subsidizing the unprofitable U.S. operation. The final decision to build an engine plant created conflict between the two divisions, IAO and NAO, and resulted in corporate paralysis in responding to Mexico's demands.

Furthermore, even though the Mexican subsidiary was proposing profitable investments, pressure from American labor made it difficult to get the approval of the parent. There was corporatewide reluctance to import auto parts into the United states from other countries. Labor pressure in America was tangible enough to prevent Mexican investment and the

[26] Author interview with senior management of the Ford subsidiary.

[27] Author interviews with senior management of the Ford subsidiary.

[28] Author interviews with senior management of the Ford subsidiary.

moving of plants overseas. As one top Ford executive explained: "Because of labor pressures, it is almost impossible to source anything from outside the U.S. It is usually cost-effective to produce in Mexico, but it has high risk in the U.S. Political labor costs in the U.S."[29] Ford faced a dilemma: an increase in investment was crucial to the survival of the Mexican subsidiary, yet proposed high risk for the Ford parent.

The General Motors subsidiary was perceived as partly exempt from such pressure. First, its commitment to large investments in Mexico was prior to the heightening of labor pressure in the United States. Second, the GM parent was also portrayed as having a management style different from Ford: it was tougher with the unions. Others emphasized that GM had a stronger bargaining position with American labor than Ford, given GM's larger U.S. operation and employment.

Ford's compromise position evolved over three long years of parent-subsidiary negotiations. The parent needed additional productive capacity for the U.S. market. Yet cash was limited for investments. Possible joint ventures in Mexico would require less of the parent's scarce resources and reduce its cost basis as well as help the subsidiary meet the requirements imposed by the Mexican government with the 1977 Decree. Since all the investments were for additional capacity, labor pressure was partially offset. Thus, the response of Ford's Mexican subsidiary was greatly affected by parent-specific issues.

As summarized in table 6–1, each of the five major Mexican subsidiaries did eventually commit itself to increasing its exports in response to the 1977 Decree. The investment decisions were the means to achieve an end: a trade balance. Getting each subsidiary to invest was a necessary precondition. However, compliance meant actually reaching a trade balance, and this required more than just an announcement of increased investments. The final measurement of subsidiary response was their compliance with the trade balance requirement.

Response to Trade Balance Requirements

During these years that all the subsidiaries were announcing their investment plans, the Mexican government was flexible: companies could borrow foreign exchange to meet the government's trade balance requirement.[30] In 1978 the 1977 Decree required, at a minimum, that exports pay for at least 30 percent of the import cost. All subsidiaries met the 1978 requirement. However, throughout 1979 and 1980, *Ford* and

[29] Author interviews with senior management of the Ford subsidiary.

[30] For an explanation of the carry-over deficit mechanism employed by the Mexican government and the rationales, see Bennett and Sharpe, *Transnational Corporations Versus the State*, pp. 238–41.

TABLE 6–1
Engine Programs of Mexican Assembly Plants

Investment plan announced	*Company*	*Engine type*	*Capacity*	*Export*	*Starts*	*Destination*
Feb. 1979	GM	V-6 2.8 liter	450,000	90%	82	U.S. Canada, Venezuela, Chile, South Africa, Australia, UK, Belgium
April 1979	VW	4 CYL. gas 50% diesel 50%	380,000	75%	81	U.S.
Sept. 1979	Chrysler	4 CYL. 2.2 liter	400,000	80%	82	U.S.
April 1980	Nissan	4 CYL. 1.6/2.2	360,000	67%	84	Japan, U.S.
June 1980	Ford	4CYL. 2.3 liter	400,000	90%	84	U.S.
	Total		1,990,000[a]			

Source: AMIA.
[a] Renault/VAM also announced an investment program for 300,000 engines, bringing the total annual production capacity for the industry to 2,290,000 engines.

especially *Chrysler* had large trade deficits and had to borrow foreign exchange, while the other three subsidiaries met the escalating trade balance requirements.

The main difference between the two borrowing companies was that while Ford had no product, Chrysler did. This did not help Chrysler, which felt it was incapable of complying without jeopardizing its very survival. As one senior Chrysler parent executive claimed: "We didn't know whether we would exist or not, so we pushed for profit for the parent. We chose short-term profit for the parent instead of long-term trade balance for Mexico. The risk, of course, is we face the need to have a trade balance in the future, but it's better for us! I don't know why Ford followed."[31] For Chrysler, delay was the only alternative.

Faced with continued trade deficits, the Mexican government in July 1981 moved to strictly enforce the 1977 Decree with the Cocoyoc Resolution, "Measures for Rationalizing the Trade Balance Deficit in the Automotive Industry." The subsidiaries would be subject to production re-

[31] Author interview with a senior executive of Chrysler USA.

ductions depending on their trade balance; import of all optional parts for luxury cars would be prohibited; and advances of foreign exchange would not be granted for the 1982 model year.[32] When the government surprised industry executives with this announcement at a weekend oceanside seminar, the senior management of the *U.S. subsidiaries* walked out of the meeting, but notably, management of the *Nissan* and *Volkswagen* subsidiaries did not follow.

Since the production reductions were based on each subsidiary's trade balance, they provided a precise measurement of compliance. As shown in table 6–2, Chrysler and Ford suffered production reductions of 7.3 percent and 25.7 percent respectively; the other three subsidiaries received quota increases, led by Volkswagen with a 17.5 percent increase.

The prohibition against importing optional parts for luxury cars hit the U.S. subsidiaries head-on. Since they dominated the very profitable luxury car market segment, how could they source optional parts locally in three months, and at what cost? As an executive from a U.S. subsidiary explained: "We make money not on the base unit, but on options. When you pull that profitability from us, you pull out the major part of the pie."[33] For U.S. subsidiaries, the new regulation cut into the heart of their profit-making strategies.

For all three U.S. subsidiaries, luxury parts had always been imported from the U.S. operations. The principal reason was small volume: there were no economies of scale. Also, a shift to the new Mexican suppliers

TABLE 6–2
The Cocoyoc Resolution: Car Production Quotas by Subsidiaries

	Production Quotas		*Change*	
	1981	*1982*	*% change*	*Vehicles*
Ford	54,594	40,575	(25.7)	(14,019)
Chrysler	58,110	53,877	(7.3)	(4,233)
Nissan	47,449	49,200	3.7	1,751
General Motors	27,357	28,800	5.3	1,443
Volkswagen	121,879	143,190	17.5	21,311

Source: La industria automotriz de México en cifras, 1982 (México, D.F.: AMIA, 1983), pp. 48–49; "Producción autorizada para 1982" (Comité Técnico Consultivo Sobre Planeación Concertada de la Industria Automotriz, AMIA, 23 Sept. 1981), Xerox.

[32] The list of optional luxury car parts included air conditioning equipment, clocks, carpets, electric windows, and electric-trunk and seat-door locks.

[33] Author interview with senior management of U.S. automotive subsidiary.

would encounter resistance from existing U.S. suppliers, even though some components could be manufactured more cheaply in Mexico than in the United States.

Ford and *Chrysler* responded first to the Cocoyoc Resolution. *Ford* management claims that the subsidiary responded quickly because it was a profit decision.[34] The parent had to accept the government regulation and so gave funds, licenses, and technological assistance to its Mexican suppliers to enable them to produce the prohibited auto parts. Likewise, *Chrysler* could not afford the damage of lost sales. United by the threat of more production reductions, parent and subsidiary management quickly agreed on a plan that could accommodate the new import prohibitions. New product plans with fewer luxury parts were devised, all of which could be produced locally.

General Motors was the last of the subsidiaries to address how to increase local content. GM subsidiary management attributed the delay to resistance from parent-division suppliers in the United States. The GM divisions wanted to continue supplying products to the Mexican subsidiary. Instead, they were being asked to provide their designs to Mexican companies, subsuming their Mexican sales. Moreover, these Mexican companies were likely to produce these parts more cheaply, and compete with them in other markets. The managing director and financial officer of the Mexican subsidiary had to push parent management to convince GM's divisions to provide their designs to local Mexican suppliers.

In this situation, the GM subsidiary, reportedly due to the Cocoyoc Resolution, began to lose money and was put on the "troubled subsidiary" list. While General Motors had been the first to comply with investment, actual changes in subsidiary policies in response to the Cocoyoc Resolution lagged. As an executive of GM's subsidiary stated: "The major risk for my company now [as the result of government regulation], is continuing not to comply: Either we would be out of business or drop lower in market share. This happened because we did not plan. Only since Cocoyoc have we tried to determine what is driving the government and their ultimate objectives; and then how we can do our planning to get into step with that program. The Mexican government is forcing us to do a better job of strategic planning."[35]

Only in 1982 did the GM subsidiary begin to change key subsidiary policies. An executive position for government relations was created to interpret government regulations and develop joint ventures that would increase local content and exports. As one senior GM executive stated: "People [at General Motors] never believed the government would apply

[34] Author interview with management of the Ford subsidiary.

[35] Author interview with the director of planning, General Motors de México.

the trade balance requirement. The government would continue to be flexible. With this position is the realization that our market share depends on exports, and the people responsible for the trade balance should report to the managing director."[36]

Roughly every three months the government-relations executive, along with the managing director, went to the parent to discuss the Mexican situation. Lobbying the parent for more resources was critical. Despite the reorganization, as of 1982 the export department employed only five persons compared with twenty-five at Volkswagen, ten at Ford, nine at both Chrysler and Nissan. The head of the export department felt frustrated: he had written a memo on the need to increase exports that was ignored. His request to hire another four persons was now being reviewed by the parent. The purchasing department also sent a request to the parent: it wanted to increase its employment from sixty-seven persons in 1982 to ninety-two in 1983.[37]

However, finally, by year's end 1982—well after the Ford and Chrysler subsidiaries—the General Motors subsidiary was implementing a new plan that, according to the director of planning, was producing "incredible results." The product program had been completely altered. Before, U.S. models had been automatically accepted in Mexico with no consideration of implications in terms of increased import volumes or decreased local content. As the result of Cocoyoc, the choice of models for the Mexican market was no longer a decision solely made by the parent, but one decentralized to the Mexican subsidiary. The subsidiary would look for new models with the same platform as its current models. Second, sourcing strategy was no longer completely driven by the MNC's global strategy. Before, imports from the U.S. were not questioned by subsidiary management. Now the subsidiary was seriously studying how to reduce import costs. Compressors were given as an example of a part now sourced locally: "We had a good supply [of compressors] from a U.S. supplier. We could have switched before, but we never thought of it. Now we have—only because of Cocoyoc."[38] Furthermore, due to the Cocoyoc Resolution, the parent was contributing its resources to help the subsidiary meet the government's regulations. In order to help the Mexican subsidiary export more, GM's Overseas Division was trying to sell Mexican components and vehicles to Central and Latin America.[39]

[36] Author interview with senior management of General Motors de México.

[37] Author interviews with management of export and purchasing departments, General Motors de México.

[38] Author interview with senior management of General Motors de México.

[39] However, the difficulty of winning export markets from the parent was often cited: "It is impossible for the subsidiary to export vehicles when the parent exports vehicles. We are

The Cocoyoc Resolution led to further differentiation of the subsidiaries' compliance to the trade balance requirements. By mid-year 1982 it was clear that further production reductions were required: the export plans submitted for the first production reductions were not being met. In 1981 the automotive deficit was 1.5 billion dollars, representing 58 percent of the country's trade deficit. *Nissan* was the only subsidiary to meet its foreign-exchange requirement. This time *Ford*'s deficit was larger than that of *Chrysler*, both followed, respectively, by *General Motors* and *Volkswagen*. In May 1982 the Mexican government requested further production reductions: *Chrysler* (38 percent); *General Motors* (28 percent); *Ford* (27 percent); and *Volkswagen* (25 percent).[40] *Nissan*, the only subsidiary to meet the trade balance requirement, suffered no reduction.

As shown, the five major automotive subsidiaries responded very differently to the demands for a trade balance. In general, the non-U.S. subsidiaries—*Nissan* and *Volkswagen*—were more consistently aligned with host-government objectives than were the *U.S. subsidiaries*—General Motors, Ford, and Chrysler. Only one, *Nissan Mexicana*, was able consistently to meet the trade balance requirements, followed by *Volkswagen*. While *General Motors* was the first to announce its investment plans, it was actually the last to adapt its subsidiary policies. The *Ford* and *Chrysler* subsidiaries, however, were in greatest violation of the government's trade balance requirements.

In conclusion, (1) *parent preferences* differentiated how subsidiaries responded. Each parent's strategy—including management and product—was decisive. The *General Motors* subsidiary was able to respond with the required investment commitment, given the convergence with parent objectives. In part due to its parent philosophy, *Nissan Mexicana* consistently complied with the trade balance requirements. In contrast, *Chrysler* and *Ford* were significantly undermined by their parents' lack of response. (2) The second variable, *subsidiary relationships with key LDC groups*, highlights the difference between the relationships of the Nissan and Volkswagen subsidiaries with the Mexican government. Management at both subsidiaries emphasized their willingness to respond to

---

now trying to substitute Ecuador." Author interviews with General Motors subsidiary management.

[40] The reductions were divided between the 1982 and 1983 model years. On 11 August 1982 a new resolution ("Resolución para Racionalizar el Déficit de la Balanza en Cuenta Corriente del Sector Automotriz en el Año Modelo 1983") imposed further restrictions on automobile production during the 1983 model year. Consistent with previous measures, the terminal companies had to balance their foreign exchange budgets. In addition, before the end of 1983 the companies had to pay back deficits incurred in 1982, advances granted before 1981, and interest due in 1983. Lastly, border sales qualifying as exports were restricted to new passenger cars sold in northern border zones and free trade zones.

trade balance demands. (3) The last variable, *first subsidiary response*, is apparent in explaining differing firm behavior. In response to *General Motors'* investment announcement, the other four subsidiaries followed suit. As a result of *Nissan*'s compliance to the trade balance requirements, the other four subsidiaries were under greater pressure to comply. As "response leaders," the General Motors and Nissan subsidiaries had broken industry resistance and set the parameters of response.

If we summarize the subsidiaries' behavior from the early 1970s, the differences are accentuated. Even before the government's 1977 crackdown on trade balance requirements, there were significant differences between the trade balance policies of the five subsidiaries. The *Volkswagen* and *Nissan* subsidiaries developed high local-content policies, while the *U.S. subsidiaries* easily imported parts from their nearby U.S. operations. In terms of exports, the *Nissan* and *Chrysler* subsidiaries had to make major changes while the *General Motors* and especially *Ford* subsidiaries enjoyed the advantage of selling auto parts in their global networks, but at levels vastly lower than their imports. Only the *Volkswagen* subsidiary had a growing export role commensurate with Mexican requirements.

At the point of crisis, the five subsidiaries had different degrees of conflict with the Mexican government. First, those subsidiaries that had realigned their policies in response to earlier regulations—*Volkswagen* and *Nissan*—were as a consequence more in alignment with government demands. Second, subsidiary ability and willingness to respond was different for a variety of reasons: strategy, product development, and resources (*General Motors, Ford, Chrysler*); home-country labor pressure (*Ford*); and parent philosophy (*Nissan*). Third, the Mexican government discriminated on the basis of personal relationships (*Chrysler*), product (luxury versus popular), and parent nationality (anti-U.S.).

MNC risks and LDC benefits resulting from government demands were not uniform. First, for the automotive MNCs, the host-government's regulations cut across their operations with varying levels of risk and benefits. (See table 6–3.) The *General Motors* subsidiary responded to further its competitive advantage, by using the required investment as a spearhead for its parent's objectives of overseas growth and cheaper sourcing. The *Chrysler* subsidiary was most at risk due to its parent situation—its profits were critical to the survival of its parent, yet the parent could not afford to comply with the Mexican investment requirements. *Ford*'s delay in its investment escalated its risk: as the last to comply in an overcrowded market and with no clear rationale (as in the case of *Chrysler*), its bargaining power with the government was minimal and it even faced possible withdrawal. *General Motors* had the resources

TABLE 6–3
Summary of Reported Risks and Benefits by Subsidiaries

	Increased Investment	*Trade Deficit*	*Production Reduction*	*Product Change*	*Increase in Local Content*
GM	b	r	r	r	r
Ford	r	r	r	r	r
Chrysler	b	r	r	r	r
VW	—	—	r	b	b
Nissan	r	—	b	b	b

Source: Questionnaire given to managing directors of subsidiaries.
Note: r = reported as risk; b = reported as benefit; — = not cited as risk or benefit.

to invest, yet it lacked actual responsiveness until pressured very specifically to change its policies; meanwhile, it was losing money. Despite their resistance, therefore, all three U.S. subsidiaries eventually had to modify their strategies in accordance with the Mexican government's demands, the response depending largely upon their parents. In contrast, the *Volkswagen* and *Nissan* subsidiaries performed best under the strict government measures.

Likewise, from the point of view of the Mexican government, the subsidiaries did not respond the same way to its demands, but the benefits it derived from the 1977 Decree were multifold: *General Motors* broke the industry's resistance and initiated a landslide of investment; *Nissan* and *Volkswagen* pioneered a further increase of local content and set the pace for the American MNCs to follow. The dynamics were the same as for the Brazilian case: The *General Motors* subsidiary led the other subsidiaries into making Mexico a major sourcing location for engines in their global MNC networks. Then *Nissan*, and to a lesser extent *Volkswagen*, achieved a breakthrough with the first automotive trade balance in Mexican history and, by doing so, forced the other subsidiaries to follow suit. The subsidiary characteristics that explain the differing risks and benefits are best documented by opening this study to an examination of each company's entire multinational structure and showing how it related to its surrounding environment.

CHAPTER 7

Determinants of Differing Subsidiary Behavior: Relationships within the Changing Regulatory Environment

As IN THE Brazilian case, the Mexican automotive subsidiaries behaved differently in response to a changing host-country environment, with those differences creating significant diverse risks to the MNCs and benefits to the host country. In both cases, regardless of whether it was a local issue (labor policy) or a parent issue (investment and sourcing policy), the subsidiaries possessed distinctive characteristics that shaped their behavior. This chapter will analyze the Mexican case study following the same comparative framework outlined for the Brazilian case study: *how can subsidiary relationships further explain the wide variance in individual subsidiary behavior?* First, the relationship of each subsidiary with the Mexican government is studied. Then, the subsidiaries' internal organizations are compared, followed by an examination of each subsidiary's relationship with its parent company. Finally, the relationships among the subsidiaries themselves are explored.[1]

Subsidiary Relationships with the Host Government

The management of all five automotive subsidiaries felt that the relationship with the Mexican government was critical to the success of their operations. From the point of view of both subsidiaries and the Mexican government, this relationship was primarily concerned with government regulation. However, as discussed in the previous chapter, the implications of government regulation were not uniformly perceived by the five subsidiaries. The managing directors of all three *U.S. subsidiaries* thought it was likely that at least one of the subsidiaries might withdraw from the Mexican market as a result of government regulation. In contrast, Nissan's managing director felt this possibility was improbable. All five subsidiaries claimed they had increased investments and exports as

[1] Except where stated otherwise, the information on subsidiary behavior in this chapter was obtained from extensive interviews with subsidiary management and Mexican government officials, and from answers given by the managing directors of each of the five subsidiaries to detailed questionnaires. See the Appendix for a list of interviewees.

a direct result of government regulation; yet the amounts and timing differed over four years. For the *General Motors* and *Ford* subsidiaries, government regulation was the only reason given for increasing local content; the other three subsidiaries stated additional factors. Therefore, the type and level of challenge presented by government demands was subsidiary-specific.

From the Mexican government's point of view, regulation was also the major component of its relationship with the five subsidiaries. Again, however, the underlying dynamics were perceived as varying greatly between the five subsidiaries given the significant differences in their willingness to comply. According to government officials, *Nissan* compromised the most; second, *Volkswagen* more than *General Motors*; and finally, *Ford* and *Chrysler* the least. Government officials also perceived the subsidiaries' responses to regulations as very different. The *Nissan* subsidiary satisfied all regulations ("It was Japanese"). The *Volkswagen* subsidiary was an effective negotiator but was also willing and able to compromise, largely as the result of "better planning." The *General Motors* subsidiary, with its parent's enormous new investment commitment, had been rated third in its willingness to compromise, but it would now change from a "second-rate company to one of the most important in Mexico." The *Ford* and *Chrysler* subsidiaries were rated "not serious," but *Ford* was "unique in its crisis management."[2]

Even after the Cocoyoc Resolution, the *Ford* and *Chrysler* subsidiaries were cited by several government officials as resisting compliance more than the other subsidiaries. Ford's subsidiary management was seen as pressuring the Mexican government the most by insisting on interviews with officials and asking for papers documenting rationales. Government officials expressed dismay at the behavior of the Ford and Chrysler subsidiaries. Inconsistencies and unfilled promises were cited as commonplace: "They [Chrysler and Ford management] say one thing, then change. For example, they say they will export a certain amount at a certain time; then, when that time arrives, they say they can't export."[3] In general, management was perceived as unwilling to compromise. So-called company mistakes were not perceived as part of a negotiating strategy, but rather as gross mismanagement and disrespect for government regulations: "It is strange how these two very large companies make so many mistakes, for example forgetting import licenses. It seems like they don't have good coordination within management. Production doesn't

[2] Author interviews with senior government officials responsible for regulating the automotive industry.

[3] Author interviews with senior government officials responsible for regulating the automotive industry.

know what is going on in sales." In contrast, the *General Motors*, *Volkswagen*, and *Nissan* subsidiaries were perceived as being more "professional and serious."[4]

What were the subsidiary/government relationships underlying the regulatory interplay? Over the years, each subsidiary had developed its own distinctive relationships with the Mexican government, with different implications for subsidiary behavior. The different variables reported as key were: (1) the subsidiaries' individual *government relations executives*, (2) the use of high-level *Mexicans on Boards of Directors*, (3) *parent philosophy*, (4) *product*, (5) the use of *intermediary parties* to pressure the Mexican government, and (6) the Mexican government's *affinity with the parent nationality*. Briefly, the *Volkswagen* subsidiary was seen as enjoying the strongest government relationship, modeled on the prototype of a national Mexican company. The *Chrysler* subsidiary, despite its failure to comply with government regulations, had a strong bargaining position with the Mexican government, primarily by using its Mexican chairman of the board and its extensive network of Mexican dealers. The *Nissan*, *General Motors*, and *Volkswagen* subsidiaries' relationships with the Mexican government were distinctively shaped by their parents' philosophies. The long close relationship of the *Ford* subsidiary with the Mexican government had deteriorated dangerously, with the MNC aggressively seeking support from the U.S. government to strengthen its bargaining power. Last, the Mexican government was reported as having a special affinity toward Japan and Germany in its unstated objective to reduce its dependence on the United States.

The Government-Relations Function

Even before the 1977 Decree, the subsidiaries differed in how they managed their relationships with the Mexican government. All five subsidiaries had a high-level executive in charge of government relations, but the importance assigned to the position and the effectiveness of the individual varied. In addition, two subsidiaries—*Volkswagen* and *Chrysler*—used a Board of Directors structure to communicate with the Mexican government.

Despite numerous changes of personnel in each subsidiary and in the Mexican government, government-relations positions had been filled for the most part with the same individuals for over twenty years. In 1982 the *Ford* subsidiary held the record (thirty-six years) for the longest-em-

[4] Author interviews with senior government officials responsible for regulating the automotive industry.

ployed government-relations executive, followed by *Volkswagen* and *Chrysler*, whose government-relations executives had represented their subsidiaries for approximately twenty years. *Nissan*'s government-relations executive, who had previously worked for Ford, had also been in the business twenty years. Only *General Motors*' government-relations executive had a term as short as seven years. With the exception of the GM subsidiary, all government-relations executives had negotiated government regulations since the 1962 Decree with four different Mexican government administrations.

In terms of subsidiary management, the sole government-relations executive who had worked for only one managing director was at the *Volkswagen* subsidiary. Changes in managing directors occurred most often at the *Ford* and *Nissan* subsidiaries, followed by the *Chrysler* and *General Motors* subsidiaries. As one of the most prominent government officials explained: "It is harder to change the government-relations guy than the managing director. His character can affect all the negotiating with the government."[5] Government relations had become a career in the Mexican automotive industry, with each of these individuals commanding their own relationships and techniques for advancing their respective subsidiary's causes.

Government officials agreed that these Mexican government-relations executives varied in their effectiveness as negotiators. The executives of *Volkswagen* and *Chrysler* were consistently cited as the most effective. They had been the focus of negotiations between the government and

[5] Author interview with senior government officials responsible for regulating the automotive industry. However, while the government-relations executives historically had monopolized much of their subsidiaries' relationships with the Mexican government, the government officials increasingly contacted others within the subsidiaries. Over the years, the Mexican government had enlarged its knowledge base, assembling a technical staff and tools to measure subsidiary compliance. Government officials felt that the subsidiaries' government-relations executives had not made the same progress. The government-relations executives were sometimes seen as impediments who had to be circumvented because they lacked the necessary expertise to ensure subsidiary compliance. As one government official explained: "Sometimes they can't understand the economic problems or technical problems or planning issues. They have problems understanding the companies' plans. But we the [Mexican] government have information on all the companies and a vision of their objectives. There is a problem of them not knowing the companies they represent . . . and the government has more information than they do. They don't have the details but only the general knowledge. They should coordinate the technical staff. Instead, I call directly the purchasing department, or any department necessary." All subsidiaries did report extensive government contact directly between the Mexican government and those departments concerned with exports, imports (customs), and engineering. With the increase in government regulation, therefore, the government-relations monopoly in negotiation had been eroded with more concrete, technical measurements of subsidiary compliance. Author interviews with senior government officials responsible for regulating the automotive industry.

their subsidiaries since the very beginning of manufacturing under the 1962 Decree. In contrast, while *Ford*'s government-relations executive was also senior in the industry, government officials felt he was ineffective, largely because of his personality. Often characterized as "a fighter," he was seen as having "very powerful friends," but many thought he enjoyed antagonism more than advancing his subsidiary's interests, and that his own interest had declined as he approached retirement. In 1980, Ford hired at "very considerable cost" the former president of the industry association to share the responsibility of government relations. Considered effective, but much less so than Volkswagen's or Chrysler's, *Nissan*'s government-relations executive was portrayed as "overly accommodating" in that he would do "anything" to please government officials. Lacking the stature and power of Volkswagen's or Chrysler's executives, he was nevertheless considered an aggressive negotiator. The behavior of the government-relations executive of *General Motors de México*, on the other hand, was in line with its parent's emphasis on ethical behavior.[6]

The subsidiaries' independent perceptions of themselves and of each other were consistent with these government perceptions. The management of the *Ford*, *Chrysler*, and *Volkswagen* subsidiaries emphasized government relations much more than the *Nissan* subsidiary or, especially, *General Motors*. A Ford executive explained the difference between the Ford and GM subsidiaries as "*Ford* believes it has to adapt, while General Motors doesn't."[7] The Ford subsidiary, like Chrysler and Volkswagen, would play the Mexican game of negotiation. *General Motors*' government-relations executive was seen as restrained from negotiating by his own management: with strict rules on entertainment and gifts set by the parent, the subsidiary could not compete.[8] The *Nissan* subsidiary, however, would follow the Japanese doctrine of compliance.

Board of Directors

Out of the five subsidiaries, *Volkswagen* and *Chrysler* had Boards of Directors that were particularly suited for negotiating with the Mexican government. Both boards had Mexican members. In the case of Chrysler, the chairman of the board was the former Mexican owner of Chrysler. This individual was considered by both competitors and government officials as Chrysler's "competitive advantage" in government relations: the benefits previously bestowed on Automex (the name of the Mexican

[6] Author interviews with senior government officials responsible for regulating the automotive industry.

[7] Author interview with key Ford executive management.

[8] Author interview with executive management of General Motors de México.

company before it became Chrysler) were partially preserved as the result of this individual's continued close ties with high echelons of the Mexican government. One Mexican government official explained: "The government has continued to give benefits to Chrysler after the de-Mexicanization of its capital. The company uses the former owner for relations with the government. He is the special strength of Chrysler. Even the VW board doesn't have that."[9] Therefore, as summarized in figure 7–1, the contact points between the subsidiaries and the Mexican government varied considerably, with both the Volkswagen and Chrysler sub-

FIGURE 7–1
Comparative Avenues of Government Relations: Subsidiary Management and the Mexican Government

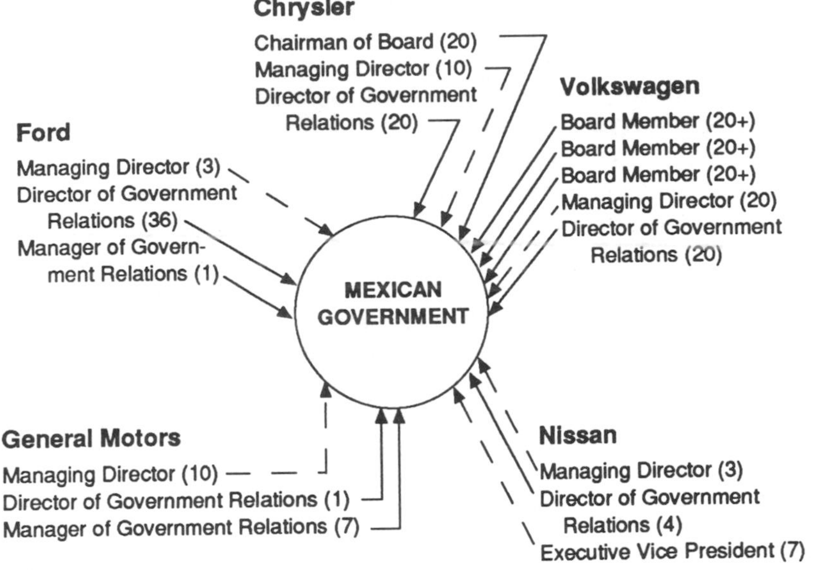

Source: Compiled by the author on the basis of information obtained in company interviews.

Notes: After each position, the number in parentheses represents the approximate number of years (up to 1982) the individual has been in a position of that subsidiary related to government relations. To avoid confusion from the diverse range of actual titles, the same generic names for positions are used for all companies.

Dotted lines drawn between a management position and the government indicate that the position is held by an expatriate. *Solid lines* drawn between a management position and the government indicate that the position is held by a Mexican.

[9] Author interview with senior government officials responsible for regulating the automotive industry.

sidiaries employing long-tenured and high-level Mexicans who promoted their companies' interests with the Mexican government.

Parent Philosophy

Parent philosophy was also reported as shaping the government relations of three subsidiaries: *General Motors*, *Nissan*, and *Volkswagen*. At *General Motors* and *Nissan*, management instilled parent values into the subsidiary's policies: GM's parent philosophy was seen by subsidiary management as a constraint imposed by the parent, whereas Nissan's was a part of their Japanese cultural duty. However, for *Volkswagen*, the parent philosophy meant only that subsidiary management was expected to adapt their values to the Mexican environment.

Several senior executives at *General Motors*' subsidiary felt that the parent policy of strict ethical behavior when it came to managing entertainment expenses put the Mexican subsidiary at a disadvantage. The other subsidiaries spent considerably more resources in maintaining close contact with the government, and as a result would always know of government actions before the GM subsidiary. Asked to name the GM subsidiary's most important company weakness in bargaining with the Mexican government, the managing director listed as second "General Motors' impeccable code of ethics."[10] Relative to its competitors, the GM parent set strict rules for presents, dinners, and trips.

According to its senior management, the *Nissan* subsidiary complied with government regulations largely because of parent philosophy transmitted from Japan. The opinions both of government officials and automotive executives were unanimous: of all the subsidiaries, Nissan set the pace for compliance. The Mexican government could always depend on Nissan's response to use against the other subsidiaries. In contrast to General Motors, Nissan's managing director felt his most important company strengths in bargaining with the government were sincerity and honesty.

Nissan management claimed that it had paid dearly in order to comply with the Mexican government's regulations, by sacrificing additional sales because it did not want to import more for increased production if that would mean violating government regulations on trade balance. Unlike its competitors, Nissan's objective was to balance its trade first and increase market share second. As one of its senior executives explained: "We have to observe honestly and strictly the regulations of this country. We are not strong enough to survive if we don't observe the rules. Nissan

[10] Answer given by managing director of General Motors de México in questionnaire. However, to a significantly lesser extent, GM's managing director also felt the company's ethics represented a bargaining advantage.

Mexicana is a Mexican company that has to be obedient to regulations. It is a duty."[11] Another Nissan executive attributed this distinctive approach to the differing historical development of government relations in their respective home countries. "In Japan, government has been the top since the seventh century. Government officials dominate society. You have to obey the government; you cannot resist the government. This is not the case in the U.S., where government is the servant of the public. You tell government to obey you!"[12] The management of Nissan Mexicana was therefore very sympathetic to host-government objectives. Mexican government officials had the noble cause of protecting and promoting their country's welfare, and Nissan management wanted to support this legitimate mission. "Sometimes we have to negotiate, but usually we agree with them. Mexican government officials can feel if a company is against them, like the U.S. subsidiaries. But we feel their country does not belong to subsidiaries."[13] The U.S. companies were also felt by the Japanese to have overstepped their rights when, after the 1977 Decree, they asked Mexican government officials to speak with U.S. government officials in Washington: "From our criteria as Japanese people, this is not understandable."[14] They could not understand how one had the right to debate governmental roles aggressively. For the Japanese at Nissan, the lines of compliance with government regulations were clear-cut and not to be ignored, even if it meant changing the subsidiary's strategy and losing sales.

The philosophy of the *Volkswagen* parent, unlike that of General Motors and Nissan, was reportedly for its subsidiaries to operate as local companies. As one government official commented: "Its strength lies within the Mexican operation. Its root is already so strong in the ground, that the government cannot touch it easily."[15] The success of the Volkswagen subsidiary served as a model to the Nissan subsidiary. As one senior executive of Nissan explained: "Volkswagen has developed many Mexicans [in management] and accomplished the social integration necessary for success in overseas business, as well as contributed to the culture of the country [Mexico]."[16] For some, the Volkswagen subsidiary's ability to "separate" from the parent company was an example of how to become integrated with the host-country environment as a local company.

[11] Author interview with senior executive of Nissan Mexicana.

[12] Author interview with senior executive of Nissan Mexicana.

[13] Author interview with senior executive of Nissan Mexicana.

[14] Author interview with senior executive of Nissan Mexicana.

[15] Author interview with the former Mexican government official responsible for automotive regulatory policy.

[16] Author interview with senior executive of Nissan Mexicana.

Product

As discussed in the previous chapter, the differences in the subsidiaries' products also affected government regulations. The *Volkswagen* and *Nissan* subsidiaries had products that were to their and the government's political advantage: popular cars sold to the increasingly powerful middle class. As one Volkswagen executive stated: "Our product represents a philosophy. The image of the Beetle as a Socialist car of the people. The origin of Volkswagen in Germany spread to Brazil, Mexico [and elsewhere]. Now Volkswagen has become a world concept."[17] Likewise, the Nissan subsidiary felt the adaptability of its product was a major bargaining strength with the Mexican government. In contrast, the *U.S. subsidiaries* were vulnerable to political attack for their luxury car models.

Use of Intermediaries

Throughout the period of conflict, the difference in the depth and nature of government contact became magnified. Intermediaries, inside and outside Mexico, became involved in the subsidiary/government relationship. Again, conflict amplified differences in subsidiary behavior: *Volkswagen* did not use outside relationships to deal with the Mexican government. To a minor extent, *Nissan* did use an outside relationship—that of its parent management—not as an entity of pressure, but as an instrument of dialogue. The *U.S. subsidiaries,* however, relied extensively on external intermediaries to negotiate with the Mexican government, but differed substantially, in degree and effect, among each other.

In regard to the 1977 decree, there is no evidence that the *Volkswagen* subsidiary involved any external agent to leverage its relationship with the Mexican government. Indeed, the Volkswagen subsidiary *was* characterized as often pressuring the Mexican government, but directly through channels established by the decades-long relationships between its managing director, the government-relations executive, and the board. As one government official explained: "Volkswagen uses its relationships to exert pressure just as if it was Mexican. . . . It wants to act like a Mexican enterprise. Perhaps it is more effective."[18] The managing director of Volkswagen was reported to be a powerful negotiator, capitalizing on his ability to make strong relationships with government officials. Supposedly, refused his first audience with the Mexican president, he humbly persisted until he succeeded in arranging an interview, throughout which he used "his charm and astuteness," so that it was the Mexican

[17] Author interview with senior executive of Volkswagen de México.

[18] Author interview with senior government official responsible for automotive policy.

president who asked for a second meeting.[19] However, the Volkswagen managing director was also reported as quick to remind the Mexican government of how certain regulations could result in unemployment, lost exports, and so on.

In the case of *Nissan*, in the aftermath of the 1977 Decree, parent management was reported to have communicated directly with Mexican government officials. The purpose, however, was not to contest the Mexican government's actions but rather to seek explanations and promote Nissan. The Nissan parent wanted to underline its current and future success as a Japanese company.

On the other hand, the *U.S. subsidiaries*, particularly Ford, complicated relationships with the Mexican government by involving third parties, including the American Chamber of Commerce of Mexico and various agencies of the U.S. government, including the Secretary of Commerce, the Secretary of Treasury, and President Jimmy Carter.[20] As one Mexican government official stated: "The problem of U.S. [subsidiary] compliance is the power of the U.S. government, and how it sees the intentions of the Mexican government."[21] Again, however, the U.S. subsidiaries differed in the degree to which they evoked these intermediaries.

Both *Chrysler* and *Ford* sought to increase pressure on the Mexican government. As one key government official commented: "Chrysler and Ford thought the [Mexican] government would always be flexible. They think they are stronger [than the Mexican government] partly because of the U.S. government. . . . Effective government relations may have added to this delusion."[22] The American Chamber of Commerce of Mexico was also reported as putting pressure on the Mexican government because it was very strongly influenced by Chrysler and Ford. The *Chrysler* subsidiary's convincing argument was couched in terms of its overall survival: the cost of compliance could mean its demise and that of its U.S. parent. The attitude of the *Ford* subsidiary, however, was less convincing: "It costs to comply. While laws require compliance, you don't want to do better than your competitors."[23]

However, the Ford and Chrysler subsidiaries differed in that *Chrysler*

[19] Author interview with senior executive of Volkswagen de México.

[20] In several discussions between the Mexican and American presidents, Carter was reported to have brought up Mexico's automotive policy. Author interview with senior government official responsible for automotive policy.

[21] Author interview with senior government official responsible for regulating the automotive industry.

[22] Author interview with senior government official responsible for regulating the automotive industry.

[23] Author interview with senior executive of Ford de México.

relied more on Mexican intermediaries, namely its very effective government relations in addition to its network of Mexican dealers. Many observers claimed the effectiveness of *Chrysler*'s government relations was due to its strong personal links with the Mexican government, and the souring of *Ford*'s government relations to its leadership in lobbying for U.S. government pressure. As one top-level Ford executive stated: "The [Mexican] government doesn't need all seven companies. If five of the seven auto companies announce investments, the other two companies are open for penalties. The bargaining power of the government is up enormously, and the companies' is down. The government doesn't need my company."[24] The probability of one automotive subsidiary's actually withdrawing from Mexico, perhaps within a year, was high, and as one executive said, the problem would probably be the subsidiary's inability to comply with the government's export requirement.

The response of the *General Motors* subsidiary was distinctly different in behavior and rationale: certain ethical benchmarks were unnegotiable despite the competitive cost, and, after all, it was in GM's interest to comply. Unlike Ford and Chrysler, General Motors did not take an aggressive role in using external intermediaries, such as the U.S. government or the American Chamber of Commerce of Mexico. It had no reason to apply pressure; it *wanted* to conform. In fact, the government regulations was to its competitive advantage in that it complicated the lives of its competitors. The same regulation that represented risk to Ford and Chrysler—perhaps to the extreme of losing the entire market or forcing withdrawal—benefited General Motors. And if Ford and Chrysler's negotiating was successful, General Motors would have the benefits without the problems.

Nationality Differences

The expanded use of intermediaries in MNC subsidiary/government relationships underlined the foreign origin of each subsidiary: to differing degrees, they served as conduits for home-country governments, values, and products. And, on the other side, the Mexican government had different preferences for and against subsidiaries, partly as a result of national origin. In the undercurrent of the subsidiary/government relationships was the Mexican government's silent hope to reduce its reliance on the "Big Three" U.S. companies. The key MNC competitors to the United States—*Japan* and *Germany*—offered preferable alternatives: their subsidiaries would not serve as conduits for home-government pressures against Mexican regulations.

[24] Author interview with senior executive of Ford de México.

In 1978, Mexican government officials and automotive executives made a trip together under the auspices of the automotive association, AMIA, to *Nissan*'s parent headquarters in Tokyo. According to the management of the Nissan subsidiary, the dialogue between its parent and the Mexican government was a turning point: "The parent was confident [of the Mexican government] after the conversations permitted by this trip with [Mexican] government officials."[25] The Nissan parent was assured of the rationales and measures underlying the 1977 Decree. The visit changed the Nissan parent's attitude toward Mexican regulation. Senior parent management felt more comfortable with the new game rules.

On their part, Mexican government officials developed an understanding of the Japanese automotive industry. A Nissan executive explained: "After their trip, their feelings and knowledge changed drastically. We had talked with government officials many time and they were very tough, but underneath we found a friendship. In order for them to understand our situation, we invited them to Japan. They now understand the industry in Japan."[26] According to Nissan's Mexican management, Mexican officials were impressed with Japan's industrial growth after World War II and wanted their country "to walk in the same path." Mexico wanted to be more independent of the United States and to develop deeper relationships with countries such as Japan where "there is no dependency."[27]

AMIA also arranged trips to *Renault* in France and to *Ford* and *General Motors* in Detroit. These trips, in contrast with that to Japan, were not reported as increasing the Mexican government's understanding of the U.S. or French parents. Mexican government officials continued their trips to Japan, with another visit in September 1980 under the auspices of AMIA and in February 1982 as *Nissan*'s guests. The 1982 trip was to see the new Nissan motor that would be manufactured in Nissan's recently approved investment in Mexico. While no Mexican official would confirm that the Mexican government discriminated against the U.S. as a matter of policy, many officials repeatedly expressed resentment of the U.S. government and its subsidiaries' aggressive contesting of Mexico's automotive laws, but acclaimed Nissan's respectful behavior.

A senior Japanese executive explained how Nissan executives dedicated their efforts on a full-time basis to developing this special affinity between their home country and Mexican government officials: "Humans are ruled sometimes by feeling. . . . In Japan, human relations are very

[25] Author interview with senior executive of Nissan Mexicana.

[26] Author interview with senior executive of Nissan Mexicana.

[27] Author interview with senior executive of Nissan Mexicana.

important. We have tried to get their [Mexican government officials'] sympathy—not just politically. We have the desire for them to have a better understanding of Japan."[28] Nissan executives perceived themselves as more than businessmen; they were emissaries bringing the message of Japan's success.

Volkswagen's subsidiary management also claimed to have a special relationship with the Mexican government because of national affinities. Developing a stronger relationship with Germany, like Japan, was a means for Mexico to reduce its dependence on the United States. As one senior German Volkswagen executive stated: "Mexico likes Germany. There is antagonism with the U.S. and we provide an alternative."[29] Volkswagen management claimed that this affinity was a competitive advantage, enabling a closer host-government relationship.

In summary, a close comparative look at subsidiary/government relationships reveals important differences (see table 7–1). The *Volkswagen* subsidiary had the strongest government relations, reaping advantages largely due to its integration with the Mexican environment: an effective high-level Mexican government-relations executive, Mexican directors on its board, and its powerful managing director. In addition, it reportedly benefited from its popular car models, "a German-Mexican affinity," and a parent philosophy that emphasized local adaptation. The *Chrysler* subsidiary also had strong government relations due to its integration with the Mexican environment: an effective government-relations executive, a vocal network of Mexican dealers, and above all its former owner, the Mexican chairman of the board, were all very influential. The Chrysler subsidiary's relationship with the Mexican government was, however, negatively affected by its U.S. origin and its luxury products. The intercession of the U.S. government and the American Chamber of Commerce of Mexico were seen as a mixed blessing. In the case of the *Nissan* subsidiary, its relationship with the government was driven largely by the parent philosophy of compliance, and principally for this reason it was the industry leader in conforming to the dictates of the local government. While the *General Motors* subsidiary also transmitted its parent philosophy, the parent imperatives of ethical behavior and the de-emphasizing of government relations dominated, hindering the subsidiary's ability to establish effective government relations. Last, the *Ford* subsidiary had the weakest relationship with the Mexican government: with its abrasive government-relations executive and its call for the intervention of the U.S. government, the subsidiary found itself at the fringes of dialogue.

[28] Author interview with senior executive of Nissan Mexicana.

[29] Author interview with the government relations executive of Volkswagen de México.

TABLE 7–1
Key Variables in Subsidiary/Government Relationships

	Effectiveness of Gov't Relations Executives	*Use of Boards*	*Parent Philosophy*	*Product*	*Use of Inter-mediary Parties*	*Parent Country/ Host Country Affinity*
VW	+	+	+	+	N/A	+
Chrysler	+	+	N/A	−	−/+	−
Nissan	+	N/A	+	+	+	+
GM	N/A	N/A	−/+	−	−	−
Ford	−	N/A	N/A	−	−	−

Note: − = reported as negative influence; + = reported as positive influence; N/A = not reported as positive or negative influence.

The Internal Organization: Relationships within the Subsidiary

What were the distinguishing characteristics of the subsidiaries' internal organization that influenced management's response to the Mexican government's investment and sourcing requirements? As in the Brazilian case, (1) *size* and (2) the *mix of expatriates to nationals in management positions*, were reported as key differentiating factors.

Size

The number of employees was reported as affecting a subsidiary's bargaining position with the government—in general, the more workers the MNC employed, the greater its bargaining power. The size of the subsidiaries varied from *Volkswagen* with a total of 13,076 employees to *Nissan* with 3,462 employees. The other three subsidiaries were in a comparative size range—*Chrysler* (with 7,928 employees), *Ford* (7,728), and *General Motors* (6,463).[30]

In fact, the managing directors of both *Chrysler* and *Ford* said that after 1962, one of the most important objectives of the Mexican government has been to increase national employment, and that their key contribution as companies in Mexico has been to increase employment at their subsidiaries. Asked to name their most important strengths in bargaining with the government, *Chrysler*'s managing director felt its high employment figure to be its strongest attribute, while *Ford*'s managing director cited it as its third most important asset. *Nissan*—with the lowest number of employees—and *General Motors* also listed employment as a major contribution to the country, but neither considered it a bargaining strength.

Expatriate / National Mix

As in the Brazilian case, the most distinctive contrast between subsidiary structures was the mix of expatriates to nationals in management positions. The Mexican case, like the Brazilian one, supported the findings of others that European subsidiaries generally have fewer expatriates remaining in-country for longer time periods and employ more nationals in high-level management positions. As the only major European MNC, *Volkswagen* had both Germans and Mexicans in high-level management subsidiary positions. The managing director and his three German direc-

[30] AMIA, *Diez años del sector automotriz en México 1971/1980* (Mexico, D.F., 1981), p. 74.

tors had been in Mexico for two decades since the establishment of the subsidiary in 1962. As in the Brazilian case study, the management of the Volkswagen subsidiary included high-level nationals. Of the six members of the Board, half were Mexican. Approximately half of the German expatriates stayed for three to five years; the other half indefinitely. As in Brazil, the German managing director represented one alternative career path for Volkswagen expatriates: remain committed to the subsidiary in Mexico and never return to the German parent.

The *Ford* and *General Motors* subsidiaries also conformed to the U.S. pattern: Americans dominated high-level subsidiary positions and were rotated from one subsidiary to another, usually remaining in Mexico for under three years.[31] Of the eight directors of the General Motors subsidiary, only one was Mexican, and the position, director of public relations, was only established in 1982 as a result of the Cocoyoc Resolution.

The expatriate management of *General Motors*' subsidiary felt that their ability to hire and promote Mexicans was hindered by the parent's policies. First, there were few highly skilled Mexicans suitable for senior management, and these individuals were aggressively sought-after by foreign companies. For example, one incident was described in which a Mexican was offered the position of director of government relations at the General Motors subsidiary. He rejected GM's offer, however, in favor of the same position at another automotive subsidiary. The other offer was more competitive than what GM was allowed to offer under parent guidelines. Second, the General Motors subsidiary managing director could only recommend candidates for high-level positions; the parent made the actual selection. Historically, the parent had limited exposure to GM's Mexican management and preferred to fill high-level subsidiary positions from its own internal selection of in-company executives. It was also the parent's policy to rotate American GM executives every two or three years; indeed, a longer stay usually indicated corporate failure.[32] Therefore, high-level positions at the General Motors subsidiary were predominately occupied by Americans on the fast track.

In the case of the *Ford* subsidiary, several Mexican government officials felt American expatriates were rotated more often than at the General Motors subsidiary. The managing director had been in Mexico for three years. The problem of rotating the managing director was somewhat offset, however, by each newcomer's having to rely on the Spanish executive vice-president, who had been employed by the Ford subsidiary

[31] One notable exception, however, was the managing director of General Motors, who had been in his position since 1973.

[32] The overall General Motors policy of rotation is discussed in John B. Schnapp et al., *Corporate Strategies of the Automotive Manufacturers* (Lexington, Mass.: Lexington Books, 1979), pp. 145–59. Schnapp et al. emphasized GM's commitment to "growing managers slowly within the General Motors system," rarely hiring from outside the company.

for over two decades. It is interesting to note that this was the same support structure employed by both the GM and Ford subsidiaries in Brazil. The Ford subsidiary, claiming a policy of Mexicanization, had other Mexicans in high-level positions, a parent-groomed Harvard Business School graduate from Mexico as finance director, as well as Mexican directors of manufacturing, purchasing, sales, and public relations.

While high-level management of the *Nissan* subsidiary was integrated with that of parent management through rotation policies, it had also a systematic interface with its Mexican environment. In terms of head-office integration, all but one director and all technical staff were Japanese because "they must know Japanese politics."[33] The only exception was the director of government relations who, since he was the key interface with the Mexican government, was an experienced Mexican previously employed by another automotive subsidiary for the same purpose. The parent made a general policy of shifting its Japanese managers from their position at the parent to a related position at the subsidiary, and vice-versa. The purpose of expatriate policies, as explained by a Nissan executive, was to keep the entire company, the Mexican subsidiary and the parent, unified with one policy. Like the General Motors and Ford subsidiaries, most of the high-level meetings were in the expatriates' native language. For example, the weekly meetings of the directors were conducted in Japanese. However, the greater difficulty of learning Japanese rather than English created a large communication gulf: while all middle Mexican management at the U.S. subsidiaries could speak English, none in Nissan's could speak Japanese.

However, Nissan countered this focus from the head office by developing a parallel management structure that enabled it to manage better in the Mexican environment. Each Japanese director had a Mexican subdirector for interpreting Mexican events. Twice a month there were meetings conducted in Spanish that included Mexican subdirectors, Japanese directors, and the managing director. Therefore, while the Nissan subsidiary mirrored its parent, it had built in a systematic interface with the Mexican environment.

Compared to the Volkswagen subsidiary, the *Chrysler* subsidiary had fewer expatriates, with most rotating as in the U.S. subsidiaries, and more high-level Mexicans filling most key positions. The managing director was an American expatriate who had arrived in 1972 and worked himself up to his position. Unlike the management of the General Motors, Ford, and Nissan subsidiaries, that of *Chrysler*, like Volkswagen, conducted the majority of its meetings in Spanish. Only the finance function of the Chrysler subsidiary was excluded from the Mexicanization policy, and as in the General Motors subsidiary, fast-track Americans

[33] Author interview with senior executive of Nissan Mexicana.

were sent from the head office or sister subsidiaries to fill this one position. Two reasons were given—the position necessitated communications with the U.S. operation, and the nonavailability of Mexicans qualified for the job. The finance function was especially important to the parent given the Mexican subsidiary's critical role in supplying needed profits.

The reasons the expatriate policies of the Chrysler subsidiary differed from those of General Motors and Ford were historical and parent-related. First, Chrysler had had a policy of Mexicanization of subsidiary management since 1970 when the parent assumed majority control. When Chrysler increased its position from minority partner to majority partner, Mexican management with whom the parent had worked over the years was already in place. Second, given the agreement with the former owner, the parent was obliged to cooperate: parent intervention would have created difficulties. Third, the parent lacked the resources to bring in more expensive American management. As a matter of explicit policy, the Chrysler subsidiary retained "as much as possible from Automex. . . . Tactics, strategies and people were largely untouched."[34] In line with this policy, the former Mexican owner was made chairman of the Chrysler subsidiary's Board of Directors.

Chrysler management claimed its policy of Mexicanization was a competitive advantage over its U.S. competitors. As one of their executives claimed: "Look at the quotas for 1982. The usage of local talent helped Chrysler finish before General Motors. . . . We use local pride and know how to get around. We didn't have to go to school and learn the language."[35] Even GM's managing director felt that the *Ford* and *General Motors* subsidiaries suffered from their expatriate policies: "Adapting is easier for other subsidiaries. They have more participation of nationals."[36] One prominent government official claimed the parent promotion policies of General Motors and Ford had a significant impact on the ability and willingness of subsidiary management to respond to government demands. "The U.S. MNCs' promotion policies determine the attitudes of subsidiary management. The expatriates here in Mexico only care about pleasing the parent. They don't learn Spanish; they communicate with the parent in English. They are isolated in English. They are isolated from the country and don't integrate government objectives with parent objectives."[37] One high-level Mexican in an American subsidiary explained how he thought expatriates impaired his company's operation: "Most of the people the corporation sends to the subsidiary are specialists, and not managers, and they are five to seven levels down. . . . They

[34] Author interview with the managing director of Chrysler de México.

[35] Author interview with senior executive of Chrysler de México.

[36] Author interview with the managing director of General Motors de México.

[37] Author interview with senior government official responsible for regulating the automotive industry.

use the subsidiary as training. Instead of receiving an education, you [a Mexican employee] are giving an education. You never have the resources to keep up. You don't have the talent to think corporationwide. You are managed by functions, and you expect only the managing director to think corporationwide. You lose flexibility."[38] Human resources policy was critical: because American expatriates were being trained, they looked to the parent for verification of answers. The rotation policy affected motivation; each expatriate's future was based overwhelmingly on the final judgments of parent management, not subsidiary management.

The rotation policy also affected perception: expatriates were more likely to judge Mexican events on the basis of their American views and the views of those with whom they consulted at the parent. GM's and Ford's subsidiary management were seen as having distinctly American biases that reduced their understanding of the Mexican regulatory environment. They were perceived as unsympathetic to the needs of government regulation and as resentful of efforts to direct their activities. One Mexican executive employed by an American subsidiary explained how the managing director perceived the latest government regulation: "My company is to blame for not taking the [Mexican] government seriously. When the Cocoyoc Resolution happened, the [American] managing director sent a telegram to the U.S. He said he thought the Mexican government was crazy, and that we couldn't comply. His perspective is short. He forgot the 1977 Decree. It is he who is crazy."[39] The Mexican executive claimed it was impossible to convince the American managing director that all Mexican-made components were not by definition low-quality. Because U.S. expatriate management was closely controlled by parent policies, subject to parent management's judgments, and tended to orient their discussions toward parent concerns (with their Mexican subordinates likely to support these efforts), they were more apt to express parent preferences and biases, while being less able to understand the critical issues and attitudes underlying Mexico's regulatory environment.

A long-term commitment by expatriates to Mexico was seen as differentiating the response of the *Volkswagen* subsidiary from that of the other subsidiaries. These expatriates were not perceived as an impediment to subsidiary response. Germans were sent to the subsidiary *to manage*, and not to be trained. A Mexican executive at Volkswagen claimed that "Europeans are more independent because they are more educated. They don't feel a need to consult the parent. The Americans

[38] Author interview with senior Mexican executive of U.S. automotive subsidiary.
[39] Author interview with senior Mexican executive of U.S. automotive subsidiary.

consult because of insecurity, not because of policy."[40] As one experienced government official explained: "When the parents are involved, the subsidiary does what is best for the parent. It is hard to break the pattern of allegiance. Volkswagen, however, is special. It is . . . a mixed company where the Germans speak the language of Mexico."[41] The internal organization of the Volkswagen subsidiary served to integrate expatriates into the Mexican environment, whereas the great majority of the expatriates of the three *U.S. subsidiaries* and *Nissan* were rotated within the parent's overall network.

Therefore, as summarized in table 7–2, expatriate and national personnel policies were reported as significantly influencing subsidiary behavior. The long-term commitment of *Volkswagen*'s expatriate management facilitated a deeper understanding of the Mexican government (that led to greater influence with the Mexican government); it also fostered independence from the parent's viewpoint so that management took Mexican interests into consideration when formulating subsidiary policies. *Chrysler*'s Mexicanization policy encouraged effective government relations, but did not diminish the parent's influence on the finance function or change its allegiance to the parent's imperatives. In contrast, the *General Motors* and *Ford* subsidiaries were managed by short-term American expatriates who, dependent on parent management, were seen as transposing parental judgments and expectations onto their perceptions of the Mexican environment. There were important differences, however, with the *General Motors* subsidiary reported as having greater difficulty in hiring high-level Mexicans because of its parent's guidelines and direct involvement. The *Nissan* subsidiary, moreover, combined a management structure modeled after its parent with an interlocking Mexican submanagement structure.

Clearly, each of the five subsidiaries had a particular internal organization—with differences in history, structure, and parental influences—that differentiated how its managers perceived and responded to the Mexican government's demands. As in the Brazilian case study, differences in internal organization included the obvious (such as size) as well as the more subtle but important differences in management structure.

Parent-Subsidiary Relationships

The timing and type of subsidiary behavior in response to Mexican government demands were greatly affected by the parent and, in the case of one subsidiary, other key actors outside of Mexico. As in the Brazilian

[40] Author interview with senior Mexican executive of Volkswagen de México.

[41] Author interviews with senior government official responsible for regulating the automotive industry.

TABLE 7–2

Managing Characteristics of the Mexican Automotive Subsidiaries

	No. of Years Managing Director Employed in Mexico[a]	*Nonexpatriate Executive VP*	*High-level Expatriate Policy of Rotation*	*Policy of Mexicanization*	*Mexicans on Subsidiary Board*	*High-level Meetings Language*
GM	10		+			English
Ford	3	+	+	+		English
Nissan	3		+			Japanese/ Spanish
Chrysler	10		+	+	+	Spanish
VW	20			+	+	Spanish

Source: Compiled by the author on the basis of information obtained in interviews with management at the subsidiaries indicated.

[a] The total years worked in Mexico include time worked in other positions or other companies up to 1982.

case, the impact of the parent relationship was broad. Three aspects of the relationship were key: (1) *the degree of subsidiary autonomy/centralization*, (2) *the global network*, and (3) the *politics of subsidiary-parent negotiations.*

Degree of Autonomy/Centralization

Throughout the previous chapter we have seen that subsidiary autonomy from the parent, while a key variable, was not the only determinant of the subsidiary's responsiveness to host-government regulatory demands. The *Volkswagen* subsidiary was very independent in developing its trade balance policies and did comply more with government regulations than any other subsidiary, excluding *Nissan.* However, centralization in some cases was associated with greater parent responsiveness. For example, Nissan's parent participated closely in the development of its Mexican subsidiary's trade balance policies; yet it complied more with the trade balance requirements than any of the other subsidiaries, including Volkswagen. Indeed, in the case of *General Motors*, the parent played a decisive role that resulted in massive support for its subsidiary and an enormous investment in response to the 1977 Decree. Conversely, in the case of *Nissan*, parent involvement resulted in lengthy parent-subsidiary discussions and a three-year investment delay. Subsidiary autonomy or centralization was not the sole determinant guiding subsidiary responsiveness. Other subsidiary-specific factors were also important.

As in the Brazilian case, Mexican subsidiary-parent relations in crisis were distinctly different from routine day-to-day relations and blurred the lines of defined authorities, revealing the internal dynamics of each MNC. The influence of the parent on subsidiary behavior is revealed by viewing the contextual issues surrounding the parent. The first critical variable was the degree of inherent conflict between the Mexican government's regulations and the subsidiary's role as envisioned by the parent: Would the subsidiary have to change parent strategy? If so, what was the subsidiary's willingness and ability to convince the parent?

The situation depended on the degree of conflict and the parent's perceived costs and benefits as well as on the subsidiary's skill in influencing that perception and the parent's ability to respond. The entire scope of the parent-subsidiary relationship was important: The *role of the Mexican subsidiary within the global network* was critical, encompassing not only product, supplier and sourcing strategies, but also the parent's current global competitive position and strength. Also key was the *politics of subsidiary-parent negotiations*, which was affected by several factors that will be discussed in later sections.

The Global Network and the Role of the Mexican Subsidiary

While all five automotive MNCs had global strategies, the role of each Mexican subsidiary in its parent's global strategy was not uniform. Did compliance with the Mexican government's trade balance requirements force the parent to modify significantly the role of its Mexican subsidiary within its global strategy? The answer was yes for *General Motors*, *Ford*, *Nissan*, and *Chrysler*—and no for *Volkswagen*. Of all five subsidiaries, only the Volkswagen subsidiary would have a role to play within its parent network that was largely consistent with the trade balance requirements of the Mexican government.

Conflict between government requirements and the *Volkswagen* parent was undisputedly the least because of the unique role delegated by the parent to its Mexican subsidiary. A major reason was the parent-defined autonomous product strategy for the Mexican subsidiary, including product type and its suitability to the environment. The Mexican subsidiary was the major producer of Volkswagen's most economical product—the Beetle car—within its global network, and was thereby responsible for exporting it to markets worldwide. Mexico was considered an optimal manufacturing site for the Beetle, given the suitability of the product for the growing popular car market in Mexico, and the cost advantages resulting from cheaper Mexican wages. With a product not subject to annual model changes, the Mexican subsidiary could therefore increase local content cost-effectively, and given its near production monopoly it could also be assured of vehicle export markets, the most important being West Germany. Between 1976 and 1981, Volkswagen de México exported 63,385 Beetles to its home country. The Mexican government's regulations on increasing local content and exports, therefore, did not present conflicts with Volkswagen or its Mexican subsidiary, but instead reinforced the benefits of its already established role of producing Beetles within Volkswagen's global network.

The strategy of the Volkswagen parent was deliberately to provide the Mexican subsidiary with greater autonomy than its competitors. As one senior Mexican executive of Volkswagen explained: "U.S. companies are integrated with the parent strategy so their activities are always controlled by the parents. Volkswagen [de México] is more autonomous since it can decide export policy itself independent of its parent. It has a survivor policy; if the parent was liquidated, the Mexican subsidiary could survive. This is a basic strategy of [the] Volkswagen [parent]. If the American or Japanese parents disappear, so do their subsidiaries."[42] Therefore, the Volkswagen subsidiary enjoyed a separateness from its

[42] Author interview with senior executive of Volkswagen de México.

parent within the context of the overall parent strategy. With its near production monopoly of the Beetle car, it was not tied solely to parent-dictated model changes that would affect its level of imports, development of suppliers, or export markets. In this case, autonomy did enable subsidiary responsiveness and a closer alignment of subsidiary strategy with host-government objectives.[43]

The Volkswagen subsidiary prospered in this environment, its success increasing both its autonomy from the parent and its flexibility in responding to the Mexican government's regulation. Success also increased its bargaining power with its parent. By winning a large market share in Mexico, the Volkswagen subsidiary not only had reached significant economies of scale, but had also become the parent's second-largest overseas subsidiary.

Furthermore, Volkswagen's Mexican subsidiary competed successfully against its sister subsidiaries (including the Brazilian) for the largest auto-parts export market in the world—the United States. Volkswagen de México had the advantage of being located at the entry point to the United States, and having recently established a subsidiary in the U.S., Volkswagen was putting together its strategy of how to increase its penetration of the American market. The 1977 Decree fit very well into Volkswagen's global strategy: of the 1,600 engines produced daily in the new Mexican plants, 1,200 would be exported to the Volkswagen assembly plant in Westmoreland, Pennsylvania. As the Volkswagen subsidiary's government-relations executive stated: "We competed with the plant in Brazil to obtain the engines contract for the Pennsylvania plant. Our price was right and we are closer."[44] With a high level of vertical integration, the utilization of relatively cheap labor, and economies of scale just across the border, Volkswagen de México was able to offer competitive auto-parts exports. Volkswagen's Mexican subsidiary, therefore, was positioned to grow within the parent's quest for the U.S. market.

For the other four subsidiaries to comply with the Mexican government's trade balance requirement, however, each parent had to modify to a great extent the role of its Mexican subsidiary within its global strategy. In the case of the *Nissan* subsidiary, its parent had not given it a significant export role within the global strategy. In fact, the primary weakness in bargaining with the Mexican government cited by the Nissan

[43] This analysis is consistent with the Schnapp study of Volkswagen's decision-making process (Schnapp et al., *Corporate Strategies of the Automotive Manufacturers*, pp. 173–78). They also state: "Volkswagen is not as tightly controlled a company as General Motors. . . . Financial criteria are applied in a flexible, non-dogmatic fashion."

[44] Jane Bussey, "Gearing Up to Export Three Million Engines to Auto Plants Abroad," *R & D Mexico* (Feb. 1982): 20–23.

subsidiary's managing director was the "subsidiary's poor capability for exporting."[45] As discussed in the previous chapter, in response to the 1969 and 1972 export regulations, the Nissan subsidiary had successfully lobbied its parent for vehicle markets. Now again, the 1977 Decree required the Nissan parent to enlarge the sourcing role it had previously defined. Should the Mexican subsidiary, like that of Volkswagen, supply engines to the newly established Nissan subsidiary in the United States?

THE VALUE OF MEXICAN SOURCING: PRODUCT STRATEGIES, SUPPLIER STRATEGIES, AND SOURCING STRATEGIES

The issues, however, were not the same: the advantages of sourcing from each Mexican subsidiary had to be analyzed within the specific global operation of each MNC. In the case of *Volkswagen*, the Mexican subsidiary had for many years effectively supplied parts for the U.S. market, and it was the cheapest source of engines for the U.S. operation. In the case of *Nissan*, however, the cheapest source of engines was not its Mexican subsidiary, but the parent in Japan. Furthermore, Nissan Mexicana had many quality problems that needed to be resolved. The size of operations also differed: Volkswagen expected to produce more vehicles, thus requiring naturally more engines than Nissan. In order to meet the export requirement, the Mexican subsidiary would also have to export engines to Nissan's Latin American subsidiary *and* the Japanese parent. Given Mexico's quality problems and transportation costs, how could Mexican-made engines be cheaper and better than the world's cheapest and best, Japanese-made engines?

On the other hand, in terms of its global strategy, Nissan saw its Mexican operation as a means to offset what was described as "U.S. country risk": should further restrictions be imposed on Japanese imports into the United States, Nissan could import from its Mexican subsidiary.[46] The Mexican government's regulations forced the Nissan parent to reevaluate the role of its Mexican subsidiary.

To what degree were the roles of the *U.S. subsidiaries* within their global MNC networks in conflict with the Mexican government's trade balance requirement? For all three U.S. subsidiaries, the first and foremost objective was to penetrate the Mexican market, which was viewed as an extension of the U.S. market. The same models were sold, changing annually to follow U.S. model changes. The U.S. subsidiaries targeted the luxury end of the marketplace, which provided the most profitable margins. As a result, the U.S. subsidiaries in Mexico were important cus-

[45] Author interview with the managing director of Nissan Mexicana.

[46] Author interviews with senior executives of Nissan Mexicana.

tomers of their U.S. parents and suppliers. Within their prescribed roles as Mexican subsidiaries, they were to import U.S. auto-parts, while keeping Mexican auto-parts purchases to a minimum.

However, with the hardening of the Mexican government's demands for a trade balance, the U.S. parents faced different options in redefining the roles of the Mexican subsidiaries in their global networks. *Chrysler's* financial difficulties and the selling off of its other overseas subsidiaries meant the Mexican subsidiary was the only option for sourcing cheaper auto-parts to meet the global challenge of decreasing production costs. In fact, the managing director of the Mexican subsidiary felt the subsidiary had two equally important roles within the overall strategy of the Chrysler parent: to accomplish the penetration of the Mexican market as well as to be a global sourcing base.

The role of the *General Motors* subsidiary was slightly different in the eyes of its managing director: the first objective was to penetrate the Mexican market; the second, to be a regional sourcing base; the third to extend U.S. manufacturing operations; and the fourth, to be a Latin American center for exports.[47] While exports were small, the GM subsidiary had developed a dual export role. When it was in the U.S. assembly division, Mexico was used to decrease production costs of labor-intensive car parts, with the transfer of select U.S. operations to the border in-bond assembly plants. Since 1981, the subsidiary had been part of the overseas division, and could now be an independent exporting base for other overseas subsidiaries. GM's Mexican subsidiary therefore had the potential to increase exports within the overseas sourcing network in addition to supplying labor-intensive auto parts for U.S. operations.

In contrast, the role of *Ford's* subsidiary within its parent's network had always been with the overseas division. Its primary objective was limited to penetrating the Mexican market. While the Mexican subsidiary did have a minor role in supplying auto parts to the U.S. and Latin American operations, it was not perceived as a major sourcing operation.

PARENT GLOBAL STRATEGIES AND COMPETITIVE POSITION

Within these closely integrated roles in their parents' global networks, important differences existed between the parents of the three *U.S. subsidiaries* in global product, supplier and sourcing strategies as well as in the parents' global competitive position. Previous chapters have referred to the availability of products and financial resources from the parents as preconditions for the Mexican subsidiaries' compliance to the trade balance requirement. The *General Motors* subsidiary could respond be-

[47] Response of the managing director of General Motors de México to questionnaire.

cause of its parent's global competitive position: strategy had been formulated, products developed, with resources at hand. The *Chrysler* subsidiary also had a product developed but suffered from its parent's financial difficulties. However, unlike General Motors and Ford, Chrysler had greater flexibility in designing products for the marketplace. The *Ford* subsidiary suffered from its parent's lack of both cash and product. However, Ford was more flexible than General Motors in responding to local-content issues largely because its U.S. operation was less vertically integrated than GM's: it was easier for the Ford subsidiary to discontinue buying auto parts from its U.S. suppliers than for the GM subsidiary to discontinue buying from parent U.S. divisions.

Therefore, as summarized in table 7–3, the five automotive subsidiaries had different roles within their respective parents' networks that conflicted in different ways and to varying degrees with the Mexican trade balance requirement. The *Volkswagen* subsidiary enjoyed a role largely consistent with Mexican trade balance demands: significant export markets, high local content, plans to use the Mexican subsidiary in supplying its new American subsidiary, and the availability of parent resources and product to follow through. The role of the *Nissan* subsidiary, however, was not consistent: while local content was high, large export markets did not exist; the use of the Mexican subsidiary in supplying the new American subsidiary was not yet decided. The *U.S. subsidiaries* all had conflicts with the Mexican government because they imported substantially more from the United States relative to their exports. However, only the *General Motors* parent had no constraints and was actively seeking new overseas markets and cheap sourcing. In summary, although at first glance one would be tempted to conclude that the Mexican subsidiaries had the same or similar roles in their parents' global networks, important differences resulted in differing risks and consequent abilities to respond to host-country demands.

Politics of Subsidiary-Parent Negotiations

The subsidiaries had to confront their parents with the Mexican government's demands, explaining that subsidiary compliance would require changes in their parents' strategies—namely, the role of the Mexican subsidiary within the overall global network. What would influence each Mexican subsidiary's ability and willingness to convince its parent to change that role? The key factors affecting subsidiary-parent negotiations were: (1) corporate culture, (2) evaluation of the Mexican government's demands, (3) reporting and decision structures, (4) the decision-making process, including the degree of centralization, individual personalities,

TABLE 7–3
Role of Mexican Subsidiaries within their Parents' Global Networks

	Large Direct Exports	*Large Imports from Home Country*	*High Local Content*	*U.S. Entry*	*Parent Position*	
					Product	*Resources*
VW	+		+	+	+	+
Nissan		+	+	+	+	+
GM		+			+	+
Ford		+				
Chrysler		+			+	

Source: Questionaires given to managing directors of subsidiaries.

and the subsidiary's bargaining power, and (5) home-country pressures on the parent company.

But in order for each subsidiary to negotiate with its parent, it first had to be willing to ask the parent to make company changes on behalf of the Mexican government. Not all subsidiaries were willing to argue with their parents. So the initial key factors were the MNC's corporate culture and the evaluation of Mexican government's demands.

CORPORATE CULTURE

The *Nissan* subsidiary was the only subsidiary willing to comply completely, the reason largely being the corporate culture shared by both subsidiary and parent: compliance to host-government regulations was a legitimate and necessary principle that should frame policy. As discussed in the previous section on parent philosophy, Nissan's parent and subsidiary management was willing, unlike other subsidiaries, to restrain Mexican sales, or in other words to give up market growth and profit. What was inconceivable to many companies, Nissan's parent and subsidiary management preferred to give up profits rather than violate Mexican government regulations. Compliance was a given; the debate between parent and subsidiary management was instead over whether to increase its investment.

The *U.S. subsidiaries*, however, were for the most part not willing to lobby their parents aggressively because of their corporate culture and their evaluation of the Mexican government's demands. In order to convince parent management, the subsidiaries themselves had to take the Mexican government's regulations seriously. First of all, unlike Nissan, many U.S. expatriate managers did not believe in the legitimacy of Mexican government regulations, and those who did had difficulty convincing their parent management. Second, as shown in the previous chapter, experience had taught them the pragmatic value of resistance: in the past, after the Mexican government had announced regulations, extensive negotiation had in fact resulted in greater flexibility.

As was seen earlier, the arguments set forth by *Chrysler*'s subsidiary management were that its parent was unable to modify its role immediately but would when it could; time would be needed. The *Ford* subsidiary, however, delayed arguing with its parent; it was more concerned with winning its parent's objective of resisting the Mexican government. The *General Motors* subsidiary was willing to invest for exports, but it was still not willing to make the local-content changes needed to comply with the trade balance requirement. The *U.S. subsidiaries* were captives of their parents and preferred to argue for flexibility with the Mexican government rather than for modifying their roles with their parents. Indeed, American executives at both GM and Ford explained that in conversations with parent management they often blamed the Mexican government when explaining local problems, and conversely in conversations with the Mexican government, they often blamed their parents.

EVALUATION OF HOST-GOVERNMENT DEMANDS

Irrespective of an antiregulatory corporate culture, the subsidiaries' willingness to lobby their parents was also affected by their evaluation of the potential impact of host-government regulations. The management of the *General Motors* and *Ford* subsidiaries admitted they miscalculated the impact of government regulations: the Ford subsidiary held out unsuccessfully for later negotiations; the GM subsidiary, despite its commitment to massive investments, failed to actually make timely local-content, product, and export changes until after the Cocoyoc Resolution. Can this be explained by differences in how the Mexican subsidiaries evaluated Mexican government demands and shared those evaluations with parent management?

None of the five subsidiaries felt their parent staff was helpful in analyzing the Mexican government. As the managing director of Nissan said, "As in war, headquarters doesn't know much about the front."[48] However, the *Chrysler* and *Volkswagen* subsidiaries were given total responsibility by their parents for evaluating the government, whereas the *General Motors* and *Ford* subsidiaries had special head-office units devoted to country-risk assessments. The *Nissan* subsidiary had an independent political-risk unit at the parent, and was formally responsible for reporting its evaluations to this unit as well as its overseas division.

The parent units dedicated to country-risk assessment at *Ford* and *General Motors* employed well-respected analysts dedicated to helping subsidiaries manage pressures in their operating environments. As *General Motors*' well-known political analyst stated: "The strident anti-multinational rhetoric of the 1970s is giving way in many cases to carefully structured measures that enable governments to control foreign investor activity without sacrificing the benefits of a continued role for multinationals. *In this more pragmatic environment, analysis of regulatory policy becomes more important than questions of regime stability or political turmoil.* . . . As an outsider, you have to play by the rules, and not let yourself get caught moving in a direction different than the country decides to go. *Your problem is to understand the rules, and also to anticipate when they might change.*"[49] It is striking how the GM analyst's em-

[48] Author interview with the managing director of Nissan Mexicana.

[49] Gordon Rayfield, "General Motors' Approach to Country Risk," in *Assessing Country Risk*, ed. Richard Ensor (London: Euromoney Publications Ltd., 1981), p. 132; and Gordon

phasis on regulatory policy encompasses this case study of the Mexican automotive industry. Yet, head-office staff at the parent was not cited as a source of information by the Mexican subsidiary during the entire crisis period from 1977 to 1982. To the extent subsidiary management even *knew* of this head-office unit, impressions were that its efforts were directed at collecting information from subsidiary management and supporting head-office decisions, not toward subsidiary planning or offering recommendations.

One of *Ford*'s political analysts would seem to agree that the major function of the Ford head-office political unit was also to support overseas subsidiary evaluations and decisions: "I think that if we have any really important function in the company, it is to *recommend prescriptions for dealing with issues*, not merely to diagnose the problem. The task is to reduce the difficulties for Ford to broaden the opportunities and to do it in a way that is seen by the foreign governments involved as being as beneficial to them as it is to us."[50] However, while the managing director of Ford's subsidiary praised this head-office unit, he felt the need to have input from his own subsidiary management for subsidiary planning and recommendations to the parent. The current situation was inadequate: he had no staff and any analysis done by the subsidiary had to be performed by him, but he felt "too close" to the situation.[51]

Therefore, in the case of both *Ford* and *General Motors*, neither head-office political unit was reported as aiding the subsidiary in its evaluation of government demands; moreover, neither subsidiary reported conducting its own systematic evaluation. In contrast, the *Volkswagen*, *Chrysler*, and *Nissan* subsidiaries were explicitly given total responsibility for evaluating and reporting to their parents on government regulations.[52] Consequently, the *Ford* and *General Motors* subsidiaries suffered a disadvantage in lobbying their parents since they lacked the resources and the explicit mandate to evaluate their environment.

ORGANIZATIONAL FACTORS: THE REPORTING AND DECISION STRUCTURE

Once subsidiary management did decide to lobby its parent to change its role within its parent's global network, the reporting and decision

---

Rayfield, "Political Risks: Doing Business in a Changing World" (unpublished manuscript), 7. Emphasis added.

[50] "Integrating Political Risk: Ford Unit Uses Several Levels of Analysis," *Business International* (22 June 1984): 197. Emphasis added.

[51] Author interview with the managing director of Ford de México.

[52] For information on Volkswagen's "Environmental Scanning" process and the subsidiary's role, see Schnapp et al., *Corporate Strategies of the Automotive Manufacturers*, pp. 176–78. Nissan's from-the-bottom-up decision-making process is also discussed in pp. 164–67.

structure was cited as an important factor. The reporting structure was the vehicle for communication. In 1977 the inclusion of the Mexican subsidiary in the domestic operations of *General Motors* and *Chrysler* was cited as aiding their respective investment decisions. Their own domestic operations, after all, were the buyers of the Mexican-made engines. As discussed, one major reason given for *Ford*'s delay was the disinterest of its reporting division, international, in supplying engines to another profit center, the U.S. division. Much negotiation between the two Ford divisions was required to determine how profits would be assigned. Therefore, when the reporting structure was *not* to the particular division within the MNC that would benefit, intra-MNC negotiation and delays resulted.

The importance of the reporting structure was underlined time and again by *General Motors* subsidiary management. When GM's Mexican subsidiary reported to the U.S. division, it had the benefit of a powerful and profitable area able to respond with an investment commitment, but its American orientation also hindered its ability to tailor specific subsidiary policies such as local content to the particular demands of the host country. It was treated like any other U.S. assembly operation, rather than as a separate and integral in-country manufacturing subsidiary. After 1981, when the GM subsidiary reported to the overseas division, it had the opportunity to compete for more overseas markets and overseas support from personnel acquainted with the difficulties of manufacturing in LDCs.[53]

THE DECISION-MAKING PROCESS

Regardless of the reporting structure, the success of each subsidiary's investment lobbying was also affected by each MNC's particular decision-making structure, including the degree of centralization, individual personalities, the subsidiary's bargaining power, and home-country pressures. The *General Motors* and *Nissan* subsidiaries reported the greatest amount of parent involvement in their investment decisions. The *Chrysler*, *Ford*, and *Volkswagen* subsidiaries claimed to have the least.

A high degree of MNC centralization enabled the *General Motors* subsidiary to engage quick massive investment from the parent, while in the case of the *Nissan* subsidiary it resulted in prolonged discussion. Centralization worked to the advantage of the *General Motors* subsidiary because it had a necessary precondition: at the parent the subsidiary had a strong supporter who argued that increased investment and a modified role for the subsidiary fit into and advanced the parent's overall global objectives. The head of the domestic division, to which the GM subsid-

[53] Author interviews with senior management of General Motors de México.

iary reported, fought for the investment proposal at the head office. As one senior General Motors executive explained: "The market outlook was great for Mexico, and GMAD [the U.S. division] was powerful, taking over divisions. From 1969 to 1979 we sent investment proposals to head office to expand capacity. Then all of a sudden, the head of General Motors GMAD really pushed for the decision. He was stubborn, a real fighter. What you need is this—one guy to move things. Regardless of what you see, everything is very, very centralized."[54] GM's centralization enabled the Mexican subsidiary to change from one of the parent's smaller, less important subsidiaries to one of the MNC's major sources of engines worldwide.

However, a high degree of centralization worked against the *Nissan* subsidiary. The main reason given was the particular decision-making process at Nissan: not only was it consensus in the widely acclaimed Ringi Japanese style, but also conservative due to Nissan's particular corporate culture.[55] In fact, the managing director of the Nissan subsidiary felt this was a major competitive disadvantage. The subsidiary's plans had to be communicated to all related functional areas at the parent, including the overseas, political-risk analysis, marketing divisions, etc., which "fiercely and enthusiastically" discussed the issue with the subsidiary and each other at great length until there was shared agreement. This need for complete agreement delayed important subsidiary decisions.[56]

However, in terms of actual policymaking, centralization was less of a liability for Nissan than General Motors. Again, the reason had to do with the legitimacy of adapting policies according to host-government dictates. Both subsidiary and parent management at Nissan felt compliance was a duty; therefore, while functional subsidiary-parent decisions were shared, the need to comply with local demands was a given.

For *General Motors*, centralization interfered with individual subsidiary responsiveness. Before the Cocoyoc Resolution, GM's subsidiary and parent management geared their decisions not to the Mexican environment but to the parent's operating needs. Local-content and product decisions were usually made on the basis of criteria totally external to Mexico. Therefore, many decisions that affected the GM subsidiary were centralized in the parent's domain and, unlike Nissan, did not have input from the Mexican subsidiary itself.

[54] Author interview with a senior executive of General Motors de México.

[55] The study by Schnapp et al. (*Corporate Strategies of the Automotive Manufacturers*) highlighted Nissan's conservative nature, suggesting as one reason the dominant number of senior executives with banking backgrounds (p. 165). Also, the managing director of Nissan's American subsidiary testified that his individual consent was imperative for any imports from Nissan's Mexican subsidiary.

[56] Author interview with the managing director of Nissan Mexicana.

General Motors' subsidiary management cited their lengthy "bureaucratic" parent decision-making process as a major disadvantage vis-à-vis their competitors.[57] As one senior executive stated, "Other companies have a shorter chain of command; they can get decisions overnight."[58] GM's subsidiary management felt dependent on only one contact at the parent, and if that individual was on vacation, it was next to impossible to get a decision. As a result, the personality of the individual who was the parent contact was also a determining factor in the parent's response at GM.

In contrast, *Ford* was hindered by its decentralized decision-making, while the *Volkswagen* and *Chrysler* subsidiaries were not. The *Ford* subsidiary's managing director expressed difficulty in convincing the parent of its views. Independently of the parent, the Mexican subsidiary would develop recommendations that would then be analyzed by its parent.[59] As the managing director explained, "Ford is working separately from the parent. General Motors is working with the parent."[60] In fact, Ford de México's managing director spent significantly more time—70 percent of his total work time—communicating with his parent and lobbying the Mexican government than did his counterparts at the other subsidiaries.[61] The managing director explained that he felt as if he was negotiating with two independent parties: he would first decide what he wanted to do, then how to bring both parent and host government together. In the case of Ford, the subsidiary's independence in formulating recommendations did not facilitate quick and successful agreement with the parent.

While both the *Chrysler* and *Volkswagen* subsidiaries also claimed to have independence in formulating recommendations, they were able to elicit stronger parent support. *Chrysler*'s subsidiary management felt its smaller corporate structure gave it an advantage over its competitors. As

[57] For a discussion of GM's centralized policymaking process, see Schnapp et al., *Corporate Strategies of the Automotive Manufacturers*, pp. 145–59.

[58] Author interview with a senior executive of General Motors de México.

[59] Schnapp et al. concur in the Ford parent's application of strict performance guidelines: return on investment, the key financial determinant of capital resource allocation, was set 10 to 15 percentage points higher than those of the other U.S. automotive companies (p. 142). The study also pointed out the impact of Henry Ford II on Ford's decision-making process. First, "he is not likely to make a major decision . . . unless he personally feels comfortable"; second, he "fills a direct liaison role between the Ford Motor Company and the U.S. Government" (p. 135). The present case study also confirms Ford's unparalleled and distinctive involvement with the U.S. government compared to the other companies.

[60] Author interview with the managing director of Ford de México.

[61] The subsidiary whose managing director spent the second greatest amount of his total work time (25 percent) with the parent and the Mexican government was Chrysler. (Based on questionnaire given to all managing directors.)

one manager stated, "We are smaller and can get to the top quicker than the competition."[62] The Chrysler head office reportedly gave its Mexican subsidiary a lot of attention. Decision-making at Chrysler was fast, given the lack of formal procedures and the importance of the Mexican subsidiary to the parent.[63]

The *Volkswagen* subsidiary's quick response was due to a combination of autonomy and bargaining power. Importantly, the only reason the Volkswagen subsidiary built an engine plant in Mexico instead of importing from its Brazilian operation was the Mexican government's regulation. Why was the Volkswagen subsidiary willing and able to convince the parent? As discussed earlier, the unusual degree of autonomy assigned the Volkswagen subsidiary coupled with its importance to the parent translated into bargaining power that commanded quick parent support.

EXTERNAL FACTORS: HOME-COUNTRY PRESSURES

The difficulty of convincing *Ford*'s parent management was made more complicated by the parent's vulnerability to its own external environment. As a result, the Ford subsidiary was affected significantly more than the other four subsidiaries by home-country pressures. When asked of the constraints limiting his subsidiary's exports, the Ford managing director cited pressure from U.S. labor and the press as the most important. Less important constraints, listed in order of importance, were the international recession, quality of product and high cost of local production, and the financial position of the parent. Only one other subsidiary—*Chrysler*—named home-country labor pressures as a constraint, but it was listed as far less important, after the international recession, the financial position of the parent, difficulty in selling Mexican-made products, and the high cost of local production.[64] Therefore, while the parents of the Chrysler, Ford and General Motors subsidiaries were all members of the same industry, operating in the same U.S. environment and facing much-publicized pressure from U.S. labor, the level of pressure and how it affected their behavior differed significantly for each of them, just as it did for their Mexican subsidiaries.

In summary, why were the *Nissan* and *Volkswagen* subsidiaries more successful in convincing their parents to comply with Mexican regula-

[62] Author interview with a senior executive of Chrysler de México.

[63] Schnapp et al. characterized Chrysler's decision-making process as "a high degree of informality . . . facilitated by the straightforward nature of the organization and the small number of people involved." Schnapp et al., *Corporate Strategies of the Automotive Manufacturers*, p. 128.

[64] Responses given in questionnaire. Also, author interviews with the managing directors of Ford de México and Chrysler de México.

tions? While the *Nissan* subsidiary retained relatively little independence, parent management was easily convinced of the compliance imperative. While the *Volkswagen* subsidiary was very autonomous from the parent, its bargaining power with the parent and successful track record were a strong combination. Therefore, in the case of *Nissan*, responsiveness was enabled by centralization combined with the corporate philosophy of adaptation, and in the case of *Volkswagen* by autonomy combined with bargaining power and competitive products.

The *U.S. subsidiaries* were less successful in convincing their parents to comply, but for different reasons and to varying extents. First, the *General Motors'* centralized reporting and decision structure, with its necessary linkage—a strong persistent advocate—facilitated the effective bidding for a share of the parent's new global thrust, but hampered its ability to evaluate government demands and adjust its planning in accordance with local needs. Conversely, while the *Ford* subsidiary had more latitude in planning, it was at first unwilling and then unable to win the support of its parent. Multiple reasons were cited—from lack of parent resources (including product and strategy), misjudgment of government demands, and U.S. labor pressure. In contrast, however, the *Chrysler* subsidiary had the advantage of greater autonomy in many decisions; yet, like Volkswagen, it also had bargaining power that ensured parent commitment despite its parent's weaker cash position compared with Ford. Therefore, as summarized in table 7–4, a multitude of parent characteristics were reported as influencing the subsidiary's ability to evaluate host-country demands and to comply with the trade balance requirement.

Subsidiary Interrelationships

The interrelationships of the five automotive subsidiaries became increasingly more important in the changing regulatory environment. As a tightly knit group of foreign companies facing the same host-government regulations, the automotive subsidiaries shared a joint quest for collaboration and mutual protection. Yet, increasing government pressure also provided a potential competitive advantage: playing the game well could mean greater market share. Individual subsidiary responses changed the parameters of behavior for the other subsidiaries: joint violation provided greater protection from the host government; partial industry compliance increased pressure on the remaining subsidiaries to comply. Therefore, the key ingredients of the subsidiaries interrelationships were *competitors' moves* (for those in compliance with government regulations), and for the others, *collaboration* in noncompliance.

TABLE 7–4
Parent Influences on Subsidiary Responsiveness

	GM	Ford	Chrysler	VW	Nissan
SUBSIDIARY ABILITY TO ACHIEVE TRADE BALANCE					
Increase					
Parent assignment of large export markets	+			+	
Parent investment strategy	+			+	
Centralization of decision-making and key parent individual support					
Parent growth objectives	+			+	+
Parent mandate to increase local content				+	+
Parent philosophy subsidiary independence/adaptation				+	
Parent compliance bias					+
Reporting structure to potential buying division	+				
Importance of subsidiary to parent			+	+	+
Decrease					
Weak parent position		–	–		
Lack of parent commitment		–			–
Lengthy parent decision process	–	–			–
Inflexibility in parent's sourcing strategy	–	–	–		
Parent antiregulation bias	–	–	–		
Parent vulnerability to home-labor pressures		–			
SUBSIDIARY ABILITY TO EVALUATE MEXICAN DEMANDS					
Increase					
Parent personnel policies					
[a] High-level continuity				+	
[b] Mexicanization		+	+	+	
Ease of parent-subsidiary communication			+	+	+
Parent assigns evaluation of demands to subsidiary			+	+	+
Parent philosophy of adaptation				+	

TABLE 7–4 (*cont.*)

	GM	Ford	Chrysler	VW	Nissan
SUBSIDIARY ABILITY TO EVALUATE MEXICAN DEMANDS (*cont.*)					
Decrease					
Personnel policies oriented to head office (e.g., high rotation)	–	–			–
Parent evaluates demands; no formal subsidiary role	–	–			
Parent approval in hiring local management	–				

Note: – = reported as negative influence; + = reported as positive influence.

The Role of AMIA

Established in 1951, the subsidiaries' industry organization, AMIA, provided a central meeting ground where the five subsidiaries could assemble and consult with one another. Over the years, AMIA had established various committees—such as the Committee for Imports and Exports (in 1968) and the Committee for Supplier Development and Local Content (1981)—in which its members could discuss industry issues. With the enactment of the 1977 Decree, AMIA became the major industry authority for lobbying the Mexican government. As the head of AMIA explained, with the 1977 Decree the Mexican government preferred to communicate "the same message once in an impersonal way" to AMIA, thus avoiding as much as possible the pressures of having to deal with each subsidiary's wanting to negotiate from its own point of view.[65] AMIA was used differently by the various automotive companies, with the most support coming from the *Volkswagen* and *U.S. subsidiaries.*

The subsidiaries also varied in how they rated the importance of AMIA and each other as sources of information in developing their investment plans. *Nissan*'s managing director cited AMIA as a key information source, second only to his own subsidiary staff. The managing director of the subsidiary with the weakest government relations, *General Motors*, also cited AMIA as an important information source, but listed it after the Mexican government, the parent company staff, and his own subsid-

[65] Author interview with the executive director of AMIA.

iary staff. The *Chrysler* subsidiary also cited AMIA as an important information source, equal in importance to outside consultants, home-country representatives (such as the U.S. Embassy and the American Chamber of Commerce of Mexico), and other automotive companies.

The managing directors of the two subsidiaries most in conflict with government regulations—*Ford* and *Chrysler*—spent the most time obtaining information about their competitors. *Ford*'s managing director was the exception in *not* citing AMIA as an information source; for him, information received directly from the other automotive companies was most important, followed by the Mexican government, his subsidiary staff, then the parent staff. In fact, after the new 1977 regulations, the Ford managing director reported spending 20 percent of his total work time contacting the other subsidiaries, and none of his time with AMIA. In contrast, the other managing directors spent more time with AMIA and considerably less time with the other subsidiaries, the total time for subsidiaries ranging from a high of 20 percent for the managing directors of *Chrysler* and *Ford* to only 6 percent for the managing director of *General Motors*. Therefore, information through AMIA or directly from competitors was reported as very important in the formulation of all of the subsidiaries' policies, but to differing degrees.[66]

Effect of Competitors' Moves

Clearly the need for information on subsidiary behavior was related to the changing regulatory environment, underlying the key role of each subsidiary in defining the parameters of acceptable behavior for its competitors. Even prior to the 1977 Decree, the behavior of one subsidiary, *Volkswagen*, had set the stage for a hardening of the Mexican government's demands with the 1977 Decree. The Volkswagen subsidiary was a market leader and it had simultaneously achieved relatively high exports and high local content. As one government official stated, "Volkswagen's success [in complying with the government's demands] decreased the other companies' bargaining power."[67] The *General Motors* subsidiary had been targeted by the government as likely to succumb to an opportunity to break ranks with the industry pack and commit itself to a high-export strategy. *Volkswagen*, and especially *General Motors*, initiated defensive counterinvestments by their competitors, *Chrysler*, *Nissan*, and *Ford*. Indeed, when asked what external actions had influenced the formation of their companies' investment plans, the managing directors of the *Chrysler* and *Nissan* subsidiaries listed their competitors' invest-

[66] Information in this section was based on questionnaires given to all managing directors.

[67] Author interview with key government officials responsible for regulating the automotive industry.

ments as second only to the Mexican government's regulations. *Ford's* managing director cited its competitors' investment as even more important than the Mexican government in influencing Ford's investment decision.[68]

Collaboration

After the enactment of the 1977 Decree, all five subsidiaries were initially protected by mutual resistance. After all, the Mexican government could not expropriate its entire terminal auto industry. As one automotive managing director observed, "Competition is key: as long as all the companies develop at the same time, each is safe."[69] The U.S. subsidiaries had collaborated in lobbying the Mexican government. Their alliance, however, cracked due to their differing interests. The subsidiary that broke ranks with the announcement of its massive export investment—*General Motors*—received acclaim from the Mexican government, but created pressure for its competitors, and especially the remaining U.S. subsidiaries, to follow suit.

This pressure escalated as other subsidiaries followed GM with investment announcements. The *Chrysler* subsidiary obtained some relief from its parent's very visible and much-publicized financial difficulties. The *Ford* subsidiary, feeling partially protected by joint noncompliance, followed in Chrysler's tracks. While Ford's management claimed that it was profitable to comply as little as possible, it also was well aware of its resulting weakened position vis-à-vis the Mexican government. Ford's subsidiary management was finally able to convince parent management to invest in Mexico only because all its competitors had. However, even after its announcement, Ford's managing director felt that the subsidiary's greatest weakness in bargaining with the Mexican government was due to its relative delay in investing.

Indeed, it was only after all the subsidiaries had announced their investment plans that the Mexican government reinforced the 1977 Decree with the Cocoyoc Resolution. With all bids placed, the captive subsidiaries (and their investments) now faced the trade balance test—again the early performers set the parameters for their competitors. Because the subsidiaries responded differently, the government could reward and penalize. Since the *Nissan* and *Volkswagen* subsidiaries were able to largely meet the trade balance requirement, greater pressure could be applied to the *General Motors*, and especially the *Chrysler* and *Ford* subsidiaries. Therefore, faced with the same regulations, the responses of the five

[68] Information based on questionnaires given to all managing directors.

[69] Author interview with the managing director of an automotive subsidiary.

subsidiaries became part of the competitive game, with each subsidiary's behavior contributing to the definition of acceptable behavior and raising the stakes for noncompliance.

Conclusion

Again, the argument has been amply illustrated: a multitude of different factors were reported as shaping subsidiary behavior, and as a result, MNC subsidiaries varied systematically in their will and capacity to deal with host-country demands. As shown in figure 7–2, differentiating factors encompassed the entire subsidiary organization. For example, each parent's *strategy* had particular ramifications for the ability of its Mexican subsidiary to respond to the host-government's demands, the key being the subsidiary's role within the global network. Product strategies, supplier strategies, and sourcing strategies either had to be in place or the parent had to have the global position and strength to adjust the strategic role of its Mexican subsidiary. The process by which the parent evaluated the Mexican government's demands was crucial to its decision to comply or delay. The parent's strategy was in turn potentially affected by its home-country environment. *Philosophies* transmitted from the parent, its corporate culture and home-country views, differentiated response. *Structures* were important—the way in which the subsidiaries were organized and managed affected their relationships and decisions. Likewise, *policies* in areas such as human resources had a direct bearing on management's perceptions of the regulations. *Practices* differed between subsidiaries: for example, some were willing to use intermediary parties, while others were not. *Relationships* were important. The Mexican government had differing affinities for the home countries of the subsidiaries. Some parents and their Mexican subsidiaries were subject to home-country pressures. Corporate policies affected *individuals*, who in turn, with their differing personalities and personal abilities, brought in the whole range of human relations. *Products* had different markets and levels of political importance. *Production requirements* varied as to employment needs, economies of scale, and supplier locations. Meanwhile, within the industry itself, subsidiaries were also affected by their respective *market positions*: *Nissan Mexicana*, for example, perceived its small size as reducing its bargaining power with the Mexican government. Therefore, when faced with host-government demands, diverse elements throughout the entire MNC organization were brought into play, all of which influenced the subsidiaries' abilities and willingness to respond.

This chapter has shown how these specific subsidiary characteristics shaped not only each subsidiary's relationships with key actors in its environment, but also its specific individualistic behavior in response to a

FIGURE 7–2
The Overall MNC Organization: Key Factors Shaping Response to Government Demands

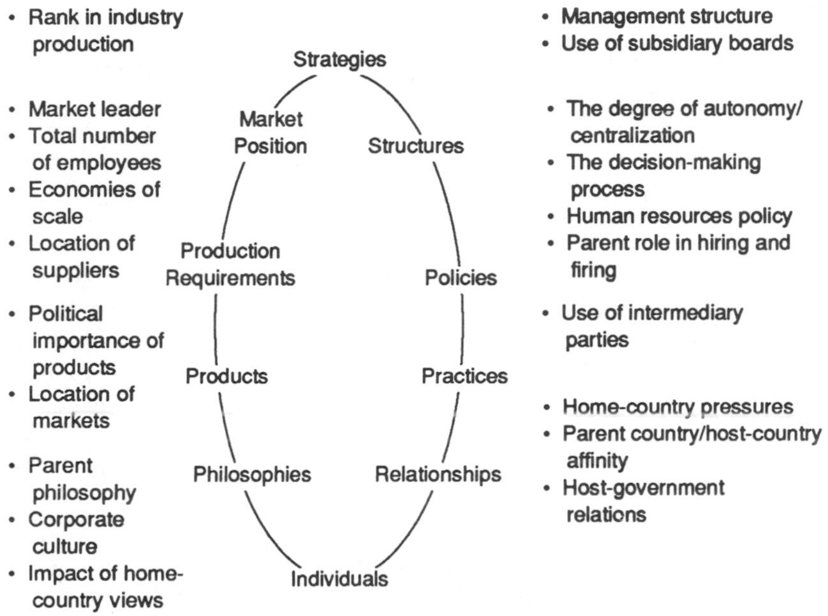

common changing environment. Summarized in figure 7–3, these relationships give us a framework for analyzing subsidiary behavior. Within this complexity, as in the Brazilian case, the implications of certain characteristics for subsidiary behavior can be assessed. Certain subsidiary characteristics resulted in a high degree of integration between the subsidiary and the Mexican government: parent philosophy (*Volkswagen*); a large number of employees (*Volkswagen*, *Chrysler*); a market leader position (*Volkswagen*, *Chrysler*); politically important products (*Volks-*

FIGURE 7–3
Key Subsidiary Relationships: Reported Factors Shaping Response to Government Demands

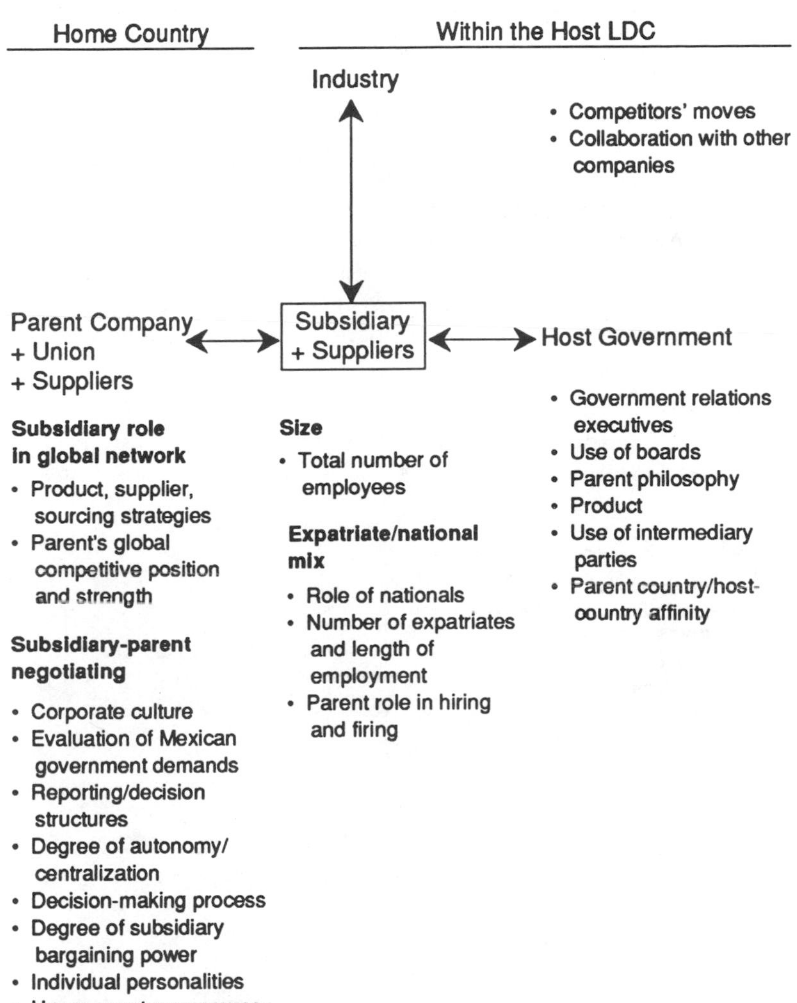

wagen); extensive personal contact between the managing director and host-government officials (*Volkswagen*); and Mexicans in top management positions and on the Board of Directors (*Chrysler*, *Volkswagen*). A different set of subsidiary characteristics seemed to reinforce a high degree of integration between the subsidiary and its parent: national and corporate culture (*Nissan*, *General Motors*, *Ford*); regular rotation of expatriate management (*Nissan*, *General Motors*, *Ford*); the role of the subsidiary as a buyer of the parent's products (*General Motors*, *Ford*, *Nissan*); and financial or product difficulties (*Chrysler*, *Ford*). Integration with other industry members was unrelated to the degree of parent or host-government integration—the two subsidiaries that relied most on industry information and behavior (*Ford* and *Chrysler*) were in greatest conflict with government demands. (See figure 7–4.)

As in the Brazilian case, the degree of integration between a subsidiary and the host government was indirectly correlated with the degree of autonomy with its parent. The subsidiaries most integrated with the host government—*Volkswagen* and *Chrysler*— were also relatively more autonomous in their parent relationship, while *General Motors* and *Nissan* were less integrated with the host government and more dependent on their parents. The *Ford* subsidiary was caught in the biggest bind, with poor government relations and weak parent support. Significantly, how-

FIGURE 7–4
Management Characteristics and the Relationships of the Subsidiary to the Parent, Host Government, and Industry

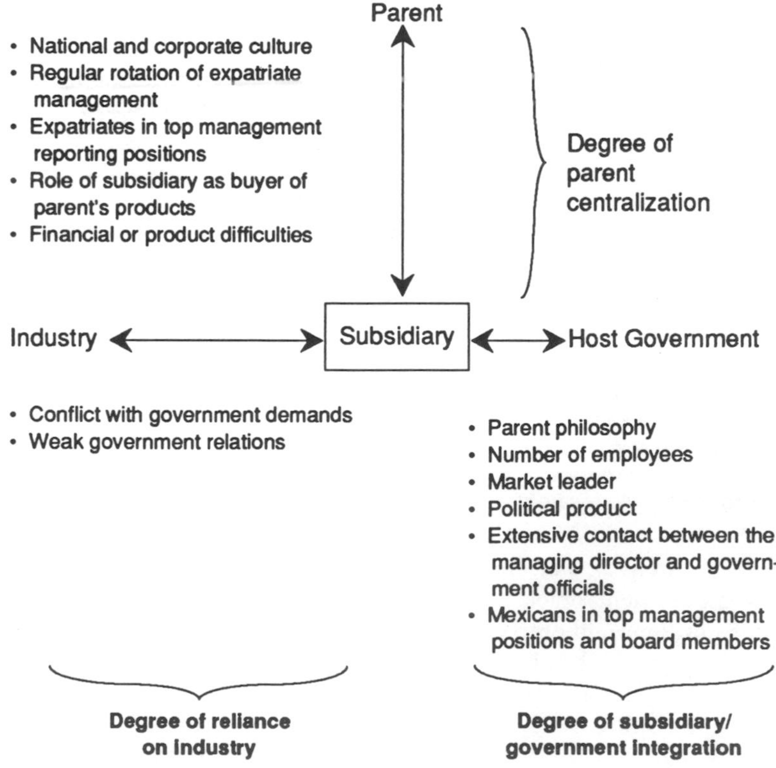

ever, whatever the degree of autonomy or host-government integration, all subsidiaries were greatly affected by external factors.

The Mexican case study demonstrates that each subsidiary's investment and sourcing policies were influenced by a multitude of varying subsidiary characteristics both from within and external to the host country. During the crisis period, as the subsidiaries developed their trade balance policies, the specific relationships between each subsidiary and its parent, the host government, and the industry became visible determinants of those policies.

The Policy Reformulation Process

The preceding examination of subsidiary relationships demonstrates the complexity of factors shaping subsidiary behavior. The relative bargaining strengths and weaknesses of the respective parties alone do not explain the complex individual responses of the five subsidiaries. Response was not just a function of conflict. Indeed, the degree of conflict was quite different between subsidiaries, as were their abilities and willingness to respond. Let us now examine certain propositions for those common key variables that differentiate subsidiary behavior.

PRE-CRISIS IDENTIFICATION OF LDC DEMANDS

The reasons why certain subsidiaries were able to identify and respond to their changing environment have become clearer. (See table 7-5.) *Volkswagen*, *Nissan*, and *Chrysler* responded first—in terms of *internal management policies*. All three subsidiaries had the specific responsibility allocated by the parent to analyze host-government regulations, while the *Ford* and *General Motors* subsidiaries did not. Further, GM did not have the resources or latitude to adjust its policy. In addition, managing directors at the *Volkswagen* and *Chrysler* subsidiaries were long-tenured expatriates, with superior language capabilities and knowledge of the country. In contrast, over the years, the *Ford* and *General Motors* subsidiaries had been managed by several expatriates. Just as in the Brazilian case studies, the General Motors and Ford managing directors were at a disadvantage in diagnosing their environments.

The evidence for the second variable—*relationships with key LDC actors*—is also more comprehensive. The *Volkswagen* subsidiary's managing director deliberately set out to establish close relations with Mexican government officials. His ability to increase his bargaining power as a "stand alone Mexican" company would be based on his ability to make the subsidiary a part of the Mexican environment. Likewise, *Chrysler* deliberately used the previous Mexican joint-venture partner as leveraged political capital with the Mexican government. In comparison, the

Table 7–5
Mexican Case Conclusions at Pre-Crisis:
The Ability of the Subsidiary to Identify and Respond to LDC Demands

Internal subsidiary management policies		
• Knowledge of country by senior subsidiary management	+	*VW*: Long-tenured expatriate management, speaks language
	+	*Chrysler*: Mexican board chairman and high-level management
	–	*Ford GM*: Expatriate rotation policy
• Resource availability	+	*Nissan, VW, Chrysler*: Subsidiary analysis of government regulations
	–	*Ford, GM*: Limited funds and personnel
• Subsidiary latitude to adjust policies	+	*VW, Nissan*: Pursued high local-content strategy
	+	*VW*: Assigned German Beetle production and markets
Relationships with key LDC actors	+	*VW* : Long-tenured managing director's close relationships with government officials
	+	*Chrysler*: Mexican chairman of the board's close relationships with government officials
Parent intervention and influence		
• Day-to-day policies	–	*GM, Ford, Chrysler, Nissan*: Subsidiary import policies designed by parents
	–	*GM, Ford, Chrysler*: Managing directors make decisions on head-office criteria
	–	*GM*: Parent role in subsidiary organization and personnel
• Participation in policy changes	+	*Nissan*: Parent philosophy of government compliance; parent gives subsidiary export markets
	+	*VW*: Parent practice of subsidiary adaptation; parent gives subsidiary Beetle production and market
	+	*Chrysler*: Parent increases ownership and invests in export products

Note: + = reported as increasing ability; – = reported as decreasing ability.

Ford, General Motors, and *Nissan* subsidiaries had to parlay government relationships within the limitations of rotating senior management; also, given their management structures, they were largely dependent on others for evaluating government demands.

The third differentiating variable, *parent intervention and influence*, is also more evident. As in the Brazilian case study, certain day-to-day policies interfered with pre-crisis subsidiary response. For all the subsidiaries except Volkswagen, the parent was the key factor in designing its import policies. However, only the parents of the *U.S. subsidiaries* restricted their criteria to include only head-office considerations. The *Nissan* parent, given its philosophy of compliance, took the subsidiary's evaluations of Mexican demands and its recommendations very seriously. Also, the GM subsidiary was reported as hindered by its parent's direct involvement in its personnel and organization. Therefore, just as in the Brazilian case study, common key variables differentiated the ability of the five subsidiaries to identify their changing environment. Subsidiary characteristics that enhanced senior management's ability to read the environment and adjust their policies accordingly with responsive parent intervention were key.

DEGREE OF CONFLICT

The explanation for the differing level of pressure on subsidiary policies is also clearer. (See table 7–6.) Subsidiaries had very different *historical policies* for trade balances largely because of differing strategies. Before the government crackdown, *Volkswagen* could export precisely because it was its role within the parent strategy to export. For *Nissan*, compliance with government regulations was also part of its already established role. In contrast, there was next to no provision for trade balance considerations within the role of the three *U.S. subsidiaries*. As the result of new investment, however, the Chrysler subsidiary had achieved the greatest export capability; but its imports were still vastly larger.

The pre-crisis response was indicative of the differing innate conflicts between subsidiary roles and the trade balance requirement. *Volkswagen*'s and *Nissan*'s high local-content strategy was linked intrinsically to their popular-product and local-supplier strategies. In contrast, the *U.S. subsidiaries* were considered expansions of the U.S. market, as clients to their nearby parents, there just to purchase auto parts for the annual model changes.

The reasons for such differing parent interests are also explained more completely by our structural examination of the subsidiaries. *Ford*'s vulnerability to home-labor pressures is at least partly explained by the company's smaller size and power relative to *General Motors*, and its weaker UAW position. The unique impact of *Nissan*'s parent philosophy is more

TABLE 7–6
Mexican Case Conclusions at Conflict:
The Level of Pressure on Subsidiary Policies

Past subsidiary policy performance		
• Pre-crisis response	–	*VW, Nissan*: Small trade deficits (role of Mexican subsidiary)
	+	*Ford, GM, Chrysler*: Large trade deficits (role of Mexican subsidiary)
• Innate conflict	–	*VW, Nissan*: High local-content strategies (products, suppliers)
	+	*Ford, GM*, Chrysler: Low local-content strategies (products, suppliers)
Pressuring-group's perception and bargaining power		
• Ability/willingness	–	*GM*: Capacity to respond
	–	*Chrysler*: Inability to respond
• Overall subsidiary value	–	*VW, Nissan*: Importance of popular car products; non-American companies
	+	*Ford, GM, Chrysler*: Oversupply of luxury cars; American companies
	–	*VW, Chrysler*: Importance of employment
Parent interests		
• Home-country pressures	+	*Ford*: Home-labor pressures (weaker UAW position)
• Parent philosophy	+	*Nissan*: Parent philosophy of compliance (history of Japanese government relations)
• Parent overall strategy	+	*Chrysler, Ford*: Parent constraints (global position)
	–	*GM*: Coincidence between parent strategy and Mexican government demands (global position)

Note: + = reported as increasing pressure; – = reported as decreasing pressure.

understandable in the context of traditional Japanese company-government relations. Likewise, an overview of the different global positions of the three American MNCs does provide the necessary framework to explain their differing abilities to increase their Mexican investment.

TYPE OF SUBSIDIARY RESPONSE

The structural examination of the five subsidiaries fleshed out the reasons for different subsidiary response. (See table 7–7.) Each of the subsidiaries was subject to parent-approval options, but their ability to influence the parent's decisions differed. A centralized strong parent enabled the *General Motors* subsidiary to take the position of "response leader." Volkswagen was undaunted by the government's crackdown, maintaining its powerful but compromising position; after all, its parent expected it to

TABLE 7–7
Mexican Case Conclusions by the Type of Subsidiary Response: Key Influences Reported

Past preferences	
• Parent-approved options	*All*: Parent export strategy (organization, resources)
• Parent practices	*VW*: Subsidiary adaptation to host-country environment, ability to stand alone
• Parent philosophy	*Nissan*: Complies consistently with trade balance requirements (Japanese government relations)
• Home-country pressures	*Ford*: Home-labor pressures against Mexican engine investment
Subsidiary relationships with key LDC groups	*Nissan, VW*: Adopts Mexican government's preferred local-content policy (historic strategy) *Ford, Chrysler, GM*: Adopts parent's preferred local-content policy (ties to U.S. parent)
First subsidiary responses in changing policy	*VW, Chrysler, Nissan, Ford*: Impacted by GM's investment announcement *Ford, Chrysler, GM, VW*: Impacted by Nissan's compliance with trade balance requirements

play the role of a Mexican company. *Nissan*, however, stole the show as the only subsidiary to consistently meet the trade balance requirement (the underlying reason being largely its parent's philosophy of compliance). In contrast, *Ford's* investment delay was the product of an unconvinced subsidiary and a resistant parent vulnerable to its own home-country environment.

The nature of parent-subsidiary relationships were also indicative of subsidiary response. From the establishment of their manufacturing operations, both the *Nissan* and *Volkswagen* subsidiaries had consciously set out to increase their local content, in part to increase their bargaining power with the Mexican government. In contrast, the U.S. subsidiaries had always been wed to auto parts supplied by their U.S. operations, and were more concerned about their relationships with their parents than about those with the Mexican government. Indeed, only the Cocoyoc Resolution forced them to loosen U.S. ties, and to win a commitment to source auto parts within Mexico itself.

Implications: Risks for MNC Subsidiaries and Benefits for LDC Governments

As in the Brazilian case study, a key difference between the MNC subsidiaries was their ability to identify and respond to the changing regulating environment. The responsiveness of the subsidiaries was related to their relationship with their parents and the host government: those subsidiaries that were more responsive—*Volkswagen* and *Nissan*—had roles in their parent's global network most in line with host-government objectives. Moreover, parent and subsidiary management at both companies believed compromise with the Mexican government was intrinsic to their policies. The degree of parent autonomy or host-government integration was irrelevant, as long as parent management was willing to accommodate host-government demands in its subsidiary's policies.

Understanding first the specific nature of the parent-subsidiary relationship and, second, the specific types of parent influences was fundamental to analyzing the potential responsiveness of any of the subsidiaries. Only in the case of Volkswagen was there sufficient autonomy to negate much of the parent's influence. For the other four subsidiaries, the dynamics of responses were complex, with each individual subsidiary transmitting its particular home-country and parent influences. Whether parent influences represented risks or benefits to the subsidiary was a function of the Mexican environment: Did parent influences increase or decrease the subsidiary's ability to achieve a trade balance? Increase or decrease the subsidiary's ability to negotiate with the Mexican government and evaluate the regulatory environment?

Subsidiary behavior was better understood within the context of its parent relationship, the complex mix of influences representing both benefits and risks to the subsidiary and the Mexican government. Parent influences significantly affected the subsidiary's internal organization as well as its relationships with the host government and other industry members—with significant implications for risks and benefits. The internal organization and all in-country relationships were affected by the parent's personnel policies, reporting and decision structures, parent philosophy, and corporate culture. To the degree that parent influences enabled subsidiary responsiveness, the host government and usually the subsidiary both benefited. The prime example was *Volkswagen*: it was able to adapt its policies and effectively negotiate a margin of compromise with the government. The exception was *Nissan*: its total compliance negated the probable benefits of negotiation with the Mexican government. Parent policies, structures, and strategies had far-reaching effects on the subsidiary's ability to evaluate, negotiate, and respond.

The Mexican case demonstrates that even when centralized MNC policies (such as import, export, and investment policies) were pressured, significant differences existed in the risks to MNCs and the benefits to the LDC. By viewing the subsidiaries within the context of their LDC environment and their parent, the underlying variables differentiating subsidiary response become clearer, providing insight into the implications of differing MNC subsidiary structures, policies, strategies, host-government relationships, and industry interrelationships. The Mexican government succeeded in utilizing the MNC automotive subsidiaries as "levers of change" by targeting subsidiary-specific variables; *General Motors* was induced to become "response leader," leading the way to making Mexico a major worldwide source of automotive engines.

CHAPTER 8

Conclusion: Strategic Implications for MNC Managers and LDC Groups

BOTH CASE STUDIES contain evidence supportive of competing theories on the role of MNCs in LDCs: As the dependency school espouses, the subsidiaries were driven in some circumstances by external parent imperatives unrelated, and sometimes contrary, to the LDC's objectives; yet, as the pro-MNCs theorists claim, subsidiaries were sometimes also engines of development establishing modernizing agendas and contributing in unique ways to those objectives. The conflicting generalizations set forth by these schools obviously contain elements of truths. However, generalizations based on a macro-oriented absolutist framework of exclusivity lead to circuitous debates without providing comprehensive pragmatic guidelines for MNC managers and LDC groups. These managers and groups need to know why and how certain MNC subsidiaries, when faced with pressures on their policies, become "levers for change, and . . . by choice or by force involved in implementing these changes."[1]

THE FIRST ARGUMENT: MNC SUBSIDIARY POLICIES AS "LEVERS FOR CHANGE"

Both case studies were prefaced with a macrohistorical chapter mapping the automotive policies—Brazilian labor relations and Mexican trade balance—within each country's development. In both case studies, neither Brazilian labor not the Mexican government was absolutely against the MNC subsidiaries; their targets were not the subsidiaries themselves, but rather specific MNC subsidiary policies. Neither pressuring LDC groups sought the unilateral withdrawal of the MNC subsidiaries; on the contrary, each perceived important benefits potentially resulting from changes in the subsidiaries' policies. In the case of Brazil, the labor union was very cognizant that the MNC subsidiaries were far more open to liberalizing labor policies than were national Brazilian firms. In the case of Mexico, the government envisioned the automotive subsidiaries as unrealized wealth potentially available for generating badly needed foreign

[1] Yair Aharoni and Clifford Baden, *Business in the International Environment* (Boulder, Colo.: Westview Press, 1977), p. 2.

exchange. As the automotive industry had led the country into import substitution, so could it lead the way toward export promotion.

The historical mapping of policies in the two cases underlines the potential role of MNC subsidiary policies in spearheading sociopolitical and economic change within LDCs. The buildup of pressure on subsidiary policy was similar in both the Brazilian and Mexican case studies: initially the subsidiary policy was conducted without interference, followed by an escalation of pressure over an extended period, the targeted policy being out of step with key trends in the economic or sociopolitical environment. In Brazil, over the years, labor policy increasingly became a major focus of the political opposition in its campaign against the military government. Likewise, in Mexico, over time, trade balance policies increased in importance as its government struggled with large trade deficits. In both case studies, the buildup of pressure did not occur suddenly or mysteriously, but rather escalated over decades with very visible signs of accelerating demands for policy changes. And significantly, these demands became targeted on MNC subsidiaries, not on national companies.

Changes in the LDC over time meant that subsidiary policies also had to be changed. Subsidiary policies had to be viewed in the context of host-country developments. Brazilian labor practices, once considered acceptable and even desirable, became unacceptable and risky. When the first massive automotive strike occurred in Brazil in 1978, the entire country was stunned. The automotive subsidiaries had aligned themselves closely with Brazil's military government. With the subsequent strengthening of labor and opposition in Brazilian politics, the government abandoned the automotive industry. The automotive subsidiary closest to the government and most akin to Brazilian companies in labor policies and attitude—Volkswagen do Brasil—had the most difficulty responding to labor demands. Likewise, in Mexico, automotive trade balance policies that had been tolerated by the government for decades were outlawed. The subsidiaries that historically had been successful in negotiating with the government were shocked by the government's insistence on a trade balance. Subsidiary policies had to be viewed in relation to the ways they responded both to the needs emerging from the LDC's development process and to the key LDC actors' perceptions of the actual and potential role of subsidiary policies in advancing their respective objectives.

No subsidiary policy was safe from pressure. LDC groups did not refrain from challenging subsidiary policies set outside their countries by the parent company. Indeed, the subsidiaries opened up the parents' policies to pressure from LDC groups. Brazilian labor formed influential alliances with groups in the subsidiaries' home countries, such as their parents' unions, which could directly pressure the parents. The Mexican government's demands directly challenged the parents' autonomy in allocating investments and defining the roles of their own Mexican subsidiaries. In both case studies, the LDC groups targeted MNC subsidiary policies, not the subsidiaries themselves, and any policy was fair game.

The Second Argument: Differing Subsidiary Responses

The first argument submitted that MNC subsidiary policies were differentiated on the basis of their role within the LDC's development process. The second argument goes further: differentiation expands as LDC demands increase, magnifying the differing ability and willingness of individual MNC subsidiaries to company with host-country demands.

The two case studies contradict generalizations about the role of MNCs in LDCs, the risks they face and benefits they provide. Each case study was composed of five MNC subsidiaries in the same industry selling similar products and facing the same LDC demands; yet under pressure, they behaved very differently. The differences become stark when comparing three aspects of the subsidiary's policy reformulation process: (*a*) identification of increasing LDC pressures, (*b*) the degree of conflict between subsidiaries and the host country, and (*c*) the type of subsidiary response.

The implications for MNC risks and LDC benefits were significant, with certain subsidiaries incurring high risks (Volkswagen do Brasil, Ford de México, Chrysler de México) and certain subsidiaries providing the pressuring LDC group with its sought-after benefits (Ford do Brasil, General Motors de México, Nissan Mexicana). Why did the MNC subsidiaries face differing risks and provide differing benefits? Why did certain MNC subsidiaries become "levers for change," and not others? Why did Ford do Brasil, and not the other four automotive subsidiaries, lead Brazil into a new era of employee relations? Why did General Motors de México, and not the other four subsidiaries, lead Mexico into its new role as one of the world's major sources of automotive engines? Why did Nissan Mexicana react late, yet was the only subsidiary to consistently comply with the Mexican government's trade balance requirement? The answers to these questions are not found in macro-oriented generalizations about the overall value of MNCs, but require instead a micro-oriented framework that relates subsidiary policies to the host-country's development, mapping policies within the country's development process, and identifying differing subsidiary relationships and characteristics that influence each individual subsidiary's behavior.

The relative bargaining power of each actor did not explain subsidiary behavior. The variables extended further, encompassing the character of the entire MNC organization itself. Indeed, in both case studies, the relevant actors numbered more than the two immediate contending factions: the LDC pressuring group and the MNC subsidiaries. Parents, as well as home-country groups, confounded any simple explanation of conflict. Even though Volkswagen do Brasil was the country's largest employer, it was the second to capitulate to labor's demands for a union-based worker-representation system. Likewise, in Mexico, differences in bargaining power did not explain why General Motors responded first, and Ford last. In both case studies, subsidiary-specific characteristics encompassing the entire MNC organization served to differentiate subsidiary behavior—varying from structures, strategies, policies, practices, individuals, relationships, philosophies, products, production requirements, to market position. Certain subsidiary characteristics, particularly parent and LDC group relationships, surfaced as critical response factors. The specific charting of each subsidiary's policy reformulation process, represented in figure 8–1, illuminates how critical response factors related to internal management policies, parent relationships, and LDC relationships, shaped subsidiary response.

Pre-Crisis Identification of LDC Demands

Before the crisis, in both case studies, subsidiaries differed in their ability to identify and respond to LDC demands. The reasons encompassed a multitude of subsidiary characteristics which can be grouped into three key variables: (1) *internal management policies*, (2) *relationships with key LDC actors*, and (3) *parent intervention and influences*. Subsidiary characteristics that fostered flexible subsidiary policies formulated by knowledgeable senior management, close relationships with LDC actors, and effective parent intervention increased the ability of the subsidiary to identify and respond to LDC demands before crisis.

INTERNAL MANAGEMENT POLICIES

In both case studies, the ability of MNC subsidiaries to identify increasing LDC demands was visibly enhanced by internal management policies that enabled senior expatriates to have superior knowledge of the country. In Brazil, the Volkswagen and Mercedes Benz subsidiaries, and in Mexico, the Volkswagen and Chrysler subsidiaries benefited from the long tenure of their senior expatriates and senior national executives.

FIGURE 8–1
Differing MNC Responses to LDC Demands: The Policy Reformulation Process

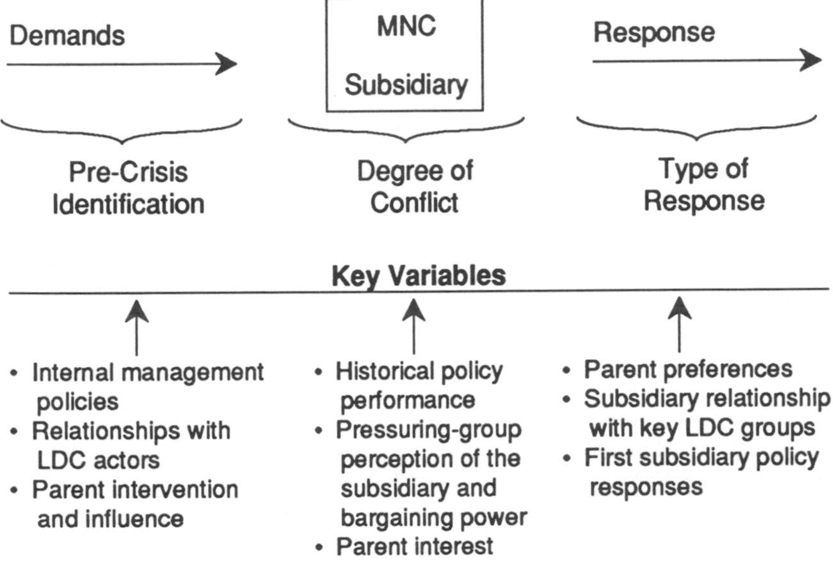

Most such expatriates adopted the host country, along with its language and customs, as their home.

In contrast, other subsidiaries had internal management policies that hindered the ability of their senior expatriates to read the changing environment and to respond appropriately. The rapid expatriate turnover of much of the Ford and General Motors subsidiary management in both Brazil and Mexico was reported as a major disadvantage vis-à-vis other subsidiaries. In particular, the Brazilian Ford subsidiary was hindered by its expatriates' lack of knowledge about Brazil and their strict adherence to the parent's performance guidelines. Expatriates were unable to directly recognize labor issues or the implications of "erratic" labor policies. Even though Ford's labor policies were decentralized, they became hostage to other centralized decisions. In Mexico, the Ford and General Motors subsidiaries suffered from the attitudes embedded in their expatriate management: despite the relatively longer tenure of several expatriates in Mexico, they misjudged the Mexican government's seriousness in enforcing the trade balance requirement. The American expatriates often harbored U.S. and parent viewpoints, transposing them over host-country developments.

A second dimension of internal subsidiary management policies reported as key was the availability of resources to subsidiary management.

Mercedes Benz do Brasil's managing director was able to create a new position to study labor policy issues; Volkswagen do Brasil's managing director also established a new group to gather information on worker attitudes. In Mexico, in the early 1970s, the managing directors of Nissan, Volkswagen, and Chrysler reported the allocation of subsidiary resources to study government regulations. Indeed, all three were expected by their parents to analyze the Mexican regulatory environment, and as a result, made changes in export markets (Nissan, Volkswagen, Chrysler), products (Volkswagen's Beetle, Chrysler's air conditioning condensers), or ownership (Chrysler). Resources enabled the senior expatriates to follow through on their superior knowledge about the host-country.

In contrast, other subsidiaries were at a disadvantage in that, while they had some access to head-office support, local resources were reportedly not available to subsidiary management. Before the strikes in Brazil, the other three subsidiaries—General Motors, Ford, and Saab-Scania do Brasil—did not conduct labor studies on their own initiative. In Mexico, before the 1977 Decree, the other two subsidiaries—General Motors and Ford—did not report conducting studies of government regulations, other than those used to lobby the government. In several interviews, management of these subsidiaries complained that they had limited funds and personnel. It was generally difficult to justify aberrations in expenditure and job positions, especially before a crisis situation had already emerged. These subsidiary managers were therefore at a disadvantage in preempting crisis.

A third dimension of internal subsidiary management policies reported as key was subsidiary latitude in adjusting the policy in question. In Mexico, subsidiary management of both Nissan and Volkswagen identified escalating LDC demands and chose to adjust their trade balance policies before crisis. Both pursued high local-content strategies. Volkswagen de México was assigned the Beetle for manufacture and export. Having the option to adjust policy before crisis, however, did not always guarantee that subsidiary management would do so. In Brazil, while Mercedes Benz and Volkswagen had identified escalating labor demands and had the latitude to adjust labor policies, they did not choose to make significant changes.

RELATIONSHIPS WITH KEY LDC ACTORS

Related to internal management policies, another variable increasing each subsidiary's ability to identify and respond to LDC demands was close management relationships with key LDC actors. In Brazil and Mexico, senior subsidiary management of certain subsidiaries had close personal relationships with key LDC actors. In Brazil, the Volkswagen and Mercedes Benz managing directors had strong friendships with high-level Brazilian government officials. In Mexico, Volkswagen's managing director and Chrysler's chairman of the board had close relationships with government officials. These individuals were cited as critical sources of information. Even if specific advance information on strikes or government regulations was not disclosed, the contacts provided invaluable insights into the attitudes, objectives, and concerns of the LDC actors. In particular, senior management friendships with individuals in the pressuring LDC groups themselves were helpful in more accurately mapping and negotiating the evolution of pressure: Mercedes Benz do Brasil's managing director was able to speak informally with labor leaders; Volkswagen de México's managing director and Chrysler de México chairman of the board could easily tap the attitudes of the government's most senior officials.

PARENT INTERVENTION AND INFLUENCES

A third variable related to both internal subsidiary management policies and relationships with key LDC actors was parent intervention and influence. If parent intervention was effective, the subsidiary's ability to identify changes before crisis was enhanced. Parent intervention encompassed two levels: day-to-day policies and the degree of parent participation in policy changes.

In terms of day-to-day policies, parent intervention was in all cases reported as interfering with subsidiary responsiveness. The Brazilian subsidiaries of General Motors and Ford were subject to the final approval of their parents. Likewise, in Mexico the parents of the General Motors, Ford, Chrysler, and Nissan subsidiaries played a critical decision role in designing their day-to-day import strategies. Any major changes in policies for any of these subsidiaries would have to be discussed with and approved by their respective parents. Unless subsidiary management could easily or tangibly justify changes, they tended (with the exception of Nissan) to refrain from involving their parents. Only after crisis became evident would contact with the parent occur, and then the parent's intervention would be massive.

Even when the parent initiated policy changes, the subsidiary did not necessarily follow through on the parent's recommendations. In Brazil, both the Saab and Ford parents intervened before the outbreak of strikes. The Saab effort was counterproductive, with its subsidiary following its recommendation in form but not in substance, thereby souring relations with the Brazilian labor union. At the Ford subsidiary, faced with contrary profit pressures, expatriate management enacted an "erratic" labor management policy. When head-office labor-relations staff intervened, implementation of its recommendation was delayed and insufficient. However, despite subsidiary resistance, Ford's parent support was reported as marginally increasing its ability to respond, but not compensating for the subsidiary's overall rigidity in labor policies.

The only cases of successful parent initiatives were those designed specifically to increase subsidiary responsiveness. For Nissan Mexicana, the parent's philosophy of government compliance combined with the Japanese consensual decision-making structure enabled the Nissan parent's participation to enlarge and reinforce subsidiary responsiveness already prioritized by its internal subsidiary management. Likewise, Volkswagen's practice of adaptation enhanced the ability of its Mexican subsidiary to comply with host-government demands. The intervention of the Chrysler parent in increasing its ownership of the Mexican subsidiary and investing in new projects enlarged its export capacity.

Therefore, a subsidiary, run by local management having close relationships with LDC actors and with decision-making authority independent of the parent, was often associated with the subsidiary's ability to identify trends in a changing environment and to realign policies before crisis. In both case studies, the subsidiaries that fit these definitions were the most autonomous from their parents. The only exception was Nissan Mexicana: autonomy was not a necessary precondition, given its parent's philosophy and consensual decision structure. In contrast, those subsidiaries with internal subsidiary management policies that hindered effective relationships with key LDC actors and facilitated parent intervention were at a distinct disadvantage in promptly identifying a changing environment and in negotiating the escalating demands to change their policies.

Conflict: Subsidiary versus Host Country

Both case studies illustrated how, at the point of crisis, the degree of conflict differed principally as a function of (1) *each subsidiary's particular historical policy performance*, (2) *the pressuring group's perception of the subsidiary and bargaining power*, and (3) *the parent's interests.* Certain subsidiary characteristics decreased the level of pressure. They had to facilitate adjustments in policies commensurate with LDC demands before crisis, as well as to elicit favorable LDC group perceptions of the subsidiary's capacity to comply. If parent interests coincided with those of the pressuring group, conflict for the subsidiary was heightened.

HISTORICAL POLICY PERFORMANCE

A key variable affecting the level of pressure on a firm was historical policy performance. Each subsidiary's past policy was a function of both its pre-crisis response (if any) and the innate conflict of its policy with LDC demands. In both case studies, those subsidiaries with policies more out-of-line with the LDC groups' demands were pressured more. In Brazil, the Ford, Volkswagen, and Saab subsidiaries were targeted in part as a result of their particular labor policies. In Mexico, the Ford, General Motors, and Chrysler subsidiaries were targeted largely because they were in greatest violations of the trade balance requirement.

Some subsidiaries identified a changing environment and, as a result, changed their policies. Consequently, they were under less pressure. In Mexico, for example, the Volkswagen and Nissan subsidiaries had "adjusted" their local-content policies in the early 1970s, years before the government's crackdown in 1977 and 1981. Thus, both subsidiaries' policies were in less conflict with the government regulations and therefore under less pressure to change.

Significantly, the innate conflict between subsidiary policies and LDC demands was also different for a number of specific MNC characteristics. For example in Brazil, the labor union perceived significant differences in the labor policies of the subsidiaries. In Mexico, the subsidiaries' historical trade policies had been shaped not only by their role within their parents' global strategies, growth objectives, products, production requirements, but also by parent philosophy. Even if none of the subsidiaries had perceived the need to change policies, there were nonetheless significant differences between the subsidiaries' policies themselves. In the face of LDC pressures, differences in subsidiary policies translated into varying levels of conflict and pressure on the subsidiaries.

PRESSURING-GROUP PERCEPTION

The level of pressure was also affected by the pressuring-group's perception of each subsidiary: Was the subsidiary willing and able to respond? Was it vulnerable? Did the subsidiary have a particular overall value in the LDC group's agenda? In Brazil, the Saab subsidiary, given its small size, was perceived as particularly vulnerable to a successful shutdown. The Volkswagen subsidiary's acquiescence had a special importance since it was the nation's largest employer and industry leader. In Mexico, the General Motors subsidiary's previous failures in meeting the government's demands were somewhat offset by the perception that it presently had the ability and willingness to comply. Conversely, pressure on the Chrysler subsidiary was somewhat lessened because the government was convinced it could not comply due to its parent's difficulties. Subsidiaries also had different levels of importance to the government: in terms of product, Volkswagen and Nissan manufactured needed popular models, while Chrysler, General Motors, and Ford primarily manufactured luxury cars; in terms of national employment, Volkswagen and Chrysler were perceived as playing an important role.

PARENT INTERESTS

In both case studies, the level of pressure on the firms was also differentiated by varying parent interests. Home-country pressures had a direct bearing on the parent's role in transmitting pressure on to its subsidiary—and that pressure could either be to comply with the LDC pressuring group or not to comply with the LDC group. To the degree parent groups reinforced the subsidiary's objectives, the less the pressure. In Brazil, however, parent labor groups served to escalate the pressure on their subsidiaries by contesting subsidiary objectives in support of the pressuring labor union. Both the Saab and Volkswagen parents exerted pressure on their Brazilian subsidiaries to comply as a result of home unions' influence on the parent Board of Directors.

Likewise, in Mexico, in part because of home labor problems the Ford parent exerted pressure on its subsidiary not to comply. However, parent philosophy also significantly differentiated the level of pressure in one case: the Nissan parent philosophy of compliance increased the pressure felt by its subsidiary to comply. The parents' overall strategies also contributed in some cases to the level of pressure on the subsidiaries: in Mexico, the global strategies of Volkswagen, Nissan, and General Motors accommodated to a large extent the Mexican government's demands, while the global strategies of Chrysler and Ford clashed with these Mexican demands, thereby enlarging the depth of innate conflict and pressure on their Mexico subsidiaries.

As a result, in both case studies the level of pressure on the MNC subsidiary was affected by past policy performance according to the pressuring-group's criterion; the group's perception of the subsidiary's ability, willingness, and overall value; and the parent's interests, including home-country issues, parent philosophy, and overall strategy.

Type of Subsidiary Response

Both case studies demonstrated that the types of subsidiary responses were differentiated primarily as a function of (1) *the parents' preferences*, (2) *relationships with key LDC groups*, and (3) the *first policy responses* initiated. Those characteristics that determined how the subsidiary would be affected by differing parent preferences also shaped its relationships with LDC groups, while the competitive repercussions of other subsidiary responses further contributed to the making of the subsidiary's own response.

PARENT PREFERENCES

The parents' preferences—regardless of whether the policy was the responsibility of the subsidiary or the parent—differentiated responses. In the case of Brazil, parents approved different options (General Motors and Ford: head-office labor review of proposals), promoted their different labor practices (General Motors: "Quality of Work Life" program; Saab-Scania do Brazil: worker committees), endorsed their parent philosophy (Ford: refused to fire workers for participating in a strike; accepted union-based worker committees), and pressured the subsidiary as the result of home-country and union pressures (Saab-Scania do Brasil: home-country press, union leaders, Board of Directors; Volkswagen: union leaders, Board of Directors). In Mexico, all the parents to varying degrees had approval roles in defining the enlarged export strategies of their Mexican subsidiaries. In fact, parent preferences in some cases were so strong that they directly participated in their subsidiaries' responses by negotiating with the Mexican government (General Motors, Ford) and aggressively engaging home-government officials (Ford).

SUBSIDIARY RELATIONSHIPS WITH KEY LDC GROUPS

The type of subsidiary response is obviously related to the specific policy change sought. The subsidiary's willingness to change policy was affected greatly by its relationships with the key LDC groups—the pressuring group as well as any other countergroups opposed to these policy changes. In Brazil, the Volkswagen subsidiary's very close relationship with the government resulted in its advancing the preferred government response to labor demands. However, when the striking union insisted, the Ford subsidiary acquiesced to labor's preferred response: a union-based worker-representative system. Ford do Brasil's aloofness from the Brazilian government enabled it to make a daring departure from Brazilian industrial-relations practices. In Mexico, the Nissan and Volkswagen subsidiaries had over the years developed high local-content strategies in conscious efforts to increase their bargaining power. In contrast, the U.S. subsidiaries were tied to the imports from their parents' operations.

FIRST SUBSIDIARY POLICY RESPONSE

The type of response was further differentiated by the first subsidiary to reformulate policy, thus establishing the parameters for the type of responses available to the other subsidiaries. "Leaders" defined the options, from which the other subsidiaries as "followers" had to choose. In Brazil, Volkswagen's, then Ford's announcement of a worker-representation system forced the other subsidiaries to analyze those particular responses, and to formulate their own approaches accordingly. With Ford's acquiescence, the other subsidiaries lost the option of *not* eventually also succumbing to labor's demands for union-based worker-representative systems. Likewise, in Mexico, General Motors' announcement of new investment also forced the other subsidiaries into "defensive adaptation," as would Nissan's compliance with the government's trade balance requirement. Analogous to the theory of "price leader" or "quality leader" in oligopolistic industrial structures, one of the subsidiaries would play the role of "response leader," thereby shaping the final outcome. As a result, each subsidiary's response was affected by parent preferences, subsidiary management relationships with key LDC groups, and the "response leader."

In summary, the case studies illustrate this volume's central theme—that, when faced with LDC demands, MNC behavior varies as a result of a multitude of differing characteristics. As summarized in table 8–1, throughout the policy reformulation process, key subsidiary characteristics related to the subsidiary's relationships with its parent and the pressuring LDC group emerged as critical response factors that enhanced the responsiveness of subsidiaries. The parent-subsidiary relationship was especially key to enabling responsiveness: subsidiary autonomy (or consensual Japanese-style decision-making), including superior senior management knowledge of the country, resource availability, and latitude to adjust subsidiary policy. Preconditions for effectiveness cut through the entire MNC organization, including parent endorsement (e.g., reinforcing parent practices or philosophy), personnel policies, parent consideration of host-country demands, and a mandated subsidiary role in analyzing its environment. These critical response factors encompassed the entire MNC organization, its policies, structures, and relationships, differentiating the responses of MNCs to host-country demands.

Strategic Implications for MNC Managers and LDC Groups

If subsidiary behavior varies because of differing characteristics and relationships, then MNC managers and LDC groups both have latitude to optimize preferred subsidiary responses. If the abilities of subsidiaries to identify a changing environment and negotiate escalated LDC demands before crisis differ, what are the implications for MNC managers and LDC groups? If the degree of conflict between the subsidiary and the host country differs, how can MNC managers and LDC groups influence the degree of conflict? If the type of response differs, how can MNC managers and LDC groups identify and negotiate potential influences to fit their respective objectives?

TABLE 8–1
Critical Response Factors

	Policy Reformulation Process		
	Pre-crisis Identification	*Degree of Conflict*	*Type of Response*
PARENT RELATIONSHIP	*Intervention and Influence*	*Interests*	*Preferences*
Critical Response Factors	• Subsidiary autonomy/consensual decision-making • Superior senior management knowledge • Resource availability • Latitude to adjust policies	• Parent interests coincide with LDC demands	• Parent preferences coincide with LDC-preferred policy
Preconditions	• Parent endorsement (practice, philosophy) • Personnel policies • Consideration of host-country demands • Subsidiary role in analysis of environment	• LDC communication with parent	• Parent resource commitment • Ability of parent to dictate subsidiary policy
Potential Influences		• Home-country pressures • Parent philosophy	• Home-country pressures • Parent philosophy
LDC RELATIONSHIP	Closeness with pressuring LDC group		
Critical Response Factors	Ability to speak language, close personal relationships		

MNC Managers

These questions are of critical importance to MNC managers as they face the dilemma of managing in a world of growing complexity with overlapping interdependencies and political pressures. Simultaneously, global competition has increased the importance of capturing growth markets and reducing production costs, both challenges magnifying the importance of effectively managing subsidiaries located in multiple host countries. The range of possible MNC subsidiary behavior in LDCs is clearly illustrated by the Brazilian and Mexican automotive cases: MNC subsidiaries were affected differently by pressure applied by LDC actors on specific policies. While the pressuring LDC groups did not intend the subsidiaries to withdraw but only to change their policies, these pressures represented risks and opportunities for the MNC subsidiaries that differed according to very specific company characteristics.

GLOBAL COMPETITIVE ADVANTAGE REDEFINED: THE CHALLENGE OF CROSS-COUNTRY MANAGEMENT

The fundamental need to manage subsidiary response results from the evolving nature of competitive advantage in global industries. As businesses become more globally integrated, so does the potential magnitude of economic, social, and political factors within the very dynamics of subsidiary management. To be globally competitive, MNC managers must explicitly identify these factors and account for them in their strategies and policies—including the organizational structure of the subsidiary and its relationship to its parent and host-country environment. In short, the strategy, structure, and management of the MNC must equal the challenge of its multiple operating environments.

This challenge cannot be met by a simple, tacked-on function such as country-risk analysis. Rather it requires an approach that encompasses virtually all the global functions of the MNC, from strategies to human resources policies to production, and even down to its very organizational structure. Each and every aspect of the MNC subsidiary, including its relationship to its parent and the host-country environment, has a bearing on its global competitive advantage.

The number of interactive issues to manage is vast, ranging from parent influence on the host country to host-country influence on the parent. In terms of the first, we have seen how subsidiaries, unintentionally, can become conduits for viewpoints, resources, and issues imported to the host country from the parent and its home country. In Brazil, the philosophies and viewpoints of home-country labor groups played a major role—even despite the opposition of Saab-Scania's and Volkswagen's subsidiary management. Thus, the policies of MNCs can become cross-country conduits for differing interest groups, philosophies, and practices—all which may themselves have an impact on the actual behavior of the subsidiary and its capacity to operate effectively in that national environment.

On the other hand, host-country demands may affect the entire corporation—in other words, not just the subsidiary is captive, but the entire MNC, its strategies and resources. The various demands emanating from host countries must be reconciled at some point within the organization—whether they be local or impinge on parent policy. The Mexican case study shows that host-country demands can modify parent policy and potentially do represent significant risks for the parent. Thus, the ability of the MNC to operate effectively in a multitude of varying host-country environments might not only result in global competitive advantage, but also constitutes a head office competitive imperative.

What does this mean for the business manager's struggle to build or protect global competitive advantage? Namely, that global competitive advantage must be redefined to include the capacity of the MNC's worldwide organization to correctly assess host-country environments, formulate corresponding strategies, and effectively coordinate operations across countries. The challenge of effective management across countries is emerging as a competitive battleground for global industries.

First, the quality of cross-country assessments, staffing, and communication is of key importance to facilitating subsidiary response. For example, we have seen in both the Mexican and Brazilian case studies the importance of subsidiary management's ability to analyze the host-country environment and to effectively communicate those assessments to the parent. Centralized parent decision-making in dependent subsidiaries impeded this process, leading to competitive disadvantage.

Second, instead of interfering with global operations, host-country regulations can enhance global strategies. MNCs that can harness national demands can reinforce their global competitive advantage. Where a fit occurs, as in the case of General Motors de México, an MNC can simultaneously gain advantages via-à-vis local and global competitors, maximizing local and global benefits in its response to local demands. In short, performance requirements may be used to leverage, rather than impede, global competitive advantage.

If the MNC's structure, staffing, strategies, or policies do not take into account the wide assortment of potential host-country demands, the organization will not be well positioned to minimize the risks and maximize the opportunities of today's global marketplace. Going forward, the practical hands-on challenge facing MNC managers is enormous, encompassing the complex day-to-day tasks of managing worldwide operations—from the administrative end to communications and staffing as well as to marketing and production strategies. All must be carefully coordinated and globalized, integrating the multitude of host-country issues.

THE MANAGEMENT OF SUBSIDIARY POLICIES: POLICY RESPONSE AS A COMPETITIVE FACTOR

Even in terms of the local national market, competition is not limited simply to the domain of investments, products, or cost, but also includes policy responses. Whether explicit or implicit, MNC subsidiaries compete against one another in terms of their responses to host-country demands. As discussed, the dynamic is similar to that of an investment, price, or quality leader: the policy "response leader" sets the pace and the parameters for response, creating a response imperative for competitors.

Just as with investment and price leaders, subsidiaries that are leaders in policy response may well gain valuable competitive advantage on multiple fronts vis-à-vis their competitors. Being a "response leader" is likely to earn the subsidiary valuable goodwill and political capital with the LDC group. The "response leader" may also be able to dictate policies to its own advantage; its competitors, having lost their latitude to reformulate (or not reformulate) their policies, may well be forced to fall into place like dominoes, with reformulated policies not of their choosing modeled on those of the initiating subsidiary. In the Brazilian case, Ford claimed benefits for departing from the country's labor traditions and introducing the first union-based worker-representation system. While one could dispute the exact nature of Ford's benefits, by being first it was able to shift its position from one of reactive defense to one of control, and therefore shape the debate to its own objectives.

The indisputable advantage of the "response leader" is in being able to set the terms and define the parameters of response for competitors. The Volkswagen subsidiary was clearly the loser. Its antiunion stance resulted in more strike days than its competitors, costing it lost sales and a drop in market share, along with the ill will of its labor force and the Brazilian government. That does not mean being a response leader is the optimal response for all companies in all situations; there are potential disadvantages and dangers associated with initiating new policies. Mercedes Benz in Brazil was able to minimize risks by maintaining a low-key profile. Chrysler in Mexico was forced by its parent's situation to delay investments, increasing its trade deficit. Making decisions on the optimal policy responses, however, requires recognizing policy as part of the competitive battleground, identifying the particular interests of the company, and mapping appropriate strategies.

POLICIES AS COUNTRY-RISK FACTORS

In summary, regardless of objectives and sometimes even contrary to MNC managers' intent, subsidiaries may play an important role in spearheading sociopolitical and economic change within an LDC. MNC managers should be fully cognizant of the potential importance of their subsidiaries' policies in LDCs and be able to recognize when particular policies may come under pressure from LDC actors. Both case studies underline the importance of analyzing subsidiary policies within the content of the particular LDC's development process.

Given the decades of escalating explicit LDC demands, subsidiary management's shock when confronted with hardened LDC demands—the Brazilian strikes and the Mexican government's crackdown—illustrates the importance of a dynamic, historical, and contextual view of subsidiary policies. Brazilian labor and Mexican government demands had escalated throughout the years, and their ability to express those demands forcefully had increased. In both cases, subsidiary management was caught unaware of the shifting power balance in their disfavor.

In Brazil, subsidiary management did not foresee the impact of the shifting political power on subsidiary labor policies. Subsidiary management had developed very close ties with the Brazilian military government over the years, but had neglected to cultivate comparable relationships with national groups such as labor, opposition parties, or the Catholic Church. Now as Brazil enters into a new stage of political development, these national groups possess renewed power and influence. The 1980 strike was clearly a political struggle between labor and the Brazilian military government played out in the arena of the automotive industry. It illustrated how a subsidiary policy, labor relations, became a focus of conflict between labor and the LDC government, with the automotive subsidiaries paying a costly price. Subsidiary management attempted to develop relationships with these national groups, but was largely unsuccessful. The strategic dilemma encountered by many managers of the Brazilian automotive industry was how to reconcile with labor and opposition groups. The automotive industry's past policies acted as constraints limiting individual subsidiaries in the formulation of new strategies.

Likewise, in Mexico, most subsidiary management did not perceive the growing dedication and commensurate ability of the Mexican government over two decades to enforce its trade balance requirements on subsidiary exporting and local-content policies. Dating from the 1962 Decree, with varying priorities, the Mexican government had visibly struggled to effectively eliminate the automotive trade deficit. With the government's crackdown in 1977 and 1981, the strategic dilemma that faced many managers of the Mexican automotive industry was how to further adjust subsidiary policies in accordance with the government's demands. To prevent costly conflicts such as these, MNC managers must take a historical view of their policies within the context of LDC developments and identify the evolution of LDC group demands and the potential implications for their subsidiaries' policies.

DIFFERENTIATING SUBSIDIARY RESPONSE CAPACITY

The two case studies also show significant differences in the ability of subsidiary management to identify and respond to a changing environment. The advisability of reformulating subsidiary policies, the timing and types of response, is necessarily the responsibility of local subsidiary management. The ability of a subsidiary to develop appropriate innovative or adaptive policies depends on the quality of local information and decision-making on host-country developments, and the role of the parent in supporting or approving new policies. The autonomy or dependency of the subsidiary has a major bearing on this ability. While either approach would seem to have basic advantages and disadvantages, the autonomous subsidiary clearly enjoys potential competitive advantages. (See table 8–2.)

The more autonomous subsidiary can innovate quickly and in many possible ways. The managing director can draw on his close relationships with the government and locals. He has considerable flexibility in hiring additional personnel, reorganizing departments, and conducting special studies. Subsidiary policies can be reformulated accordingly. By the same token, the more autonomous subsidiary is also more open to local pressures from both the government and national groups on its policies. As in the case of Volkswagen do Brasil, the subsidiary may become hostage to unpopular alliances.

In contrast, the more dependent subsidiary can draw more extensively on the resources of the parent in developing its policies. Subsidiary staff can be trained in various areas and be privy to the lessons learned by the corporation at large. Parent funds and support are more easily obtained. Such a process is likely to necessitate, however, longer periods for developing new policies and to confine underlying concepts and policies to those already endorsed by the parent.

Delayed, untimely response is often the result. The dependent subsidiaries may not respond to a changing environment until after the crisis. In the Brazil case, only the Volkswagen and Mercedes Benz subsidiaries, and in the Mexican case, only the Volkswagen and Nissan subsidiaries began to reformulate policies before the outbreak of crisis. Nissan Mexicana, despite its parent's participation in decisions, responded because of the unique corporatewide parent philosophy of government compliance.

Table 8–2
The Degree of Autonomy and Strategic Implications for MNC Managers, LDC Policymakers, and LDC National Groups

		Strategic Implications for Groups Concerned with Subsidiary		
Autonomy	*Subsidiary Response*	*MNC Managers*	*LDC Policymakers*	*LDC National Groups*
High	• **Ability to innovate quickly**	• Need to manage local pressures • Need to correctly forecast political and economic situations	• Subsidiary more responsive to pressure from goverment officials • Subsidiary may be candidate for initiating national policy model	• Subsidiary more likely to initiate dialogue
	• **Limited range of potential innovations and adaptations**	• Need to negotiate successfully with local groups • Need to control local pressures on innovations and innovate early	• Subsidiary may be targeted by national groups • Political pressure may influence type of innovation	• Subsidiary more likely to innovate in ways authorized by government • Alliances between domestic and international groups may influence subsidiary policy
Low	• **Innability to innovate quickly**	• Need to develop supportive relationship with parent for increased flexibility • Need to develop information network on local environment	• Subsidiary less responsive to pressure from government officials to innovate • Subsidiary more likely to follow policies set by industry	• Subsidiary less likely to initiate dialogues or make meaningful contact • Relationships with subsidiary staff may influence subsidiary policy
	• **Greater range of potential innovations or adaptations**	• Need for effective parent support in training and program direction	• Subsidiary more apt to introduce parent practices/resources • Pressure on the subsidiary may result in parent intervention	• Subsidiary less likely to innovate • New policies may be very innovative

Dependent subsidiaries are usually at a disadvantage in identifying changes due to subsidiary management policies (e.g., high turnover), weak management relationships with key LDC actors, and parent intervention. The result may be that the more autonomous subsidiaries (such as Volkswagen in both countries) develop policies aligned with the changing environment that, after the eruption of crisis, the more dependent subsidiaries (such as Ford do Brasil and General Motors de México) are forced to adopt only after parent approval.

MANAGEMENT OF CROSS-COUNTRY RISK

A precondition to effective management across countries is being able to make environmental assessments that are integrated into parent and subsidiary decision-making. While many MNCs do systematically analyze changing LDC environments, often such efforts are divorced from local subsidiary management and decision-making. In the study, for example, the more centralized MNCs, General Motors and Ford, had political-risk analysis performed by corporate staff at the parent; the more autonomous subsidiaries, Mercedes Benz, Saab-Scania do Brasil, Volkswagen, and Chrysler made a decentralized analysis of the LDC environment. The challenge of either a centralized or decentralized approach would seem to be identical: to organize the specific structuring of a subsidiary's relationships with the host government, the parent, and the industry in order to maximize and maintain control of local policies while minimizing any associated risks. In either case, the subsidiary must have the primary role of assessing its environment and, in concert with the parent, the responsibility for developing appropriate policies, strategies, and relationships.

Second, any MNC strategic response to such assessments requires intrafirm communication, coordination, and consensus on objectives and overall strategies. We have seen, that faced with crisis, groups related to the parent may join the pressuring LDC actor as an ally and significantly increase pressure on the subsidiary to change its policy. Or conversely, the subsidiary may want to comply, but lack parent support.

These case studies provide guidance to MNC managers of the variables potentially affecting the responses of their parents and their competitors. Key variables are (1) the *centralization of decision-making* as well as (2) *parent characteristics* (such as philosophy, practices) and (3) *home-country pressures* (such as labor). The more centralized MNCs will need reporting structures between the parent and subsidiary that will allow for comprehensive support in the formulation of local policies and strategies. Specific strategies for increasing parent communication and responsiveness as well as subsidiary management's ability to read the environment are key. In contrast, the more autonomous subsidiary needs to have parent guidance on keeping the local operations and relationships within set parameters, and identifying what parent-related influences may unintentionally affect subsidiary policies.

Absolutely essential, however, to effective cross-country management of host-country demands is the subsidiary's own autonomous response capacity. The case studies showed how individual subsidiaries differed in their abilities to identify and respond to host-country demands. Even the degree of conflict differed. We saw the importance of subsidiary organization, its internal management structure, historical policies, and relationships with key actors.

The two cases also provide lessons for subsidiary management on variables that determine the degree of conflict between the subsidiary and the host country. The case of Brazil illustrates the latitude for managing the degree of conflict. Mercedes Benz was subject to less pressure from the local union and local government officials than Volkswagen. The reasons given included the earlier efforts of management at Mercedes Benz to open a dialogue with the union. Volkswagen's enormous role in the economy and its close relationship with the government were significant constraints on its flexibility in formulating local policies.

Host governments may find it of utmost importance for an industry leader to adopt new policies. Other interested parties, such as unions, national groups, and the parent are also likely to concentrate on the most visible company. The managerial implication for industry leaders is the special need to formulate relationship strategies that insulate them from undesired external pressures. In order to maintain their policy prerogatives, it may be very important for these subsidiaries to take the initiative in responding to host-country demands before the host country or parent themselves become interested in determining the nature of the subsidiary's policies.

The case studies also illustrate the need to manage the unchangeable—those characteristics that are undeniable elements of an MNC, with undeniable competitive consequences. For example, certain parent characteristics can translate into cross-country competitive advantage. The Mexican case study showed how differing national origins could result in preferential treatment, even if unstated, by the host government. Chrysler de México was partially immune to anti-U.S. bias, given its origins as a Mexican company, the continuing strong associations with Mexicans, and minor Mexican capital participation. While Chrysler largely inherited this mitigating factor, the example illustrates the advantages of consciously creating or taking advantage of such circumstances.

In sum, the Brazilian and Mexican cases suggest basic guidelines for enabling MNC subsidiaries to manage more effectively host-country demands. First, the subsidiary must build an assessment capacity. Subsidiary management should identify the historical policy demands of the host government and key interest groups, and consider how possible shifts in political power could result in escalation of those demands. The parent and the subsidiary must come to agreement on how the subsidiary is to fulfill its responsibilities, on required resources, and management changes. For the pertinent policies, a strategy must be devised for developing diverse sources of information in order to keep abreast of political developments.

Second, the subsidiary must build a response capacity. Management has to formulate policies in collaboration with its parent so as to hedge for uncertain political developments. Relationship strategies should be laid out. For example, the subsidiary may need to develop strategies to distance itself from the present regime without losing lobbying power. Objectives would be outlined, with specific tasks assigned to key subsidiary personnel. A strategy for industry collaboration must be devised. Management should map out lines of effective communication with the parent company, the local industry association, and other industry firms. In the event the subsidiary is the industry leader, methods to protect its policies from government pressure must be constructed. If the subsidiary is not the industry leader, management has to devise a strategy for isolating it from the influence of the industry leader. The parent and subsidiary will need to define in which areas the subsidiary has the option of localizing policies, and what flexibility the managing director might have in introducing new policies.

LDC Groups

While the development objectives of LDC government policymakers and national groups such as labor may well be conflicting, all LDC groups share a common interest in understanding and influencing the behavior of MNC subsidiaries in their country. The range of potential behavior of MNC subsidiaries in LDCs is clearly illustrated by the Brazilian and Mexican automotive cases: regardless of previous subsidiary policies, pressure on those policies resulted in benefits for the LDC pressuring groups. In Brazil, to varying degrees MNC subsidiaries introduced parent practices, ideas, and programs that were innovative in the context of Brazilian labor relations. In Mexico, MNC subsidiaries' investments transformed the country into a major source for automotive engines, and the subsidiaries transformed their trade deficits into trade surpluses.

OPTIMIZING CROSS-COUNTRY CONVERGENT INTERESTS

LDC groups should view each MNC subsidiary as an individual and particular entity in the context of its parent and home country, and potentially capable of transmitting resources, ideas, and options commensurate with the group's development objectives. This research demonstrates that subsidiaries, irrespective of day-to-day policies, are open to parent influences, and that those influences can be of benefit to the LDC group. In both case studies, while day-to-day subsidiary autonomy was important in enabling the identification of a changing environment and influenced the type of subsidiary response, it did not necessarily mean that in crisis the parent would not have an influence on subsidiary policies. Indeed, in the Brazilian case, those subsidiaries that were on a day-to-day basis most autonomous in labor policies were also influenced greatly by their respective parents. In crisis, parent influences external to routinized contact between the subsidiary and the parent became key determinants of subsidiary response. This phenomenon suggests that the structural day-to-day autonomy of MNC subsidiaries is not indicative of the potential parent influence on subsidiary policies, and that subsidiary policies should always be analyzed within the context of each entire underlying MNC structure.

The strategic implication is significant: LDC policymakers and national groups can potentially influence in different ways the policies of MNC subsidiaries on a variety of levels, both domestic and international. As LDC groups become better educated and more informed, their effectiveness increases multifold. Both case studies illustrate the importance of the LDC groups' knowledge of each subsidiary's overall global structure. In the Brazilian case, for example, the success of the local unions was at least partially due to the support of outside groups associated with the subsidiaries' parents, such as the International Metalworkers Federation and the home unions of the parent company. Local labor leaders in Brazil were able to influence subsidiaries through meetings with labor representatives on the parent Board of Directors. Both the Brazilian and international press publicized the viewpoints of labor and influenced public opinion in the home countries of the subsidiaries. Identifying and enlarging cross-country alliances was a critical task for Brazilian labor leaders in ensuring the effectiveness of their demands on MNC subsidiaries for changing their labor policies.

In the Mexican case, the success of its government was also largely due to its understanding of the overall global structure for each of the five automotive subsidiaries, and how it affected the respective ability and willingness of each to comply with the government's demands. A deep understanding of each subsidiary's relationship to its parents was critical, especially in regard to the overall strategy of the parent and the role of the Mexican subsidiary. Based on an accurate perception of General Motors' global and Mexican strategy, the Mexican government was able to enlist the subsidiary's compliance, thereby initiating defensive investments by the other subsidiaries.

In studying the individuality of each subsidiary, LDC groups should therefore analyze how differing subsidiary characteristics and relationships might affect subsidiary behavior in response to pressure on their policies. In both case studies, certain variables were associated with certain subsidiaries' greater responsiveness to LDC group demands as well as with the resistance of other subsidiaries. Parent philosophy was cited as a key variable in Ford do Brasil's ultimate acceptance of a union-based worker-representation system as well as in Nissan Mexicana's adherence to the Mexican trade balance requirement. Yet, parent philosophy was also cited as a key variable in the U.S. subsidiaries' resistance to Mexican regulations. LDC groups should take note of each parent's inherent philosophy, whether it be a function of the home country or corporate culture, and evaluate what influence, if any, it may have on the parent's and expatriate management's views about changing their subsidiary's policies. Other external variables, including home-country pressures, should also be analyzed.

DEFINING PARAMETERS FOR SUBSIDIARY RESPONSE

The definition of each subsidiary's relationships with key actors will also clarify the potential responses to policy pressures. The responsiveness of each subsidiary will be influenced by its specific relationship with key actors in its environment, i.e., its autonomy with respect to the parent, its integration with the host government, and the reliance on the industry. In the case studies, the more autonomous subsidiaries were usually more aligned with the host government than the more dependent subsidiaries. Each group of subsidiaries demonstrated distinctive characteristics in their propensity to adapt or innovate that may prove to be useful guidelines for the strategies of both policymakers and national groups.

The more autonomous subsidiaries were more responsive to pressure from government officials as well as more likely to initiate dialogues with national groups. From the perspective of LDC government policymakers, an autonomous subsidiary may be a more suitable candidate for initiating a policy model for other MNCs or national companies. Since the more autonomous subsidiary is usually closely integrated with the host government, it may be more open to government persuasion. Unlike national firms, an MNC subsidiary has access to resources, ideas, and techniques external to the LDC that might be usefully diffused to national companies. Furthermore, since the more autonomous subsidiary has more latitude in the design of its in-country policies, the host government may have, depending on other home-country pressures, less parent intervention countering its own preferred policy. The host government may therefore more directly influence the timing and types of innovative policies of the more autonomous subsidiaries.

From the perspective of LDC national groups, the close relationship between LDC government policymakers and autonomous subsidiaries may be of particular concern. As in Brazil, national groups may form alliances in and out of the country and also pressure the autonomous subsidiaries. National groups may want to systematically identify subsidiary/government alliances, and to develop their own cross-country alliances that might be useful in counterpressuring the subsidiary's policy.

In contrast, the more dependent subsidiaries of centralized MNCs were less responsive to pressure from government officials as well as less likely to initiate dialogues with national groups. Correspondingly, neither policymakers nor national groups had a comparable degree of influence on the timing or type of innovative policies. If the more dependent subsidiaries are not forced to innovate, they are generally likely to follow policies set by the industry. On the other hand, subsidiaries under tight parent control may also be able to engage—provided the parent is convinced—substantial external resources and accomplish the transference of parent practices. The case studies illustrate that the more dependent subsidiaries are less likely to identify and respond to a changing environment, but more likely to import parent practices, programs, and resources when they do. Therefore, LDC policymakers may want to directly pressure the more dependent subsidiaries when they want to encourage the intervention of the parent or the transference of certain programs, practices, or resources from the parent.

National groups, on the other hand, may find the more centralized MNCs of greater value than the more autonomous ones. In the Brazilian case, the more dependent subsidiaries introduced parent policies that were very innovative in the context of Brazil. Subsidiary management of more dependent subsidiaries may be well versed in the industrial-relations practices of the parent, and therefore able and willing to adopt parent policies. National groups interested in diffusing such policies may be interested in developing relationships with subsidiary staff members who may be useful in influencing subsidiary policies.

Therefore, both LDC policymakers and LDC groups should perceive MNC subsidiaries as actual and potential conduits for the introduction of new practices, programs, and resources to their countries. The ideas, practices, and programs innovated by the automotive subsidiaries in response to labor demands, will be gradually diffused to national Brazilian companies. In the Mexican case, General Motors' commitment to its very large engine investment was a success for the Mexican government: the four other major subsidiaries made similar investments, with important implications for the country's exports, employment, and supplier industries. If LDC policymakers and national groups want to effectively influence MNCs' contributions to their countries' development, they must better understand the process by which MNC subsidiaries adopt and innovate policies, and the role key variables play in determining their distinctive responses.

In sum, as MNCs further encircle the globe, an awesome challenge faces practitioners and scholars of international business—simultaneously to enhance global competitiveness while meeting the demands of host countries. Within the MNC itself, the economic imperatives of globalization must be reconciled with the political imperatives of multiple nation-states. Deciphering this complex interaction can reveal distinct systematic differences between MNCs in their will and capacity to respond to host-country demands. Despite the complexity of understanding these subsidiary-specific differences, in the day-to-day realities now unfolding—utilized or not—these differences constitute an additional reservoir that offers new competitive advantages for MNC managers and potent effective strategies for LDC groups.

Appendix: Interviewees

From 1980 to 1984, three hundred interview sessions were conducted with more than eighty people. Interview sessions were lengthy, often lasting two hours or more. Many people took part in several sessions, principal sources in most cases participating in more than six sessions. Managing directors of all the subsidiaries provided answers to an in-depth questionnaire. All evidence used in the study was confirmed by at least a second interviewee or a reliable published source.

Brazil Case Study

Ford do Brasil

Lloyd Halstead, President
Donald Kummer, Director of Labor Relations
Osmar Valentin, Labor Relations
Salvadore Evangelista, Jr., Labor Relations
Diego Alarcón Clemente, Labor Relations
Larry Kazanowski, Director of Strategic Planning

General Motors do Brasil

Joseph Sanchez, President
André Beer, Executive Vice-President
Herbert Brenner, Director of Labor Relations
Ereudy Fernandes, Labor Relations
Antonio Alcántara, Labor Relations
Antonio Romeu Netto, Director of Public Relations
William Losh, Director of Production

Mercedes Benz do Brasil

Werner Fritz Gerhard Jessen, Managing Director
Louis Scheur, Director of Labor Relations
Pedro Proseurcin, Labor Relations
João Corduan, Director of Public Relations

Saab-Scania do Brasil

Gunnar Lindquist, Managing Director
Inge Lunnerdal, Director of Labor Relations
Claudio Orlandi, Labor Relations
Mario Lima, Director of Public Relations

Volkswagen do Brasil

Wolfgang Sauer, President
Karl-Heinz Gerber, Vice-President and Finance Director
Admon Ganem, Labor Relations
Laura Magalhaes C. Amorim, Labor Relations
Mauro Marcondes Machado, Labor Relations
Luiz Antonio Guimardes Silva, Labor Relations
Jens Kook-Weskoot, Director of Strategic Planning
Paulo Dutra, Director of Public Relations
Horst Richer, Public Relations

ANFAVEA

Jose Roberto, staff
Salvador Rocha, staff
Osmar Masson, staff

Labor Union Officials

Jair Meneguelli, President of the São Bernardo Metalworkers Union
Miguel Huertas, São Paulo Metalworkers Union
Anésio de Araujo Correa, Technical Director of the São Paulo Metalworkers Union
Esteban Torres, São Paulo Metalworkers Union
Osvaldo Rodrigues Cavignato, DIEESE

Other

Alencar Naul Rossi, Secretary of Labor Relations, Ministry of Labor, Brazilian Government
Maria Helena Moreira Alves, expert on Brazil's labor unions
John Humphrey, expert on Brazil's labor unions
Cassio Mesquita Barros, lawyer for General Motors do Brasil

Mexico Case Study

Chrysler de México

Jack Parkinson, Managing Director
Claudio Mayoral Gasio, Director of Government Relations
Thomas Gilman, Director of Planning and Investments
David de León Moore, Corporate Planning
Alberto Castrejón, Director of Finance
Gilberto Cantu G., Commercial Director
Michael Philips, Comptroller's Office

Ford de México

Michael Hammes, Managing Director
Abelardo Padín, Director of Government Relations
Carlos Bandala Serrano, Manager of Government Relations
Jacob Hanneman, Manager of Business Planning and Development
Juan Antonio Salazar, Finance Department
Fernando Mendoza Butron, Manager of Supplier Development

General Motors de México

William Slocum, Managing Director
Mario Silva, Director of Government Relations
Carlos Nava Perea, Manager of Government Relations and Customs
Stuart Maitland, Director of Corporate Planning
Walter Noch, Export Director
David Arguelles, Purchasing
Alfredo de la Fuente, Assistant to the Managing Director

Nissan Mexicana

Issei Yoshino, Managing Director
Gustavo Baz Gonzalez, Director of Government Relations
Kiyoshi Sekiguchi, Director of Commercial Relations
Hiroshi Yoshioka, Coordinator of Commercial Relations
Masataka Ebato, Assistant Director of Project Development

Nissan Motor Manufacturing Corporation, USA

Marvin Runyon, President

Volkswagen de México

Hans H. Barschkis, Managing Director
Armando Carrillo, Director of Government Relations
Tomas Reigadas, Director of Market and Product Planning
Horst Kreimerman, Director of Purchasing

Asociación Mexicana de la Industria Automotriz

César Flores, Executive President
Alfonso Ponce Robles, Prior President and Consultant
Antonio Olmedo Zamarripa, Head of Economic Studies
German Saavedra Gonzalez, staff

*Mexican Government Officials**

Ruben Beltran Guerrero
Alfonso Chavez Torres

* The positions of Mexican government officials are not given because many of them have served in various capacities in different administrations.

Gabriel Fernandez Sayago
Luis Alberto Perez Aceves
Raul Salinas Lozano
Hector Vazquez Tercero
Amado Vega
Juan Wolffer P.

Other

Alain Hayat, General Secretary of Renault de México
Jose Rodriguez Garca, Director of Official Relations of Renault de México
Claude Dessert, Director of Purchasing and Exports of Renault Industrais Mexicana

Index